smart bites for baby

smart bites
for baby

*300 Easy-to-Make, Easy-to-Love Meals
that Boost Your Baby and Toddler's Brain*

Mika Shino

Preface by Meirav Sakalowsky
Foreword by Lisa Stern, MD
Nutritional Consultation and Foreword by Bonnie Modugno, MS, RD, CLE

Photographs by Beatrice Peltre

Da Capo
LIFE
LONG

A Member of the Perseus Books Group

Design and production by Eclipse Publishing Services
Set in 11 point Joanna and 10 point Zapf Humanist

Cataloging-in-Publication data for this book
is available from the Library of Congress.

First Da Capo Press edition 2012
ISBN: 978-0-7382-1555-6
eISBN: 978-0-7382-1584-6

Published by Da Capo Press
A Member of the Perseus Books Group
www.dacapopress.com

Da Capo Press books are available at special discounts for bulk purchases in the U.S. by corporations, institutions, and other organizations. For more information, please contact the Special Markets Department at the Perseus Books Group, 2300 Chestnut Street, Suite 200, Philadelphia, PA, 19103, or call (800) 810-4145, ext. 5000, or e-mail special.markets@perseusbooks.com.

Note: The information in this book is true and complete to the best of our knowledge. This book is intended only as an informative guide for those wishing to know more about health issues. In no way is this book intended to replace, countermand, or conflict with the advice given to you by your own physician. The ultimate decision concerning care should be made between you and your doctor. We strongly recommend you follow his or her advice. Information in this book is general and is offered with no guarantees on the part of the authors or Da Capo Press. The authors and publisher disclaim all liability in connection with the use of this book. The names and identifying details of people associated with events described in this book have been changed. Any similarity to actual persons is coincidental.

10 9 8 7 6 5 4 3 2 1

contents

preface

Meirav Sakalowsky, mother of a three-year-old

When the time came to introduce solid foods to my first child, I was feeling frustrated. My instincts told me that feeding my child prepared food from a jar just didn't seem right—I don't like to eat processed food, so why would I give my baby something like that? But I didn't know what else I could do that was realistic. Meanwhile, I was amazed at how other moms in my circle of friends were struggling to get their children to eat. They seemed to dread mealtime. So there I was—unsure of where to start when I began talking with Mika, whom I met in a parenting class. We bonded quickly, and I told her how I was apprehensive about the entire approach to feeding.

It was then that Mika shared with me that there indeed were alternatives to the baby food jar, starting with several ways that other cultures introduce foods to their infants. The concepts, she explained, were simple and made sense to me:

- Feed babies and toddlers seasonal, fresh foods to maximize absorption of nutrients.
- Provide a variety of different textures during every meal to stimulate the mind.
- Offer different colors of food during meals to interest the child.

As a person who loves to eat healthy, fresh foods myself, I knew I wanted to try this at home with my baby, now that I knew this was a possibility.

Not only did Mika share this incredibly logical concept in theory, she also showed me how to actually live by it. Once we got started, I was so surprised at how easy these foods were to prepare. With Mika's help and recipes, we were eating foods that were full of vitamins, stimulating to the mind, and just fun to serve. My baby daughter ate foods that I grew up eating myself and loved—tahini, eggs, sesame seeds, soba noodles, lentils, sweet potato, beets, and spinach. In some cases, I had never before tried the foods I was serving, like kelp, tofu, and daikon radish, but, to my surprise, they were delicious.

I cannot stress enough how uncomplicated this philosophy was to live by. I remember one time we traveled to visit family in Philadelphia, and it was so easy to continue giving my daughter, 10 months old at the time, her varied meals. We stayed with my sister-in-law, who is French, comes from a family of professional chefs, and loves to cook. She was amazed by what I was feeding my daughter. As a mother herself, she had never even thought to feed her daughter fresh, homemade "mini meals" like what I was serving. Now with her second child, she has followed this approach and is so thrilled.

I am so grateful for having met Mika when I did. In my three years of parenting, I have been very fortunate that eating has not been a struggle I have had to face with my daughter, and I truly believe this has to do with her early introduction to different textures and flavors. Now, I can't lie. Today at three years old, my daughter doesn't eat *everything*, but she is very comfortable trying new foods. And since she was introduced to variety from the start, today I serve the same meal for the whole family and don't have to "hide" vegetables, proteins, or anything for that matter in her food. I encourage all moms interested in offering a better way to feed their young children to try *Smart Bites for Baby*.

foreword

Lisa Stern, MD, pediatrician

Organic, calcium-fortified, high antioxidants, no nitrates . . . argh! It is so easy to get overwhelmed by the simple task of going to the supermarket. The act of eating literally consumes us: three meals a day plus snacks. Add in shopping, preparing, and cleaning up, and you have nearly a full-time job just to feed your family. And yet, hard as it is to imagine, this job has gotten increasingly easy. Yes, I did say *easy*. On one hand, we have never had so many food choices or such ease in obtaining high-quality, delicious foods. On the other, we have never had so many food dilemmas—starting from the earliest age.

I am a pediatrician who grew up in a family of foodies. When I began my pediatric training 20 years ago, I followed the guidelines fed to me: *Start rice cereal at 4 to 6 months, wait four to five days before introducing a fruit or vegetable; begin proteins at 9 months.* As a young doctor, I became uncomfortable repeating this rhetoric. As time went on, I looked back on my upbringing and began combining the experiences I had in my childhood with the information I was learning from the ethnically diverse patient population I was seeing on a daily basis. The families that I knew growing up in New York City all ate ethnic foods, and their children were expected to do the same. My family tradition was Sunday night dinner in Chinatown. As a treat we would go to the lower east side for Indian food. Little Italy was always a favorite. I remember my youngest sister, eight years my junior sitting in a highchair, her face and hands covered in smashed won-tons. These early memories shaped my ideas about the importance of exposing children to different types of foods before they begin to reject them.

Dietary trends and food fads come and go, and the most recent guidelines from the American Academy of Pediatrics (AAP) have reversed much of what I was taught during my training. But I wondered, what did people in other countries do? After all, children around the globe eat, grow, and thrive.

After my residency training, I joined a private practice in Santa Monica and had the continued good fortune of meeting families from all over the world. I asked mothers and fathers from diverse backgrounds, "What are the first foods given in your culture?" I was surprised by some of the answers. I learned that in Vietnam babies are fed a broth made of vegetables and then, later, of meat. As the baby grows, the broth becomes thicker and more substantial. In Sweden all babies eat a special porridge, which is such an important baby food in Swedish culture that the many Swedish families I took care of (nearly the entire Swedish population in Los Angeles!) would have it shipped to them. All these families taught me so much! As time passed, I evolved a hybrid philosophy of early feeding practices. Yes, I still start with rice cereal or a fruit or a vegetable, and I do recommend waiting a few days before introducing the next new food. But after a baby has experimented with a handful of simple foods, I feel comfortable exposing her to a wider selection of flavors and then textures. The more I learned about babies' diets from around the world, the more I realized that the rigid approach to early feeding practiced by American families leads to the diet of pizza and hot dogs preferred by so many children. Along the way, I had the opportunity to practice what I preached with my own two children who became my own living, eating lab rats.

Twenty years later I have built a pediatric practice that takes a holistic approach to all aspects of child-rearing, especially feeding and nutrition. I have always felt that part of my job as a pediatrician is not just to teach families the logistics of starting solid foods, but to have a dialogue about planning adventuresome meals that will enhance a child's physical, psychosocial, and emotional development.

Picky eating, obesity, and eating disorders are just some of the common food issues facing American families these days. I believe that *Smart Bites for Baby* is a wonderful first step in getting us on track to solve these problems. Infancy and early childhood are fantastic periods of growth and development. Infants will double their birth weight at about 4 months of age and triple it at a year! Imagine if we continued to gain weight at that pace—we would have 180-pound three-year-olds! During this crucial period of growth, the nervous system is rapidly myelinating (insulating), which requires cholesterol and fat as building blocks. The developing brain goes through an amazing process, akin to pruning a tree, reinforcing crucial neural connections and obliterating redundant ones. Exposing young children to healthy, tasty, flavorful foods stimulates the brain and offers a veritable feast. During this period, untold numbers of neural pathways are established that lay the foundation of how we will respond to a lifetime of sensory input.

We are due for a revolution in pediatric nutrition. Being attuned to developmental cues, introducing foods with varied colors and textures, and stimulating the palate from an early age are a smart approach to feeding your children and are the underlying principles in Mika Shino's *Smart Bites for Baby*. Introducing meals that incorporate global flavors and textures is not only enriching, it can foster a lifetime of good eating habits. With the help of *Smart Bites for Baby*, we can raise a healthier, happier next generation.

foreword

Bonnie Modugno, MS, RD, CLE, registered dietician

Feeding our children can be an overly anxious and emotionally charged task. Mika Shino brings a calming clarity to the challenge.

Food is a rich medium with many tangents. Social and cultural norms influence beliefs and behavior. Science infuses the discussion with concerns about calories and essential nutrients. The medical world measures growth and other markers of development. With this book, Mika Shino opens the discussion to a richer and wider realm, bridging the gaps.

Babies and children learn through food and with food at every stage of their lives. Breast-feeding and bottle feeding begin the adventure.

The Role of Solid Foods

Solid foods are typically introduced about 6 months of age. These early foods are a natural medium—and feeding time is a perfect opportunity—to explore each developmental stage. There is learning for everyone: baby, mother, father, and all other caregivers as well.

During feedings, babies, toddlers, and older children get to explore the rich colors, tastes, smells, and textures of food with their hands and their mouths, your hands and mouth, a spoon, a cup, and sometimes with their skin, their clothes, and even your clothes.

Babies learn to open and shut their mouth around their hand, a finger, and every object within reach. Older infants explore with food. Soon they learn to grasp at "finger foods" and begin to feed independently.

Each feeding lends itself to the large and small motor skills development needed for more sophisticated tasks that lie ahead, including verbal communication and play. Your baby's brain is very busy creating new neuronal pathways and networks.

Feeding is a time for children to explore a mix of sweet, sour, salty, and bitter tastes of food. But they also get to explore wet, dry, sticky, lumpy, and slick. Children will explore cold, warm, and, eventually, hot. If we let them, this is a time for young children to experience mild and spicy, sweet or savory, crunchy, crumbly, and mushy. Visual presentation and colors expand their horizons. This is the essence of *Smart Bites for Baby*.

Celebrating the Process

Introducing a new food, and every new feeding method, represents a milestone. Each attempt can be celebrated, no matter the outcome. Some babies readily accept different tastes, textures, smells, and colors. Others will benefit from enormous patience, repeated exposure, and carefully timed practice. Every new taste, smell, or texture constitutes a learning experience—especially those times when the food at hand doesn't quite make it inside the mouth or actually get swallowed.

Each time we slow down the process and calm our expectations, we allow our babies and children to tell us about themselves. Feeding during these tender years is about much more than just quieting hunger. It is not always easy or possible to engage in the process, but it is helpful to appreciate the opportunity at hand.

We get to learn what our children like—and what they don't. We get to observe what is easy and what is difficult. We get to see how they handle frustration. We get to encourage them as they build their resilience. We learn how to soothe and can help them learn how to self-soothe when they get overwhelmed. And we get to do it again and again. This is the essence of feeding our babies "brain food."

On Nutrition

Mika Shino's recipes are fabulously varied and inventive. Each one contributes nutrient density with the goodness of whole foods and champions essential nutrients, especially the often elusive Omega-3 fatty acids.

Experiment with different mixes of protein- and carboyhydrate-rich foods and vary the fat content. See what you learn about your child's energy needs and metabolism. A balanced mix of foods provides our children the energy they need to grow and develop. A good mix can positively influence a child's mood and disposition, while a poor mix of foods can contribute to an emotional tumble.

Smart Bites for Baby celebrates food's rightful place during a child's early years. How your baby responds to food is like a puzzle or code that you get to solve. All behavior is communication. *Smart Bites for Baby* is a warm and wonderful resource for the journey ahead.

Introduction

The birth of my baby boy was an elating experience, filled with joy and wonder.

But even as I welcomed Magnus into the world, I faced not only the anxiety of new motherhood, but the added stress of knowing that Magnus had been born with an abnormal liver. His doctors initially feared it was a rare disease called alpha 1-antitrypsin deficiency that often leads to complete liver failure, requiring a liver transplant. While, fortunately, this turned out not to be the case, the first months of his life were spent in hospitals and clinics, going from one specialist's office to another.

Like many parents of a child with a serious health condition, I felt frustrated at the lack of control I had in keeping him healthy. In those early days, we depended solely on the views of doctors and specialists. I summoned the courage to face the visits to the hospitals day after day, but I felt helpless during his painful interventions and blood work, sonograms of his organs, and the constant fasting he had to endure for the numerous tests; it was easy to give in to despair. But as Magnus grew stronger by the month, thriving first on breast milk and then on solid foods, I realized that there *was* something that I could determine and take control of for my baby's health. Besides providing love, support, and care for him, I saw that I could do my best to give my son the most nutritious foods possible to improve his overall health and growth.

I began to look fervently for resources for cooking for babies. What I found was only a handful of books of what I thought was underwhelming quality. Some had very few recipes; some were quite dated; others were extremely confusing; and still others were very limited in the range of flavors they presented. Many featured bland foods that I would not eat myself. Moreover, while I found multiple support systems for breastfeeding mothers, there was little available for new mothers who had to learn how to feed their babies beyond breast milk. I could not find a comprehensive book on feeding babies and toddlers, especially one that provided essential information on food safety, a very basic feeding guide, and reasons behind why certain foods should be introduced at different stages for a baby's growing digestive system. I struggled to find information in a variety of resources, which took energy and time that I did not have much of when my baby was 4 months old and ready for solids. I knew that I could not be the only mother who was concerned about infant nutrition.

The more I searched to find good nutritional information for my son's growing body in the existing literature, the more I became aware of the need for a holistic approach to food for a growing infant and child. What the infant eats nurtures his entire little body——his organs, bone structure, eyes, mouth, and brain. I was convinced that my son's condition could not be dealt with by simply feeding him foods aimed only to fortify his liver. He would have to take in vitamins and minerals that would strengthen his entire being.

The search for nutritious meals led me to learn about certain "superfoods"—foods that provide *more* than the essential nutrients found in protein, fats, and carbohydrates. They benefit specific human functions, such as blood circulation, bone growth, and the immune system. I was particularly inspired by the information in the field of cognitive developmental research about particular foods that support healthy brain function and development. I began to call certain foods that provided particularly brain-beneficial nutrients "brainfoods"—and for my son's food, "baby brainfoods." From that point on, I became much more conscious of everything I cooked, and I tried to include essential foods for healthy body and brain function in everything I made.

As I pored over the existing cookbooks for recipes for baby and toddler food, my most striking discovery was that all of them virtually ignored the importance of a meal's textures, flavors, scents, and visuals for a developing brain. In other words, no book that I found addressed how important food is as the principal source of brain stimulation. The oral senses are a major component in an infant's learning and growing process. Anyone with an infant knows that everything goes into the mouth; this is how an infant understands and connects with the new world around him. It's a fundamental part of a baby's life.

Between birth and 2 years of age, the human brain experiences exponential growth that will never repeat itself. This is the prime time to provide mental stimulation and enhance the receptivity of the palate. It makes perfect sense to approach nourishment from this perspective.

What surprised me the most was that in the last 15 years, the United States has undergone a significant shift in its eating and cooking culture, which includes a renewed emphasis on organic foods and receptiveness to world cuisine. But this great cultural transformation was only benefitting adults.

What Is *Smart Bites for Baby?*

Smart Bites for Baby is an alternative and original approach to cooking for and feeding babies and toddlers, focusing not just on fresh organic ingredients, but also on foods that scientific research has proven to enhance development and stimulation of the brain, mouth, and eyes. It entails an entirely different vision of food for young children—as a source of learning, physical and mental development, sensory stimulation, and fun. Eating, tasting, and feeling are developmental tools in and of themselves, and the entire process of feeding babies and children should be approached as such.

I wanted to cook foods for my baby that could stimulate his senses, boost his physical and mental development, and awaken his palate to appreciate a diverse array of flavors. I wanted to provide the foundation for him to experience food as an inspiring and exciting part of daily life.

I wanted to build up his resistance and, at the same time, allow him to have an open spirit toward food. The experience of eating, sharing, and sampling new flavors with loved ones is, for me, one of the most intimate and joyful activities we have as social beings. On the practical side, I also wanted to give him fresh, organic, and vitamin-packed meals without spending hours in the kitchen.

I began to experiment and research recipes from my Japanese cooking culture and realized that cooking for a baby and toddler in Japan always takes into consideration texture, color, and flavor to enhance mealtime experience and simultaneously stimulate the brain, eyes, and mouth. Some of those "brainfoods" also happen to be the main components of Japanese food—fatty fish, seaweed, and soy. Omega-3 fatty acids could be included in most meals after 8 months of age. It was natural, then, for me to turn to the basics of Japanese food when creating my recipes. It is also a Japanese approach to emphasize vegetables and fruits that reflect the flavor, color, and scent of the changing seasons. Following nature in this way allows the body to replenish itself with vitamins and minerals from seasonal ingredients that can specifically target the weather (for example, watermelon in the summer to cool the body, or chestnuts in the fall for complex carbohydrates).

This, in turn, inspired me to delve in to other countries' food cultures— starting with my husband's culture (Norway); then France, where I lived for over 15 years; then other European cultures; and then to Asian, African, and Latin American cultures. As I researched different cooking traditions, I found that all over the world, babies were being introduced to more variety and intensity in textures and flavors much earlier than babies in the United States, including spices and aromatics, as well as a diversity of tangy, tart, salty, and sweet tastes. In other words, babies' taste buds and palates were being challenged and stimulated in different ways all over the world while many children in the U.S. were being given the standard pureed food out of a jar, then on to chicken nuggets and mac-n-cheese on a daily basis.

As a result, the recipes in *Smart Bites for Baby* draw on world flavors, with the intention of introducing as much variety to the new, developing palate as possible and as early as possible. The ingredients call for organic, fresh, seasonal, and local produce.

I know that all parents want to provide optimal conditions for their babies and children so they grow up healthy and strong. How to give them the most well-balanced, nutritious meals possible, prepared with care, is what I have tried to share with my friends, and what I share with you now.

How to Use This Book

Chapters are organized by months, from the initial solid food feedings—sometime between 4 and 6 months (depending on the recommendation of your pediatrician on when you start solids for your baby), up to 3 years and beyond.

The first 8 months of a child's life are specifically geared toward your child's journey from experiencing simply breast milk or formula to a whole new world of sensations, looking at food as a sensory adventure in taste, texture, temperature (at this point, cold, warm, room temperature), touch, and smell. This is the time for your child to explore food to the maximum. According to registered dietician Bonnie Modugno, this phase has two objectives:

1. To introduce and increase the variety of foods in a safe and measured way.
2. To approach eating and food as developmental tools.

The physical aspect of eating marks a critical step in improving a child's motor skills, muscle development, and hand and eye coordination. These, in turn, all enhance the capacity for verbal communication.

As we move on toward 12 months and beyond, we will use recipes and quantities that are for family meals—recipes for kids and adults alike. These recipes are meant to help your child become receptive to a variety of flavors and textures, while not "overdoing it." While every stage of eating for a child presents challenges—introducing new sensations can mean dealing with phases of fussiness—it is important to remember that every phase also presents opportunities.

The recipes from 24 months on strongly emphasize variation in flavor combinations, surprising your child's palate with unexpected mixtures of tastes, smells, and textures. The recipes may seem to be more intricate, but it is mostly because of the unusual ingredients I use. Don't get discouraged; it is a lot simpler than it may first appear.

In this book, you will see a lot of recipes containing salmon, sardines, walnuts, flaxseeds, chia seeds, soybeans, seaweed, and eggs, among others. This is because these particular ingredients have the highest DHA Omega-3 fatty acids. I also thought it would be helpful to give options in cooking these Omega-3 rich foods, especially since many mothers often ask me for different ways to prepare the salmon that they so often just stick in the oven and then serve. You can use any other kind of fish, however, in the recipes that call for salmon, herring, cod, or sardines. When you see some of these key ingredients, you may wonder with a tinge of skepticism, "Seaweed? Will my baby eat seaweed?" You may be surprised. The key is to be open-minded about foods that you may not be familiar with yourself and allow your baby to be exposed to all kinds of foods.

If you are ever in doubt about any aspects of this book, talk to your pediatrician and follow the medical guidance. If your pediatrician recommends a different kind of diet for your baby, by all means, please follow his or her advice.

Thinking about Balance

In using this book, which contains recipes with varying nutritional focus—some centered on protein or on complex carbohydrates, others on fruits and vegetables, some on desserts/treats—it is important to be mindful of balance when feeding your child. Balance can mean several things: attention given to not overfeeding or underfeeding; the balance of protein, vegetables, and carbohydrate in a meal; and a balanced intake of vitamins and minerals from food.

For almost all of the recipes in this book, I use unprocessed whole foods, which are naturally rich in vitamins and minerals. I try to point out the nutritional value of an ingredient whenever it is first introduced in the book. Keep in mind, however, that while a recipe may primarily focus on a protein, carb, or a vegetable, a child should consume a balance of all three. To this end, nutritionist Bonnie Modugno suggests giving your baby one tablespoon of each—protein, vegetable, carbohydrate—and then when your baby has finished all of that, providing the next round of tablespoons. This helps prevent your child taking in only protein or only carbs, for example. Later on, as your child grows and begins to eat independently, you may find that your child will focus on eating one kind of food—say carbohydrates—for one meal or even for an entire day. But children will usually balance out their diet and consume protein the following meal or day, as well as vegetables, so rather than force your child to eat each food group in one sitting, you should allow your child to have some decision-making power on this (unless, of course, your child wants to eat only sweets all day long).

You will notice that I introduce desserts at the 9 to 11 month period, mostly with brown sugar or agave nectar used as sweeteners. I realize that many mothers today do not want to give any sweets to their young children, but I tend to think that sweets are a joyful part of life if made with unprocessed sugar and other healthy ingredients. I included many recipes I use for weekends and special occasions.

Brain Growth and World Flavors

There are many approaches and methods to feeding babies and toddlers, and I encourage everyone to learn and read as much as possible and to make choices that are right for them. For my part, with this cookbook, I wanted to go beyond thinking about food in its purest utilitarian form as simply calorie intake. For children, food is about joyfully exploring, discovering, and learning.

It is a scientific fact that children from birth to the age of 2 experience incredible brain growth and maintain an openness to trying new things that is unlike any other period in their lives. The opportunity is ripe to introduce foods that will nurture not only their physical growth, but their intellectual growth as well by tapping into the receptivity of their palate.

Moreover, introducing world flavors is also a way to connect your child to the richness of other cultures and traditions all over the globe. It is important for me to raise my child to be a world citizen, to be resilient when faced with challenges, curious to novelty, and enthusiastic about diversity. This is a small, but concrete, way for me to show him to not fear embracing new things, different cultures, and "foreign" places. It is all right there in our kitchen: we eat what the people of Morocco, Portugal, Senegal, Peru, and Thailand all eat. Food is a universal heritage that connects all of us. It doesn't matter where you go in the world, people bond by breaking bread together, and I want to share this heartening perspective with my son.

All of this inevitably means that you will have to spend a little more time and energy thinking about what you feed your baby, shopping for ingredients, and, of course, trying new recipes and getting accustomed to a new way of cooking and feeding. But if you have picked up this book, you are certainly someone who cares deeply about what your baby or toddler is eating. You are also ready to make a commitment to feed your child in ways that can have a positive impact. Not everyone can cook from scratch for every single meal, nor are they expected to do so. There is no pressure to make every meal a perfect "brainfood" meal. Parents have to find the right fit for their child, their family, as well as their time and energy. I hope that *Smart Bites for Baby* can help you in your efforts to find the right approach to food for your child.

The 5 Key Components of *Smart Bites for Baby* Recipes

Omega 3: The Essential Brain Oil

The benefits of DHA, an Omega-3 polyunsaturated fatty acid have long been known and accepted among many cultures. In Scandinavian countries, parents give daily spoonfuls of cod liver oil—a concentration of DHA—to their children from infancy. In most parts of Asia, fatty fish, such as mackerel and salmon, are part of their everyday meals.[*] Today we know that DHA is available from many sources: vegetables, seeds, sea vegetables, nuts, and fish, such as in flaxseed, walnuts, lingonberries, soybeans, seaweed, eggs, hemp seeds, blackberries, milk, and kiwi.

This fatty acid is an essential building block for the brain, as it makes up 25 percent of the total fat found in the brain. It is considered an "essential" nutrient because the body is not able to produce it in sufficient qualities to meet its physiological needs.[†] Studies have shown that children who have higher levels of DHA intake perform better in school, deal better with stress, and are able to focus for longer periods of time. There are also studies indicating they also have higher IQ scores.[‡]

The brain thrives on DHA, a fatty acid that specifically stimulates the functioning and development of the brain. The brain is 60 percent fat,

---

[*] "For centuries, fish has been considered "brain food" in cultures around the world. Generations of children were raised on a daily spoonful of cod liver oil because their parents had a general sense that "it was good for you." Recent medical research has bourn out this traditional wisdom. Today, the scientific community has come to recognize that important compounds contained in fish oils have profound benefits on human brain health, development, and behavior." Goeppe, Julius G., MD. "DHA and the Developing Brain," *Life Extension Magazine*, July 2006.

[†] Whitney, Ellie, and Sharon Rady Rolfes, *Understanding Nutrition*, 11th Edition, Thomson Learning Inc., 2008.

[‡] ". . . The astonishing effects of Omega-3 fatty acids—especially DHA—on human brain health and development have only emerged over the past 5 to 10 years, as scientists have uncovered powerful evidence . . . DHA appears to have beneficial effects after birth . . . boosting children's performance on various intelligence tests. DHA's importance in prenatal and infant brain development—and its impact on IQ, and other measures of cognition and vision are no longer in question. . . . behavioral scientists are now discovering that DHA supplementation in older children, teens, and even adults can have powerful and beneficial effects on behavior, mood, and learning. . . . DHA's stunning success in enhancing brain development and childhood IQ is likely to be a topic of intense study for decades." Goeppe, Julius G., MD. "DHA and the Developing Brain," *Life Extension Magazine*, July 2006.

and the main essential fatty acid in the brain is DHA. It is found in even greater quantities in the retina and is fundamental for the development of the eye.* Unfortunately, it has been shown that in many Western countries today, most of us are not getting even the minimum daily amount of DHA Omega-3 fatty acid required. Fatty fish, as well as other key DHA-rich foods are simply not part of the daily diet. In many recipes in Smart Bites for Baby, I've made a conscious effort to include this nutrient in your child's diet. I have also integrated other key components in brain development—iron, folic acid, anthocyanins—as well as key vitamins, antioxidants, and minerals that enhance physical growth and boost the immune system—such as beta-carotene, vitamins C, A, and D.

Varied Textures

Babies and toddlers are stimulated first and foremost by their physical receptors—mouth, fingers, hands, and skin. They understand and try to make sense of the world by feeling it. As parents, we have all seen that the oral receptors are especially critical to our infant—so much is discovered through the mouth and tongue. If an infant is constantly being fed mushy food, eating will not be a challenging or stimulating experience. Why lose out on this opportunity to wake up the senses and explore new sensations and flavors? Try to introduce different textures (when the infant is ready, of course) in every meal.

A Range of Flavors

As Dr. Lisa Stern mentions in her foreword, research has shown that diverse flavors physically stimulate the tongue and mouth in different ways. Salty, sweet, tangy—they all hit different sensory receptors located all over the tongue and the upper mouth, sending different signals to the brain, challenging it to open new neural channels with the newness of the taste.

During a child's first two years, the taste buds are wide open, waiting to sample whatever is presented. The more their taste buds are introduced to different flavors, the more their brains will be stimulated, and the

---

* Loh, Andrew. "Brain Food." www.brainy-child.com: All about Child Brain Development.

more receptive to a diversity of dishes the child will be in the future. In other words, if a child grows up eating a limited range of flavors and textures, it is only normal that, later on, they will have a more difficult time appreciating new or "unusual" foods. Studies have shown that the more a child is exposed to a variety of foods and flavors, the more likely they are to accept a wide diversity of foods later on in life.[*] These flavorful foods are safe for babies to consume because we are talking about whole, fresh organic foods and presenting a variety during one meal (the strong flavors of carrots, peas, and yogurt, for example). The key is to buy fresh and organic ingredients, locally produced when possible, and not to overcook them, as the cooking process impacts the intensity of flavor, especially for babies who cannot yet handle many kinds of raw foods.

The Visual Element
In Japan, and especially my hometown of Kyoto, food is an art form. It is as much about the way food *looks* as it is the flavor. The question of: *is it good?* is essentially linked to the question: *is it beautiful?* The presentation of the meal, the color combinations, and the attention to detail in the preparation, are all integral parts of cooking, eating, and fully experiencing food. We eat with our eyes, our nose, and our mouth. It is an entire experience. This aesthetic element to cooking produces a rich and varied visual stimulation to the brain. It also ensures that there is a variety of nutritional elements in the food.

First, for infants, a variety of colors keeps them interested in the food they are eating. It shows boundaries between foods and indicates by color the distinct taste of foods. If a 7-month-old infant is sitting in front of four small bowls containing yellow squash, green pureed peas,

[*] "Starting at around 4 to 6 months old, children become very open to new experiences and will try most any food," said Lucy Cooke of University College of London, who specializes in the development of childhood eating habits. . . . Studies, in both laboratories and natural settings, have shown that the more children are exposed to a food, the more likely they are to like it. . . . Cooke recommends using the window between 4 months to 2 years to expose children to as many different foods as possible. That way, when the pickiness of toddlerhood sets in, they are retracting from a larger repertoire." Nixon, Robin. "How to Handle Kids' Picky Eating," 24 November 2010, www.livescience.com.

white tofu, and mashed roasted red beets, it will be beautiful and amazing to look at.

Second, there is a nutritional benefit to offering colorful whole foods—a diverse array of vitamins and minerals. In the four bowls of food mentioned above, there is a range of phytonutrients and antioxidants—yellow foods (pumpkin, squash, carrots) contain beta-carotene which is a powerful antioxidant that protects cells from the damaging effects of free radicals, also boosting the immune system; green foods (spinach, collard greens) contain iron and folic acid or vitamin B9, which help with red blood cell production, enhance nerve function, and promote cell production in general; blue and violet foods (blackberries, blueberries, grapes) contain anthocyanins, which are antioxidants that can have positive effects on brain development, preventing memory loss and enhancing other cognitive capacities—for example, blueberries not only prevent the loss of brain fat, which causes brain aging, but can also *reverse* the degenerative effects of fat loss in the brain, and so on. Color is a strong indicator of the different nutritional elements contained in the food.

Deliciousness

The bottom line is that the food has to be delicious. Babies and toddlers are the first to reject a food that is not good. For a chef, children are the most demanding, trickiest, and pickiest eaters. So the foundation for every recipe in this book is that it has to be a wholesome and delicious meal that kids will enjoy, regardless of how good it is for them. They will love to eat it simply because it *tastes good*.

It is my hope that the same kind of respect and care that is routinely given to cooking for adults will be given to cooking for the smallest and youngest in our families and communities. What goes into their bodies and how it affects their budding bodies and brains is not a matter that should be taken lightly. It deserves at least the same level of careful attention, awareness, and care that we give when we prepare a meal for our most important dinner guests.

Supporting Research

Agostoni, C., S. Trojan, R. Bellu, E. Riva, and M. Giovannini. "Neurodevelopmental Quotient of Healthy Term Infants at 4 Months and Feeding Practice: The Role of Long-Chain Polyunsaturated Fatty-Acids," *Pediatrics* 38 (2) (August 1995): 262–6.

Auestad, N., D.T. Scott, J.S. Janowsky, et al. "Visual, Cognitive and Language Assessments at 39 Months: A Follow-Up Study of Children Fed Formulas Containing Long-Chain Polyunsaturated Fatty Acids to 1 Year of Age," *Pediatrics* 112 (3 pt 1) (September 2003).

Hirahama, S, T. Hamazaki, and K. Terasawa. "Effect of Decosahexaenoic Acid—Containing Food Administration on Symptoms of Attention-Deficit Hyperactivity Disorders—A Placebo-Controlled, Double-Blind Study," *European Journal of Clinical Nutrition* 58 (3) (March 2004): 467–73.

Innis, S.M. "Dietary Omega-3 Fatty Acids and the Developing Brain," *Brain* 9 (September 2008).

Itamura, M., K. Hamazaki, S. Sawazaki, et al. "The Effect of Fish Oil on Physical Aggression in Schoolchildren—a Randomized, Double-Blind, Placebo-Controlled Trial," *Journal of Nutritional Biochemistry* 16 (3) (March 2005): 163–71.

Politi, P., H. Cena, M. Comelli, G. Marrone, C. Allegri, et al. "Behavioral Effects of Omega-3 Fatty Acids Supplementation in Young Adults with Severe Autism: an Open Label Study," *Archives of Medical Research* 39 (7) (October 2008): 682–5.

Richardson, A.J., and P. Montgomery. "The Oxford-Durham Study: A Randomized, Controlled Trial of Dietary Supplementation with Fatty Acids in Children with Developmental Disorder." *Pediatrics* 115 (5) (May 2005): 1360–66.

Ross, B.M., I. McKenzie, I. Glen, and C.P. Bennett. "Increased Levels of Etane, A Non-Invasive Marker of N-3 Fatty Acid Oxidation in Breath of Children with Attention Deficit Disorder," *Nutritional Neuroscience* 6 (5) (October 2003): 277–81.

Young, G., and J. Conquer. "Omega-3 Fatty Acids and Neuropsychiatric Disorder," *Reproductive Nutritional Development* 45 (1) (January 2005): 1–28.

one

4 to 6 months
Introducing Solids

In the beginning, the best Smart Bites for your baby are organic, fresh, and, optimally, seasonal vegetables and fruits that are simply cooked for the best flavor intensity.

Each time a new flavor is introduced to the baby, it is a stimulating experience for her, and this experience is precisely what is challenging the palate and the senses. The food's consistency should be smooth and soft because the digestive system is not yet ready for texture.

You have several options when choosing what to serve initially. Some people like to start by giving their babies fruit, then vegetables; others like to stick to cereals for a few weeks before introducing anything else. Not only do different cultures feed their babies differently from the start, but even in the United States, there is no consensus on what specific food is the best to feed first. According to the American Academy of Pediatrics (AAP), "For most babies, the first solid food is rice cereal, followed by oatmeal and barley. . . . Meats can also be introduced as the first solid food, rich in iron and zinc. . . . If you started with cereal, and your baby has accepted it, you can introduce him to other foods slowly. One possible order is: meat, vegetable, fruits."[*] I followed my pediatrician's advice, which was to introduce white foods (rice, cereal, potatoes,

---

[*] American Academy of Pediatrics' The Complete and Authoritative Guide: Caring for Your Baby and Young Child, Birth to Age 5, American Academy of Pediatrics (Steven P. Shelov, M.D., F.A. A.P., Editor-in Chief, Robert E. Hannemann, M.D., F.A.A.P., Associate Medical Editor), Bantam Publishing, 2012, p. 215.

etc.) for two weeks, then yellow foods for two weeks, then greens for two weeks, and then a variety. I believe the rationale was that introducing the "white" foods, such as cereal, rice, and other vegetables, is safe because they are all very mild, both in flavor and in the digestive demands on an infant.

There are a variety of options for cooking food for your baby—steaming, poaching, roasting. At this point, any cooking method that does not add fats (oil, butter) is a good one. Use a steamer to cook fruits and vegetables until tender, or poach them in simmering water; strain them when necessary (pears, for example) and puree them with a food processor or blender. Detailed cooking instructions are provided in each recipe.

Food Safety and How to Store Food

Cooked food can be kept in the refrigerator for two or three days, and it will keep up to two to three months in the freezer. The food can be frozen in ice cube trays, stored in trays specifically designed for keeping baby food, or packaged in small individual containers. It is important to use glass containers and jars when possible, but if you use plastic, try to avoid using containers containing BPA (Bisphenol A) or POP (Persistent organic pollutant). BPA and POPs are known to disrupt metabolic functions in the body and, while there is no hard evidence on the effects of these plastics, they are considered to be harmful to babies and young children. (This is also why I avoid using canned tomatoes and other canned vegetables and fruits because there is often BPA plastic lining the cans.)

The best way to thaw foods before serving is in a bain-marie (put the food in a small pot, which is placed in a bigger pot with simmering water). Microwaving can potentially destroy some vitamins and produce hot spots in the middle of the food. It is not recommended to refreeze foods that have been thawed because this may allow bacteria to multiply in the food.

For safety, any food that is left on the plate or cup from which you are feeding your baby should not be refrigerated for later use; it should always be disposed of.

When to Introduce Solids

While there is a lack of scientific consensus on when it is best to intro-duce solids to a baby,* there are certain cues that you can observe that signal readiness. If your baby seems consistently hungry after feedings, even though he is consuming about 30 ounces per day of breast milk or formula, or your baby shows interest in whatever you or other adults are eating, you can try to introduce solids as early as the third month. It is important at this stage that your baby can hold her head upright without assistance. It is also important to note that most babies have a tongue-thrust reflex until about 4 months of age, which makes them push their tongues at anything inserted into their mouths (for example, a spoon), so 4 months is generally considered the earliest to introduce solid food. Babies develop differently, so please consult your physician before start-ing solids with your baby. Also, ask how much breast milk or formula your baby should be taking per day. For my son, our pediatrician recom-mended starting solid foods at 4 months; others might need to wait until 6 months.

How to Introduce Foods

There should be a three- to four-day waiting period when introducing new foods. Introduce one new food at a time, and then wait at least three or four days before introducing another. Use this time to monitor your child for any allergic reaction to a particular new food and to identify which food is causing the reaction. You should also pay close attention to food sensitivities in your child and watch if some foods are more difficult for your child to accept.

---

* "There is a difference of opinion on when to introduce solids. AAP says exclusive breast-feeding until 6 months, while the Committee on Nutrition supports the intro-duction of solids between 4 to 6 months." AAP Caring for Your Baby and Young Child, Ibid., p. 183.

What to Expect in the First Feedings

In the beginning, your baby will not know how to take food inside the mouth, and her meal will inevitably dribble down her little chin. My son was not able to swallow the solids for quite a long time, and everything that went into his mouth simply drooled back out, but he was happy with the new experience and enjoyed the new routine of being fed. Be patient with the first feedings (you will need a lot of patience with the feedings in general), and your baby will slowly learn to close her mouth and swallow—but it will take time. In Japan, the first feeding calls for a celebration, and the entire extended family, as well as friends, get together to watch the infant take her first "bite" and enjoy a meal together gathered around the baby. It is a joyous occasion and a big milestone for the baby.

How Much Do Babies Eat?

The quantity of food taken in a single meal will obviously vary among babies, and a lot depends on their weight, their development, and their mood for the day. An initial baby portion could be anywhere from one spoonful to five.

Feeding Guide:[*] **4 to 6 Months**
- Breast Milk or Formula: 4 to 6 feedings per day (28 to 32 ounces per day)
- Cereals: Gradually increase from 1 tablespoon to 3 to 5 tablespoons per day of single grain cereal, thinned with breast milk or formula
- Fruits: at 6 Months, 1 to 2 tablespoons per day, 1 to 2 times per day
- Vegetables: at 6 Months, 1 to 2 tablespoons per day, 1 to 2 times per day

[*] Lucile Packard Children's Hospital at Stanford University, www.lpch.org.

The key, however, is not to count exactly how many spoonfuls your baby did or did not eat but to carefully take cues from your baby regarding how much food should be given. If your baby turns her head away, or puckers her lips, or becomes antsy, it is time to stop. Any feeding beyond that point would be akin to forced feeding. The quantity that your baby eats will gradually and naturally increase with her growth.

Balance in the Meals

It is important to keep in mind the value of balance in a given meal as your child begins to wean off breast milk or formula. Once your baby is regularly eating solids and has begun to accept variety, try to provide a protein source, a carbohydrate, and a fruit/vegetable in every meal for the first year. The goal is to finish those three servings in each meal, and then add more as necessary. You can be confident that your child is not filling up on only one particular nutrient (for example, only eating carbs).

Foods You Can Introduce at 4 to 6 Months
Rice porridge
Rice cereal
Commercially sold single grain cereals
Udon noodles
Bananas
Potatoes
Sweet potatoes
Apples
Pears
Butternut squash
Peaches
Sweet peas

 porridge

Rice Porridge

Rice porridge is the foundation of Asian baby food, always made from scratch with rice that has been carefully rinsed and boiled softly until very tender. The very first feeding should be only a very small quantity (1 teaspoon) of the cooked rice with the rice liquid (1 tablespoon). You can prepare 3 to 4 tablespoons, which you should mash until it's very smooth, or puree. This recipe is for 4 to 6 feedings, depending on how much porridge your baby consumes. You should only feed your baby ¼ teaspoon at a time for her first feedings, and you may only get a total of one or two teaspoons in her mouth (although I have known several babies who began to eat their first meals with incredible enthusiasm, eating a few tablespoons—much to the surprise of everyone). With each feeding, you can slowly increase the proportion of rice to water.

> ¼ cup rice, ideally Japanese rice or any kind of short grain rice, as they are higher in starch and cook to a smoother porridge-soup consistency
> 2½ cups water

1 Wash the rice thoroughly in cold water until the water runs clear.

2 Put the rice and water in a small pot and bring to a boil; lower the heat and simmer for 40 minutes, covered, stirring occasionally. If a film develops on top, remove it using a spoon.

3 When the rice has been cooked until it has a soupy texture, remove from heat and let cool.

4 Puree in a food processor until completely smooth.

5 Serve at room temperature.

Udon Porridge

Udon noodles are thick, soft noodles made from rice powder. They are very mild, which is perfect for young bellies. You can find these noodles in most Whole Foods stores and supermarkets in the Asian foods section.

¼ cup udon rice noodles, chopped
2½ cups water

1 In a large pot, combine 2½ cups of water and the noodles and boil for 1 minute. Reduce the heat to low and simmer until the noodles are very soft, about 15 to 20 minutes.

2 Drain the noodles through the strainer; reserve some of the cooking liquid.

3 Puree the noodles in a food processor until completely smooth, adding some of the cooking liquid to thin the porridge.

4 Let cool and serve at room temperature.

Commercial Cereal

Commercially available cereal (rice, barley, millet, or oatmeal), made with water or breast milk, is an alternative to cooking porridge from scratch. The texture is definitely different. Today, cereals contain added vitamins and minerals and are a good alternative to making each baby meal from scratch. Consider alternating between freshly made porridge and dry, ready-made ones.

Prepare commercial cereals according to the instructions on the package.

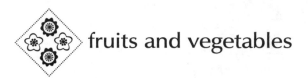 fruits and vegetables

Ripe Bananas

Bananas can be fed raw or cooked, and they are packed with potassium, vitamins A and C, folate, calcium, protein, and a good amount of Omega-3 fatty acid.

1 banana

1 Cut the banana into small pieces and mash it with a spoon until smooth.
2 Add breast milk to give a thinner consistency.
3 You can also heat the banana and milk mixture in a small pot for 2 to 3 minutes.
4 Let cool and serve.

Potatoes

Potatoes are a starch, but they also supply protein, as well as other vitamins and minerals—potassium, vitamins A and K, folate, calcium, and Omega-3 fatty acid. They are a good mild first food for your baby.

2 potatoes

1 Preheat the oven to 425°F.
2 Wash the potatoes; wrap them in foil; and bake them for 45 minutes or until tender when pierced with a toothpick or knife.
3 Scoop out the flesh of the potatoes and puree in a food processor until completely smooth. Add breast milk or water to thin, as appropriate.
4 Serve at room temperature.

ALTERNATIVE OPTION: Wash the potatoes; peel them and cut into small pieces. Put in a steamer and cook for 20 minutes or until tender. Puree in a blender, adding breast milk or water to thin as needed. Serve.

Sweet Potatoes

Sweet potatoes are packed with beta-carotene, as well as folate, calcium, and some protein and Omega-3 fatty acids. They are sweeter and more moist than white potatoes, adding a nice variety in your baby's first foods.

2 sweet potatoes

1 Preheat the oven to 425°F.

2 Wash the sweet potatoes; wrap them in foil; and bake them for 45 minutes or until tender when pierced with a toothpick or knife.

3 Scoop out the flesh of the sweet potatoes and puree in a food processor until completely smooth. Add breast milk or water to thin, as appropriate.

4 Serve at room temperature.

ALTERNATIVE OPTION: Wash the sweet potatoes; peel them and cut into small pieces. Put in a steamer and cook for 20 minutes or until tender. Puree in a blender, adding breast milk or water to thin as needed. Serve.

Butternut Squash

This delicious, sweet vegetable has a very hard skin, so be careful when peeling, or buy it peeled and cut up. It is loaded with beta-carotene, and it also contains Omega-3 fatty acids, vitamin C, folate, and calcium, among other vitamins and minerals.

1 butternut squash

1 Preheat oven to 425°F.

2 Peel the skin, and cut the squash in half.

3 Scoop out the seeds and the stringy section in the middle. Place squash on a baking sheet covered with foil, cut side down.

4 Roast squash for 45 minutes or until the flesh is tender when poked with a toothpick or knife.

5 Remove from the oven and let cool slightly.

6 Puree the cooked flesh in a blender or food processor until smooth. Add breast milk or water as necessary.

7 Serve.

Peaches

I feel the best way to peel a peach is using a French technique called *monder*—dunk the peaches in boiling water for a few seconds, and then immediately immerse them in cold ice water. The fuzzy skin will peel right off without bruising the tender flesh. If you just don't have the energy or the time, by all means, simply peel them. Peaches contain protein, vitamins A, C, K, calcium, magnesium, potassium, as well as a small quantity of Omega-3 fatty acid.

2 ripe peaches

1 Peel the peaches, either using the *monder* technique or by simply peeling them with a knife. Cut them into small pieces and place in a steamer.

2 Steam for 3 minutes or until the pieces are soft when pierced.

3 Puree in a blender or processor and serve.

Green Sweet Peas

Peas have a light outer skin that can make digestion difficult for some babies. If necessary, remove the skin by hand after the peas have been steamed to avoid gassiness. Peas contain protein, vitamins C and K, folate, as well as a good amount of Omega-3 fatty acid.

1 cup peas, fresh or frozen

1 Wash the peas in water.
2 Place in a steamer and cook for 5 to 10 minutes if using frozen peas, 3 to 5 minutes for fresh peas. (Interestingly, I have found that frozen organic sweet peas taste sweeter than fresh ones from the pod.)

Apples

I use Fuji apples most often because they are not tart, and they have more flavor than Delicious or Golden Delicious. Apples have a good amount of vitamin A, as well as potassium, calcium, and phosphorus, and they are great raw, pureed, baked, or frozen.

2 apples (Fuji, Golden Delicious, or Honeycrisp)

1 Peel the apples, and then cut them into small pieces.
2 Steam them for 4 minutes or until the flesh is tender when pierced.
3 Place the apple pieces in a blender with some of the cooking liquid and puree until smooth.

two

7 months
Stepping It Up

At 7 months, depending on when your baby was introduced to solids, you can begin to introduce more flavors and textures in his meals.

There are no absolutes that signal readiness for changes in texture in your baby's food—it's simply trial and error. If your baby responds well to a slight modification in the texture or flavor of the food, keep going and continue to diversify. If there is refusal, you can step back and proceed more slowly, delaying the introduction of new flavors and textures, and interspersing them more gradually. Following the 4-day feeding rule for introducing new foods, slowly increase the thickness of the pureed food that you are preparing.

How to Introduce Foods

This should be a very gentle process, keeping in mind that your baby's tummy is still fragile and growing accustomed to receiving and digesting solids. By the 8th month, your baby will generally be able to eat more foods that maintain their own shape (rice begins to look like rice), rather than being completely pureed into a mash. Carefully monitor your baby's reaction to the new flavors and textures and match his progress according to his unique rhythm. As always, consult your pediatrician if you have any questions or concerns.

The more variety in flavors, colors, and textures that you can provide in each meal, the more exciting the entire eating experience becomes for your baby. Instead of mashing and pureeing everything together, set up small bowls of different and brightly colored purees and alternate the spoonfuls of food by giving one spoonful of, say, tofu, then another spoonful of pureed squash. It will be stimulating for your baby to taste, smell, and see variation in the food that he is eating.

What to Feed Your 7-Month-Old

Experts differ on what you can feed your baby at various stages, and cultures vary in their guidelines for food and milk consumption. In Japan for example, we don't have strict rules on what to feed when: tomatoes are given to babies at 7 months, while in the United States, not until 12 months. In writing this book, I took a very conservative approach by listing what is considered acceptable for babies in the United States, as recommended by the American Academy of Pediatrics. But I tried many other foods beyond this list, and my son loved eating them. This is not an exhaustive list, and you should always discuss with your pediatrician what your child can eat at this stage; they, too, have their own recommendations. Everyone agrees that the obvious foods to avoid are fruits with strong flavors, like strawberries and oranges, and vegetables that could cause gassiness, like broccoli and cauliflower.

Feeding Guide: 7 Months
- Breast milk/Formula: 3 to 5 feedings per day (30 to 32 ounces per day)
- Cereal: 3 to 5 tablespoons mixed with formula/breast milk per day
- Fruits: 2 to 3 tablespoons, 2 times per day
- Vegetables: 2 to 3 tablespoons, 2 times per day
- Meats/Protein: 1 to 2 tablespoons, 2 times per day
- Juice: 2 to 4 ounces per day
- Snacks: toast, crackers, etc.

Foods You Can Introduce at 7 Months:

Brown rice
Tofu
Carrots*
Apples
Pears
Peas
Green beans
Oatmeal
Butternut squash
Potatoes
Peaches
Dried fruits
Asparagus
White fish
Chicken
Turkey
Lamb
Cereals, like millet, amaranth, and quinoa
Legumes, like lentils and split peas
Yogurt[†]
Cottage cheese
Egg yolk, cooked

---

[*] AAP warns that the following foods have nitrate risks due to the intake of naturally occurring nitrates and should be avoided before the age of 3 months: green beans, squash, beets, turnips, carrots, collard greens, and spinach.

[†] While milk is not to be introduced to your baby until at least 1 year, yogurt and other dairy products are acceptable because lactose, which is difficult for your baby's digestive system to handle, is broken down in yogurt or cheese. The culturing of yogurt or cheese removes or limits the milk proteins. Milk can, however, be used in baking after 7 months, www.babycenter.com.

 porridge

Rice Porridge

At 7 months, you can begin to slowly decrease the water used to cook the rice in order to increase the texture of the porridge. Carefully observe your baby as you introduce this textured porridge and take cues from her reaction. If she refuses the thicker consistency, keep the porridge runny (per recipe in chapter 1) and wait a few more days or even a week before trying again. There is no rush. Texture should be increased little by little, and according to the level of acceptance, which differs from one baby to another.

> ½ cup rice, ideally Japanese rice or any kind of short grain rice, as they are higher in starch and cook to a smoother porridge-soup consistency
> 2½ cups water

1 Wash the rice thoroughly in cold water until the water runs clear.

2 Put the rice and water in a small pot and bring to a boil; lower the heat and simmer for 40 minutes, covered, stirring occasionally. If a film develops on top, remove it using a spoon.

3 When the rice has been cooked until it has a soupy texture, remove from heat and let cool.

4 Mash with a spoon for more texture than the porridge served to your 4- to 6-month-old.

5 Serve at room temperature.

Udon Porridge

A similar approach to the rice porridge should be taken for the udon porridge. Pay close attention to your baby's reaction and take cues from her. Try to slowly increase texture by not pureeing the noodles, but by mashing them instead.

> ½ cup udon rice noodles, chopped
> 2½ cups water

1 In a large pot, combine 2½ cups of water and the noodles and boil for 1 minute. Reduce the heat to low and simmer until the noodles are very soft, about 15 to 20 minutes.

2 Drain the noodles through the strainer; reserve some of the cooking liquid.

3 Mash the udon noodles slightly rather than pureeing them as done in the 4 to 6 month period.

4 Let cool and serve at room temperature.

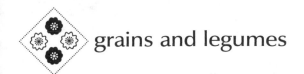# grains and legumes

Lentils

Lentils are a light legume, surprisingly high in Omega-3 fatty acids, as well as iron, fiber, protein, and vitamins A, B1, and K. They are easier to prepare than other legumes because you don't have to soak them overnight. Lentils can serve as a foundation of your child's meals, just like textured rice porridge. And similarly, the idea is to keep reducing the amount of water as your baby grows in order to provide more and more texture. At this stage, the lentils are pretty neutral in flavor, just like the other porridges, but as your baby gets older, you can integrate other elements that will add flavor, such as onions, celery, olive oil, and pancetta.

1 cup lentils
1 carrot

1 Rinse the lentils and discard any discolored pieces. Drain.

2 Wash, peel, and dice the carrot into small pieces.

3 Bring 4 cups of water, lentils, and carrots to a boil in a large pot; cover and simmer until the lentils are very tender, approximately 30 to 40 minutes.

4 Mash them with a spoon or puree in the food processor.

5 Serve warm, cold, or room temperature, along with a vegetable or a fruit compote or puree.

Brown Rice Puree

Brown rice is more difficult for babies to digest because of its bran, which contains the nutrients and fiber that white rice does not have. It is important to puree brown rice well before serving.

¼ cup brown rice

1 Bring rice and 4 cups of water to a boil, and boil uncovered for 1 minute.
2 Cover the pot and reduce the heat. Cook the rice on low heat for 40 minutes.
3 Remove from the heat and drain. Allow to cool for 10 minutes.
4 Transfer rice to a blender and puree until smooth.

Oatmeal Puree

Oatmeal is a powerful grain that contains high amounts of fiber, folates, vitamins, and minerals.

¼ cup whole oats

1 In a food processor, grind the oats to a fine powder.
2 Bring the oats and 3 cups of water to a boil. Reduce the heat and cook until the oats are soft, approximately 20 minutes on low.
3 Remove from heat and let cool. This puree can be mixed with fruit purees, breast milk, or water.

Tofu

Tofu is a great source of protein—it is considered a source of complete protein, the kind that is found in red meats—and has a neutral flavor that can be infused with many other flavors to create savory dishes, as well as sweet. Most supermarkets carry tofu in their refrigerated section near the dairy or in the international food section.

1 cup of soft tofu

1 Remove the tofu from its packaging and rinse it under cold running water. On a cutting board, cut it into small pieces.
2 Place a quarter of the tofu in a small pot, adding water to cover it completely. Store the remaining tofu in an airtight container filled with water and refrigerate for later use (keep for up to 2 days after opening).
3 Bring the pot of water with tofu to a boil and let simmer for 2 minutes.
4 Remove from heat and allow the tofu to cool, discarding the water.
5 Put tofu in a small bowl and mash it with a spoon.
6 Serve tofu by itself during the 4-day waiting period when introducing new foods. Later, you can add a teaspoon of fruit puree or egg yolk.

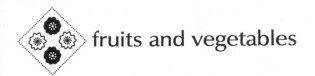 fruits and vegetables

Mango Puree

Mangos are packed with vitamin C, and its sweet flavor and wonderful bright color make it a great dish for babies.

1 fresh or ½ cup frozen mango

1 If you are using fresh mango, note that its pit is shaped like an oblong disk, making it sometimes difficult to remove the flesh. The easiest way is to cut the fruit in two pieces, slicing on either side of the pit, leaving the skin on. Turn each piece skin side down and scrape out the flesh using a spoon or by cutting it lengthwise and crosswise into squares, then removing the peel.

2 Put the flesh into a steamer and cook for 3 minutes.

3 Puree until completely smooth (mango can contain fiber-like ligaments), and then serve.

4 When the baby is a few months older, mango can be served raw, cut into small pieces.

Zucchini

Zucchini is packed with vitamins C, A, and Bs, Omega-3 fatty acids, fiber, magnesium, calcium, iron, and protein. Eliminate all of the seeds, and puree the vegetable very well to a very smooth consistency.

1 fresh zucchini

1 Wash the zucchini.

2 Cut the vegetable lengthwise, scoop out the seeds, and cut into small pieces.

3 Steam until the flesh is tender when touched with a knife, approximately 5 to 10 minutes.

4 Puree in a blender until completely smooth.

Spinach

Spinach is a superfood with vitamins K, A, C, and Bs, as well as high levels of folate, magnesium, manganese, iron, fiber, Omega-3 fatty acids, zinc, protein, and copper. The brighter green the leaves, the more nutritious they are, so choose the most vibrant spinach you can find.

2 cups fresh baby spinach

1. Wash spinach leaves. Remove and discard any white stems.

2. Steam the leaves until they have wilted and soft and mushy, approximately 3 to 5 minutes. Remove the leaves and drain, reserving the cooking liquid.

3. Puree leaves in a blender until smooth, adding the cooking liquid or breast milk to thin the puree as necessary.

Pears

Pears can sometimes cause gassiness in babies, so monitor your baby's reaction and make sure that he is responding well to the fruit. When buying pears, you should choose those that are not too overripe.

2 ripe organic pears

1. Peel the pears, and then cut into small pieces.

2. Steam until the flesh is tender when pierced with a knife, approximately 4 minutes.

3. Put the pieces with some of its cooking liquid into a blender and puree until smooth.

Avocado

Avocado is yet another superfood containing unusual amounts of carotenoids like beta-carotene, and fatty acids, like oleic acid, which is found in olives and olive oil. It also contains vitamins K, C, and Bs, fiber, potassium, folate, and copper. The most nutritious part of the avocado is the dark green flesh closest to the skin, so the vegetable should be peeled with your hands rather than cut in order to retain the maximum amount of the green portion. Just start peeling from the top and work your way down. It is a dry and brittle skin and comes off rather easily when it is ripe.

1 fresh ripe avocado

1. Peel the avocado with your hands and cut it in half, or cut the avocado in half with a knife, and then remove the skin.

2. Remove the pit in the middle and mash the flesh with a fork until smooth and "whipped."

Plums

Plums come in an array of colors and shapes and are packed with vitamin C and A, fiber, and potassium.

4 to 6 small ripe plums

1. Peel the plums with a knife, and then cut them into small pieces, discarding the pit.

2. Steam until tender when pierced with a knife, approximately 3 minutes.

3. Puree in a blender or a food processor until smooth.

Apricots

Apricots are full of beta-carotene and fiber, as well as vitamin C. The beautiful orange color is a wonderful visual for your baby. When buying apricots, choose those that are not too overripe because that texture can be too mushy for a nice puree.

4 to 6 small ripe apricots

1 Peel the apricots, either by the *monder* technique—dunking them into boiling water for 3 to 4 seconds, then immediately dunking them into ice water to loosen the skins—or by simply cutting the peel off with a knife. (This latter method can be quite difficult when the apricots are too ripe and often makes waste by cutting too deep into the flesh.)

2 Cut the apricots into small pieces, discarding the pits. Steam until tender when pierced with a knife, approximately 3 minutes. Put into a blender or a food processor and puree until smooth.

Asparagus

Asparagus is a delicate vegetable and more perishable than other vegetables. To obtain the most nutrients, it is better to consume it as fresh as possible. Make sure the asparagus you buy is not wrinkled or shriveled because that indicates it has been sitting on the shelf too long. Asparagus is packed with vitamin K, folate, vitamins C, A, and Bs, as well as protein, potassium, iron, zinc, and magnesium. When steamed or boiled and pureed, it has a bit of a slippery texture that is fun for your baby to explore.

Bunch of asparagus

1 Cut off the white ends of the asparagus stalks and discard. Gently peel the outer layer of the stalk with a peeler, only up to the beginning of the tip. Then cut the stalks into small pieces.

2 Put pieces in a steamer or boil them in a pot of water with a pinch of salt. Cook until tender when pierced with a knife, approximately 5 minutes.

3 Drain, reserving the cooking liquid in a separate bowl.

4 Puree with a small amount of the cooking liquid until completely smooth.

5 Serve 3 tablespoons of the pureed asparagus in a bowl; store the rest in the refrigerator or freezer for later use. Pureed asparagus can be served with a teaspoon of boxed cereal to give a thicker consistency.

Carrots

Carrots contain powerful antioxidants, like beta-carotene, as well as phytonutrients, which prevent oxidatine damage (damaging of cells by free radicals) to our body. It also contains vitamins A, K, C, and Bs, fiber, and potassium. I think carrots taste best steamed, so I would recommend that over boiling.

3 fresh organic carrots

1 Cut the tips off both ends of the carrot. Then peel the outer layer with a peeler.

2 Cut the carrots into small pieces and put in a steamer or in a pot of boiling water. Cook carrots until completely soft, approximately 7 to 10 minutes.

3 Puree in a blender or food processor until completely smooth.

4 Pureed carrots can be served with a teaspoon of boxed cereal or a tablespoon of tofu.

Green Beans

Green beans contain high amounts of anti-oxidants, as well as vitamins K, C, and A, manganese, fiber, folate, and iron. They taste best when in season and, while it is a bit labor intensive to pick off the ends and the fiber that runs along the bean, it's worth the effort. Green beans have the best flavor when fresh rather than frozen.

1 cup fresh organic green beans

1 Wash the green beans in cold water. Cut off the two ends of each bean, allowing the thin stringy section from one side to peel off with one end.

2 Cut the beans into small pieces and place in a steamer. Cook until the pieces are soft when pierced, approximately 3 to 5 minutes.

3 Drain.

4 Put the beans into a blender and puree until smooth.

dairy and egg

Yogurt

My pediatrician recommended yogurt and cottage cheese at this age, and my son loved the textures and flavors of both. These foods are a great way to provide extra calcium as your child begins to wean from breast milk.

½ cup yogurt (Greek strained yogurt is good for its neutral flavor)
3 tablespoons of Apple Puree (page 24) or ½ mashed banana

1 In a small bowl, combine yogurt with the fruit. Mix thoroughly with a spoon, adding ½ teaspoon of boxed cereal if desired.

2 Serve.

Cottage Cheese

Cottage cheese comes in several varieties. I prefer to buy the small curd, full-fat cottage cheese because it has good texture and rich flavor.

3 tablespoons cottage cheese

1 Mash the cottage cheese in a small bowl with a spoon and serve plain during the 4-day waiting period. After that, you can serve it with a teaspoon of fruit puree added.

Egg Yolk

While it is not recommended to give babies at this age whole eggs, the egg yolk is acceptable and contains great nutrients and Omega-3 fatty acids. You can mash it together with the other fruits or vegetables that your baby has already tried and accepted without an allergic reaction.

2 eggs
1 teaspoon salt

1 Place 2 eggs, shell on, in a pot and cover with water. Add salt (the salt is to coagulate the white of the egg if the shell cracks during boiling).

2 Bring to a boil and cook 5 to 6 minutes.

3 Remove the eggs from the pan with a ladle and immerse them in a bowl of cold water for 5 minutes.

4 Peel one egg (put the other in the fridge for later use), and remove the cooked yolk.

5 Put the yolk in a small bowl and mash it with a spoon, adding breast milk or water to modify the powdery consistency of the yolk.

three

8 months
Raw Foods and New Combinations

Your baby is now ready for more raw foods: fresh apricots, apples, melons and cantaloupes, quartered and peeled grapes, sliced kiwi, plums, and watermelon are all good options.

Your baby is also ready to experience mixed flavors, as well as more texture in the food. Dried fruit purees and compotes are great additions to fresh fruits because they contain iron, fiber, and vitamin C from the drying process, which concentrates nutrients and calories, and they have a rich and dense flavor. Choose organic dried fruits without chemicals or additives, if possible.

The goal in this phase is to introduce a broad range of foods so that your child will be ready for a diet consisting mainly of solid foods starting at 12 months. Breast milk or bottled milk will be reduced to approximately 24 ounces a day, depending on your pediatrician's recommendations, and water or juice will decrease to around 4 ounces a day. Your child will get more and more of her nutrients and vitamins from solids.

Your baby needs between 750 to 900 calories each day, and about 400 to 500 of those should come from breast milk or formula (approximately 24 ounces).[*]

---

[*] AAP, Ibid., p. 251.

Feeding Guide: 8 Months:[*]
- Milk: 3 to 5 feedings per day, 30 to 32 ounces per day
- Cereals: 5 to 8 tablespoons per day
- Fruits: 2 to 3 tablespoons, twice a day
- Vegetables: 2 to 3 tablespoons, twice a day
- Meat and Protein: 1 to 2 tablespoons, twice a day
- Juice: 2 to 4 ounces per day
- Snacks: yogurt, crackers

Sample Menu for 8- to 12-Month-Old:[†]

Breakfast: ¼ to ½ cup cereal or mashed egg yolk, ¼ to ½ cup fruit, 4 to 6 ounces formula or breast milk

Snack: 4 to 6 ounces juice, ¼ cup diced cheese

Lunch: ¼ to ½ cup yogurt, ¼ to ½ cup yellow vegetable, 4 to 6 ounces formula or breast milk

Snack: ¼ to ½ cup diced cheese

Dinner: ¼ cup diced poultry, ¼ to ½ cup green vegetable, ¼ cup noodles, ¼ cup fruit, 4 to 6 ounces formula or breast milk

Bedtime: 6 to 8 ounces breast milk or formula

This is also the time to begin introducing (always in consultation with your pediatrician) ground seeds, such as flaxseeds, and ground nuts. Almond and almond butter[‡] can be introduced at this point because almonds are botanically a fruit seed and not a nut.[§] Peanuts are different,

---

[*] Lucie Packard Children's Hospital at Stanford University, www.lpch.org.

[†] AAP., Ibid., p. 256.

[‡] There is no consensus regarding when nuts should be introduced to the baby. In 2008, AAP issued a Policy Statement that notes, "Although solid foods should not be introduced before 4-6 months of age, there is no current convincing evidence that delaying their introduction beyond this period has significant protective effect on the development of atopic disease. . . . This includes delaying the introduction of foods that are considered to be highly allergic, such as fish, eggs, and foods containing peanut protein." Frank R. Greer, MD, Scott H. Sicherer, MD, A. Wesley Burks, MD, and the Committee on Nutrition and Section on Allergy and Immunology, Clinical Report, AAP Policy, "Effects of Early Nutritional Interventions on the Development of Atopic Disease in Infants and Children: The Role of Maternal Dietary Restriction, Breastfeeding, Timing of Introduction of Complementary Foods, and Hydrolyzed Formulas," *Pediatrics* 121 (January 1, 2008): 183–191.

[§] Please check with your pediatrician before introducing all fruit nuts and nuts. While not all children/adults with potential allergies to nuts are also allergic to fruit nuts, it is safer to check first.

however; more children are prone to allergies from peanut protein, and most pediatricians recommend waiting until 12 months to introduce them. The AAP has stated that there is no evidence that waiting until later to introduce foods, even peanuts, guarantees allergy prevention. An exciting addition at this phase is kelp and other kinds of seaweeds, which are packed with superfood nutrients like Omega-3 fatty acids and antioxidants.

For textures, this is the time to go beyond smoothly pureed food. Try to cut food into small pieces after it is well steamed, in order to introduce new textures. Or, when introducing fruits that you pureed in the beginning (prunes, apricots, etc.), try combining them with textured rice porridge or other kinds of porridge. Slowly and gradually decrease the amount of water you use to prepare them. Your baby may not "get it" and not appreciate those new sensations the first few times he or she tries new textures, but keep at it, and she will soon understand that food comes in different forms, shapes, and sizes. One way to do this is to put food in separate bowls—one bowl with the varied texture of rice, udon noodles, or oatmeal porridge. Add flavors with other bowls of fruit or vegetable purees. This way, if the baby does not eat any of the textured food in the beginning, you can switch mid-meal and offer the pureed food until your baby is comfortable with the new feeling in her mouth when chewing. The idea is to use the textured porridge as a base, integrating different new flavors with the purees.

Each ingredient that is introduced will be a building block for the Smart Bites recipes. Remember to keep following the 4-day rule when introducing new foods to your baby, carefully watching for allergic reactions to any of the foods. For nuts and seeds, consult with your pediatrician first, as many children could be prone to allergies.

You will see that this month I introduce soy sauce. Buy the low-sodium kind, which is available now in most supermarkets, or dilute regular by half with water.

As you begin to introduce more solids, you should be aware of choking dangers. You should never offer peanut butter, raw carrot, whole nuts, whole grapes, popcorn, hard candies, or other hard round foods like hot dogs.[*]

Foods You Can Introduce at 8 Months:
  Ground nuts
  Ground seeds
  Zucchini
  Leeks
  Parsnip
  Wheat germ
  Cheese (mild cheese, like Mozzarella, American, Emmental)
  Kelp and other seaweeds
  Watermelon
  Stone fruits, such as plums and apricots
  Grapes
  Kiwi
  Melon (cantaloupe, honeydew)
  Broccoli[†]
  Blueberries
  Avocado

[*] AAP, Ibid., p. 252.

[†] Broccoli is safe to give to your baby at 8 months. If your baby has had digestive issues, however, it would be better to wait and introduce it at 10 to 12 months.

porridge and cereal

Textured Rice Porridge

The rice porridge will be thicker and less soupy than that served at younger ages, as your baby begins to appreciate textures. The rice will begin to look more and more like rice, and less like broth.

½ cup rice
2 cups water

1 Wash rice thoroughly in cold water until the water runs clear.

2 Put the rice and 2 cups of water in a pot. Bring to a boil, and then lower heat and let simmer for 20 to 30 minutes, covered, stirring occasionally. If a clear film develops on top, remove it with a spoon.

3 When the rice has been cooked until it has a soupy texture, yet retains some shape of rice (a puffy round shape), remove it from the heat and let cool before serving.

Textured Udon Porridge

Similar to the rice porridge, the udon porridge also will begin to take on more texture.

⅓ cup udon rice noodles, chopped

1 In a large pot, combine the noodles and 3 to 4 cups of water. Bring to a boil and boil for 1 minute. Lower the heat to low and simmer until the noodles are very soft, approximately 15 to 20 minutes.

2 Drain the noodles through the strainer, reserving some of the cooking liquid.

3 In a small bowl, mash 3 to 4 tablespoons of noodles lightly with a spoon. Add the cooking liquid to smooth the texture, then mash noodles completely to a mush.

Textured Steel Cut Oatmeal

Steel cut oatmeal takes longer to cook than dried whole oats, but it has better flavor and more interesting texture than rolled oats. Make sure the oatmeal is cooked thoroughly and is very tender before serving. Different brands of oatmeal have different consistency, so check the softness before serving because cooking times may differ according to the brands.

⅓ cup steel cut oats

1 In a pot, bring 5 cups of water to a boil. Add the oats; reduce the heat to low and simmer for 40 to 60 minutes, stirring occasionally.

2 Taste to make sure the oats have softened sufficiently and remove from heat. If you find that they are still too hard, you can add another ½ cup water and cook for another 10 minutes.

3 Repeat until the oats are sufficiently soft.

4 Let cool and serve with a fruit puree.

Textured Couscous

Couscous originated in North Africa and is still a daily staple in countries like Tunisia, Morocco, and Egypt. It has a light grain that fluffs up when cooked and absorbs sauces very well. It is high in protein, folate, and calcium, and has small amounts of Omega-3 fatty acid.

⅓ cup couscous (your choice of variety)

1 In a large pot, bring 3 cups of water to a boil. Add the couscous; lower the heat to low and simmer for 10 to 15 minutes.

2 The couscous should not be dry, but wet and runny with the grains intact but still very soft—if not, add more water to make it soupy.

3 Let cool and serve with a fruit or a vegetable puree.

Textured Pasta Porridge

Pasta porridge adds variety to the basic rice and udon noodle porridge that your baby has been introduced to. I recommend starting with elbow macaroni, as it is the quickest to cook and mashes up nicely.

¼ cup elbow macaroni

1 In a large pot, bring 4 cups of water to a boil. Add the macaroni; lower the heat and simmer until the macaroni is completely tender and soft to the touch, almost silky and fragile, approximately 15 to 18 minutes. It should be very soft.

2 Drain the macaroni and mash up lightly with a fork.

3 Let cool and serve with tofu or vegetable puree.

Tahini and Textured Rice Porridge

Tahini is a smooth paste made of ground sesame seeds. While this can be made from scratch as described below, there are also very good organic pre-blended brands of tahini available. They are usually sold next to the peanut butter.

1½ teaspoons sesame seeds
5 tablespoons rice porridge

1 In a blender, food processor, or spice grinder, blend the sesame seeds until finely ground.

2 Slowly add ¼ cup of water to the processor until the mixture is smooth. Pour the contents into a small container.

3 Mix 1 teaspoon of tahini and 5 tablespoons of rice porridge.

4 Serve at room temperature or warm.

 **stocks and soup**

Vegetable Stock

This gentle soup stock can be given to the baby as is, or it can be used with rice porridge or other porridges.

1 leek
2 carrots
1 onion
1 celery rib

1 Wash the leeks, carrots, celery, and onion and give them a rough chop.

2 In a large pot, add 4 cups of cold water and all of the chopped vegetables. Bring the mixture to a boil, and then lower the heat and simmer until all of the veggies are tender when pierced with a fork, approximately 20 to 25 minutes.

3 Strain the liquid into a bowl, removing all of the cooked vegetables to a separate bowl.

4 The stock can be used to prepare porridge, veggies, or meats. The cooked veggies can be mashed lightly with a fork and served with textured rice porridge.

Dashi Stock

Dashi means stock in Japanese, and the word is used to describe many kinds of stocks. There are three main stocks that are used for Japanese cooking—kombu dashi (seaweed stock), katsuo dashi (dried bonito fish flakes stock), and shiitake mushroom dashi (rehydrated mushroom stock). At 8 months, both the kombu dashi and the katsuo dashi can be used because they are both mild in flavor and quite neutral to the delicate digestive system of a baby. You can buy kombu at almost all health-food stores, including Whole Foods in their Asian foods section.

3 strips of thick kombu wakame seaweed

1 In a large pot, add 4 cups of water and the seaweed and bring to a boil, covered. Lower the heat and let simmer for 20 minutes. The seaweed should be plump, and the water should be a bit murky.

2 Serve the seaweed with noodles or use as a stock to cook fish, meats, or vegetables.

Katsuo Fish Stock

Katsuo, a.k.a. bonito, is in the tuna family and is rich in flavor. To make the katsuo flakes, the bonito is dried. The flakes are used to make stock, or they can be added as a topping for rice dishes, vegetable, and meat dishes. Dried katsuo flakes or dried bonito flakes are now sold at Whole Foods in the Asian foods section.

½ cup of dry katsuo fish flakes

1 In a large pot, add the dried fish to 4 cups of water and let it soak for 1 hour.

2 Then bring the water to a boil, simmer for 10 minutes, and strain the water into another bowl, discarding the dried fish.

3 Use the stock as a base for soups, noodles, or various protein and vegetable dishes.

Baby Vegetable Soup

This is a nice blend of butternut squash, leeks, and carrots, and can be given as a soup or as a puree.

1 potato
2 carrots
¼ cup cubed butternut squash
½ leek

1 Wash and peel the potatoes and carrots and place them in a large pot with 4 cups of water. Add the butternut squash and bring to a boil.

2 Meanwhile, wash the leeks carefully (dirt often hides between the layers), and cut them into pieces.

3 When the pot comes to a boil, add the leeks and reduce the heat to low. Cook until the vegetables are tender when pierced with the tip of a knife, for approximately 20 minutes.

4 Remove from the heat and mash up the vegetables with a fork. If you would like a smoother consistency, blend with a hand blender until smooth.

5 Serve by itself in a small bowl or with a tablespoon of cooked barley (page 51) mixed in.

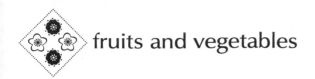 fruits and vegetables

Prunes

Prunes, as well as plums, are extremely nutritious superfoods because they contain unique antioxidants that prevent free radicals that can damage cells. Prunes also have a high concentration of beta-carotene, as well as fiber, copper, and potassium.

½ cup dried prunes

1   Soak the prunes in a cup of water for 10 to 15 minutes.
2   When the prunes have been rehydrated and are soft, drain them (reserving the soaking water) and put them in a blender or food processor. Blend until smooth, adding the water to the desired consistency.
3   Serve a small amount at any one time with textured rice or oat cereal.

Apricot Puree

Apricots are packed with vitamins A and C, as well as fiber. Here I use the dried apricots, which are available all year long, but you can also use fresh apricots when they are in season during the summer months.

½ cup dried apricots

1   In a small bowl, combine the apricots with ½ cup of water and let soak for 5 minutes.
2   Pour everything into a small pot and cook over medium heat until the apricots are tender when pierced with a tip of a knife, approximately 5 to 7 minutes.
3   Remove from the heat; puree in a blender until smooth. Thin with breast milk or water to the desired consistency.
4   Serve with textured rice porridge or cottage cheese.

Cantaloupe Puree with Mint

Cantaloupe is full of vitamins A, C, B6, and B3, folate, and fiber. Mint is also full of vitamins C and A and is often considered a tummy-soothing element. You can try giving your baby the cantaloupe by itself for 4 days, and then add the mint if you have observed that there has been no allergic reaction.

> ½ ripe cantaloupe
> 2 mint leaves

1 Cut the cantaloupe into small pieces.

2 Put into the blender with the mint leaves and mix until smooth. The mixture should be thin and smooth, but if a thinner consistency is desired, add a teaspoon of water or breast milk.

3 This puree can be served with tofu, yogurt, cereal, or rice porridge.

Kiwi, Banana, and Apple Puree

These three fruits blend well together, and as long as your baby has not had any allergic reactions to the first sets of fruits, you can begin to serve different combinations and serve them without pureeing them completely, for more texture.

> 2 kiwis, peeled
> 1 banana
> 1 apple, peeled and cored

1 Cut up the kiwis, apple, and banana into small pieces.

2 Combine and cook in a steamer until the apples are tender when pierced with a knife tip, approximately 7 to 10 minutes.

3 Mash up slightly with a fork.

4 This can be served with tofu, yogurt, cereal, or rice porridge.

Almond Butter and Apple Puree

Almonds are not a nut; they are actually the seeds of the almond fruit, and many consider them a fruit. As such, they don't trigger the same kind of allergic reaction as other tree nuts and peanuts. They are full of vitamins E and B2, as well as copper and magnesium. Almond butter is sold in many supermarkets, and there are excellent organic brands.

> 1 tablespoon organic almond butter
> 3 tablespoons Apple Puree (page 24)

1 In a food processor, combine the almond butter with the apple puree and mix until smooth and uniform in color.

2 Serve by itself or with textured rice porridge.

Apple and Carrot Puree with Tofu

This is a sweet tofu mash that combines protein with vitamin C, beta-carotine, and Omega-3.

> 3 tablespoons Apple Puree (page 24)
> 2 tablespoons Carrot Puree (page 34)
> 2 tablespoons Mashed Tofu (page 30)
> 1 teaspoon ground flaxseeds
> 1 teaspoon tahini

1 Mix the apple and carrot purees and the mashed tofu in a small bowl until well blended.

2 Sprinkle with ground flaxseeds and tahini and serve.

Broccoli

Broccoli is an incredible vegetable. It is packed with vitamins A, K, C, E, B6, B2, and B5, folate, fiber, iron, zinc, calcium, and Omega-3 fatty acid. Broccoli can be introduced at 8 months.

Bunch of fresh organic broccoli

1 Cut the broccoli florets into small pieces and discard the stems.

2 Put into a steamer and cook until the florets are tender, approximately 5 to 7 minutes.

3 Mash up slightly with a fork. Add a teaspoon of water or breast milk to thin to desired consistency.

4 Put 3 tablespoons in a small bowl and serve by itself or with tofu or rice porridge. Store the remainder in the refrigerator for later use.

Daikon Radish Puree

Daikon radish is a long white radish from Asia with a mild flavor. It has two layers of skin to peel off. Be sure you use a good peeler to scrape off the double layers of skin.

½ daikon radish

1 Peel the daikon radish and cut it into small pieces.

2 Put them in a steamer and cook until the pieces are tender when pierced, approximately 7 to 10 minutes.

3 Drain off the water; put the radish pieces into a food processor and puree until smooth.

4 Serve in a small bowl by itself for the 4-day waiting period, after which it can be served with rice porridge, barley, or tofu.

Yams and Rice

Yams add a natural sweetness, and give rice porridge a nice flavor without adding sugar. In Asia, most traditional snacks and treats are made with the sweetness of yams. It is a good way to provide beta-carotene and fiber as well.

1 yam
4 tablespoons of Rice Porridge (page 41)

1 Preheat the oven to 425°F.

2 Wash the yam, and then wrap it in foil and roast it in the oven until the middle is tender when pierced, approximately 45 minutes.

3 Scoop out the flesh of the yam and puree it in a food processor until completely smooth.

4 In a small bowl, combine 4 tablespoons of yam and 4 tablespoons of the rice porridge. Mix well and serve.

Mango Banana Mash

A great combination of mango and banana for an easy mash, this can be served with yogurt or rice porridge.

   3 tablespoons Mango Puree (page 31)
   ½ ripe banana
   1 teaspoon ground flaxseeds
   1 teaspoon tahini

1 In a small bowl, first mash the banana until soft, and then add the mango puree.

2 Sprinkle with ground flaxseeds and tahini and serve.

Seaweed Flakes

Seaweed, or sea vegetable, is a true brainfood. It is packed with DHA Omega-3, as well as iron, potassium, calcium, and vitamin B12, which is rarely found in vegetables, vitamins A, C, E, and K, and folates. There is a multitude of varieties in sea vegetables, including wakame—a thin short seaweed most often served in a miso soup, kombu—a thick dark seaweed that is used for stock, and kelp— black stubby seaweeds that are cooked as side dishes (which should be avoided for baby because they have been found to contain heavy metals). These seaweed flakes are made from the light nori seaweed sheets, which are often used to roll sushi. They are now available in most supermarkets.

   4 or 5 dried nori seaweed sheets

1 With kitchen scissors, cut the seaweed into small, flaky pieces.

2 Put the flakes in a food processor and pulse until they become flakes.

3 You can use these flakes on rice porridge, oatmeal, or even fruit compotes. Keep in an airtight container for up to 10 days in the refrigerator.

Wakame Seaweed

Because seaweed comes in many forms and shapes, it can sometimes be a challenge to figure out which kind best suits a recipe. Seaweed is sold in dried form for rehydration (like dried mushrooms) or in ready-to-eat packages, like the kind that is used for sushi. This seaweed is the dried, short version called wakame, used in miso soups. You can now find it in many grocery stores, such as Whole Foods in their Asian foods section.

   3 tablespoons dried seaweed

1 Rehydrate the seaweed in 1 cup of water for 20 minutes.

2 In a pot, bring the water to a boil with the seaweed and simmer for 5 minutes. It should become moist and slippery in texture. Add a bit more water as desired.

3 Puree in a food processor and serve a spoonful mixed with rice, purees, or tofu.

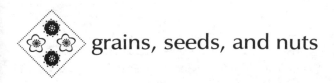 grains, seeds, and nuts

---

Wheat Germ and Tofu

Wheat germ contains high levels of antioxidants, which are not destroyed by heat and cooking. It is basically the embryo of the wheat kernel that is discarded when making refined flour, and it's where all of the nutrients are stocked, like folic acid, fiber, iron, protein, potassium, and magnesium. It is a perishable item, so you will need to keep it in the refrigerator after opening and carefully monitor that it does not go rancid by smelling it from time to time; it should smell fresh and nutty, not sour.

1 teaspoon wheat germ
3 tablespoons tofu, washed

1   In a small bowl, combine the tofu and the wheat germ. Mash together with a spoon until smooth, and the wheat germ is integrated into the tofu.

2   Serve at room temperature.

Pistachio Nut Paste and Pear Puree

Pistachio nuts have a mild flavor and are packed with potassium, protein, Omega-3 fatty acid, and vitamins A, E, and K.

¼ cup pistachio nuts, shelled and peeled of the outer brown layer
3 tablespoons Pear Puree (page 32)

1   In a food processor or, ideally, a spice grinder, add the nuts and blend until they become powder.

2   Slowly add 5 tablespoons of water into the processor and blend until the mixture becomes a paste.

3   In a small bowl, mix 1 teaspoon of the paste and the Pear Puree, and mix with a spoon until the paste is fully integrated into the puree.

4   Serve by itself or with yogurt or tofu. Store the remainder of the paste in the refrigerator in a small container for later use.

Ground Roasted Sesame Seeds and Apple Puree

Sesame seeds are very commonly used in Asian cuisine—they are packed with copper, manganese, calcium, magnesium, iron, zinc, vitamin B, and fiber that are great for your baby. It has a nutty flavor and a deep aroma that will be interesting and stimulating to try with different purees.

¼ cup sesame seeds
3 tablespoons Apple Puree (page 24)

1 Preheat the oven to 350°F.

2 Line a baking sheet with parchment paper. Pour the sesame seeds on the paper and roast for 3 to 5 minutes.

3 Remove from the oven and let cool for 5 minutes.

4 In a food processor, mix until the seeds become powder. You should be able to smell the deep scent of the sesame intensified by the roasting.

5 Place the apple puree in a bowl and sprinkle with 1 tablespoon of the sesame seed powder; mix well.

6 Serve at room temperature. Keep the unused ground sesame seeds in a tightly packed container in the refrigerator, where they should keep for up to 10 days.

Ground Walnuts

Walnuts are another incredible brainfood, a very rich source of Omega-3 fatty acids, vitamin E, manganese, copper, and other vitamins. The waxy skin is a bit bitter, but it is there that most of the nutrients are stored, so I don't remove it when serving walnuts to my baby.

2 cups dried walnuts

1 Preheat the oven to 350°F.

2 On a nonstick baking sheet, spread the walnuts in a single layer and roast them for 3 to 5 minutes until slightly golden, being careful not to burn them.

3 Remove them from the oven and let them cool for 15 minutes.

4 Put the walnuts into a food processor and pulse until they become a fine powder.

5 Store in an airtight container in the refrigerator (will keep for 1 to 2 weeks). Sprinkle the walnut powder over purees and various dishes.

Ground Pumpkin Seed Kernels

Pumpkin seed kernels are full of protein, calcium, zinc, and Omega-3 fatty acid. You can sprinkle this on many dishes, and it is neutral enough to blend into most recipes.

2 cups of the inner grains of unsalted pumpkin kernels

1 Preheat the oven to 350°F.

2 On a nonstick baking sheet, spread the seeds evenly and roast for 10 to 15 minutes until slightly golden (if using dried seeds, the baking time should be shorter— 5 to 7 minutes).

3 Remove from the oven and let them cool for 15 minutes.

4 Put the seeds into a food processor and pulse until they become a fine powder.

5 Store in an airtight container in the refrigerator (can keep for 1 to 2 weeks). Sprinkle the pumpkin seed kernel powder over purees and various dishes.

Ground Flaxseeds and Roasted Banana Puree

Flaxseeds, like sea vegetables, are another super brainfood. They are extremely rich in Omega-3 fatty acids, fiber, antioxidants, and B vitamins. You can't rely only on flaxseeds for your Omega-3 intake, but it is a great source in combination with other foods and extremely easy to integrate into recipes.

1 tablespoon organic ground flaxseeds
1 banana

1 Preheat the oven to 350°F.

2 Peel the banana and cut it in half lengthwise.

3 Place the banana on a baking sheet lined with parchment paper and roast it for 10 minutes.

4 Remove the banana from the oven, and let it cool for 10 minutes.

5 Put banana in a small bowl and mash it with a spoon, adding the flaxseeds and mixing until well blended.

6 Serve 3 tablespoons with yogurt or tofu. Store the remainder in a plastic container in the refrigerator, where it will keep for 1 day.

Millet

Millet is a fluffy little grain that is nutty in flavor and packed with Omega-3 (1 cup of millet contains 48.7 mg of Omega-3 fatty acid), as well as manganese, magnesium, calcium, iron, and potassium. As a carbohydrate, it really gives you more nutrition than most grains and rice. It is also neutral enough in flavor to use in a variety of savory and sweet dishes.

½ cup millet

1 In a pot, bring 1½ cups of water to a boil. Add millet and reduce heat to low; cook for 7 to 10 minutes, stirring constantly.

2 Remove from the heat and let cool for a few minutes.

3 Pour into a blender and puree until smooth, adding a bit of water if necessary.

4 Serve with fruit purees or with tofu.

Barley

Cooked barley has a smooth slippery texture, and, like millet, has a high amount of Omega-3, as well as folate, vitamin A, calcium, magnesium, and potassium.

¼ cup barley

1 In a pot, bring 2½ cups of water to a boil. Add barley and reduce heat to low; cook for 7 to 10 minutes, stirring constantly.

2 Remove from the heat and let cool for a few minutes.

3 Pour into a blender and puree until smooth.

4 Serve with fruit purees or with tofu.

 protein

Steamed Fish Puree

The first fish for your baby should be a very mild white fish, steamed and carefully checked for bones. It is a great way to begin providing protein for your baby.

1 fish fillet (mild white fish, such as cod, hake, sole, or haddock)

1 Cut the fillet into small pieces, checking carefully for bones.

2 Steam for 3 to 6 minutes until the fish is flaky when touched with a fork.

3 Reserve the cooking liquid.

4 Put the steamed fish in a food processor and blend, slowly adding cooking liquid until the consistency is not pasty but soft and almost fluffy. Alternatively, you can simply use a fork to mash it up slightly.

5 Serve in a small bowl by itself or with barley or millet. Since white fish can sometimes be neutral in flavor, you can liven up the taste by adding a teaspoon of carrot puree, zucchini puree, or yam puree.

Steamed Salmon Puree

Wild-caught salmon is safer than farm-raised salmon due the high levels of polychlorinated biphenyls (PCBs) found in farm-raised salmon. In addition, I think wild salmon has a lot more flavor with a denser consistency of the flesh. If you can find it, purchase wild-caught salmon.

1 wild-caught salmon fillet

1 Cut the fillet into small pieces, checking carefully for bones.

2 Steam for 3 to 6 minutes until the fish is flaky when touched with a fork.

3 Reserve the cooking liquid.

4 Put the steamed fish in a food processor and blend, slowly adding cooking liquid until the consistency is not pasty but soft and almost fluffy. Alternatively, you can mash the steamed salmon lightly with a fork.

5 Serve in a small bowl by itself, or serve with tofu, rice porridge, or barley porridge.

Steamed Chicken Puree

Chicken is another great source of protein for new eaters, and it is mild with little fat compared to other meats. It is good to start with chicken tenders because that is the mildest and softest part of the chicken.

2 thin strips of chicken tenders

1 Lay the strips flat on a cutting board and check to make sure there are no white veins or ligaments. If there are any, pull them out carefully with the tip of a knife. Then cut the strips into small pieces.

2 Place chicken pieces in a steamer and cook for 7 to 10 minutes or until the pieces are completely white with no pink tint in the middle of the flesh.

3 Reserve the cooking liquid.

4 Place the steamed chicken pieces in a food processor and puree, slowly adding the cooking liquid until the consistency is smooth and not pasty.

5 Serve the puree in a small bowl by itself or with tofu, rice porridge, or barley porridge. You can even mix in sweet purees, like mashed banana or apple puree.

Cottage Cheese with Apple and Flaxseeds

An easy recipe that contains protein, calcium, vitamin C and Omega-3.

2 tablespoons cottage cheese
2 tablespoons Apple Puree (page 24)
1 teaspoon ground flaxseeds

1 In a small bowl, mix the cheese, Apple Puree, and flaxseeds together until well blended.

2 Serve.

Green Eggs— Whipped Avocado and Egg Yolk

This is a great flavor combination and full of vitamins and Omega-3 fatty acids.

3 tablespoons Whipped Avocado (page 32)
½ hard-boiled egg yolk (page 35)

1 In a small bowl, combine the avocado and egg yolk, and mix well with a fork until well blended.

2 Serve immediately.

four

9 to 11 Months
More Texture, Bolder Taste

Your baby should now be more interested in food and even trying to eat on his own.

He may be putting his fingers into his foods more often, trying to feel the textures by hand. Finger foods are perfect for this stage. Many babies become very curious about what they are eating, and this is a fun and active phase. It is important to be patient and not get too worried about the mess that the activity of eating can make. (And there will be messes!) Try to see it as an enriching activity for your child. Mealtime is not just about the utilitarian purpose of eating—it is a time to interact with your baby and help him have a wonderful sensory experience.

For my son, this was a time when he refused to be spoon-fed, and he decided that he only wanted to eat what he could pick up himself and put into his mouth. I had to come up with an array of finger foods that he could eat by himself. This phase lasted quite a while, so I did develop an interesting variety of finger foods, as you will see in many of these recipes.

At this stage, it is great to introduce a wide diversity in flavors, colors, and textures because, by now, your baby is ready for more substance, and his little tummy has evolved quite a bit since the initial months of feeding. So don't be afraid. Remember, you are creating a platform on which your child can grow strong and healthy, resistant to challenges to his palate and digestive system. It is safe to include more dairy products, like cheeses, because the milk solids and lactose are broken down in the cheeses and yogurts and therefore do not strain the baby's still-developing digestive system. Milk, as you will see, can be introduced at 12 months.

By 9 months, breast milk or formula should still be the main source of nutrients for your baby, but as he begins to be more active—crawling, exploring, playing—you will need to enrich his food intake through snacks—one to two snacks a day—and diversify the kind of snacks you provide your child (can't do cheese sticks every day!). It is important to provide a variety of different foods to munch on between meals to maintain his energy level.

Feeding Guide: 9 to 11 Months:[*]
- Breast milk or Formula: 3 to 5 feedings per day, 30 to 32 ounces per day
- Cereal: 5 to 8 tablespoons, any variety with breast milk or formula mixed in
- Fruit: 2 to 4 tablespoons, 2 times per day, strained or soft
- Vegetables: 2 to 4 tablespoons, 2 times per day, mashed, bite-sized soft, 2 times per day
- Meat and Protein: 2 to 3 tablespoons, 2 times per day, soft and tender
- Snacks: finger foods, toast, yogurt

Foods You Can Introduce at 9 to 11 Months:
Beets
Parsley
Brussels sprouts
Dark leafy greens, like spinach, kale, etc.
Eggplant
Red peppers
Different kinds of mild fish, like cod, haddock, tuna, etc.
Ground meats, like beef, lamb, chicken

[*] Lucie Packard Children's Hospital at Stanford (www.lpch.org).

Many of these recipes are made for two to four people, meaning two to four adults, with the intention of cooking for the entire family from 9 months and onward. Your baby can now eat more table foods just like the rest of the family. You can either make the extra portions and keep them in the freezer for your baby or begin to make these foods for a family meal.

 porridge

---

Rice

2 servings

Now rice will look and feel more like cooked rice, rather than a soupy porridge.

> **1 cup rice, ideally Japanese rice or any kind of short grain rice, as they are higher in starch and cook to a smoother porridge-soup consistency**
> **1½ cups water**

1 Wash the rice thoroughly in cold water until the water runs clear.
2 Put the rice and water in a small pot and bring to a boil; lower the heat and cook, covered, for 20 minutes.
3 When the rice has been cooked, remove from heat and fluff with a fork.
4 Serve warm or at room temperature.

Udon

2 servings

Udon noodles can now be served as noodles, and not as a mush. This opens up a whole new area in creating noodle dishes, which are usually loved by toddlers.

> **1 cup udon rice noodles, chopped**
> **2½ cups water**

1 In a large pot, combine 2½ cups of water and the noodles and boil for 1 minute.
2 Reduce the heat to low and simmer until the noodles are very soft, about 10 minutes.
3 Drain the noodles.
4 Serve warm or at room temperature.

Textured Rice Porridge

In providing more and more texture to your baby, the key is to gradually reduce the amount of water until you have a 1:1½ ratio of rice to water by 12 months. That is the ratio of normal cooked rice.

½ cup cooked rice
1½ cups water (alternatively, ¼ cup uncooked rice, 2 cups water)

1 In a pot, bring water to a boil. Add the cooked rice and lower the heat.

2 Cover and cook until the rice has absorbed the water but retains some texture.

Brown Rice Ginger Porridge with Cod

2 to 4 servings

In Korea, adults eat hot porridge in the morning with spicy pickles and preserved condiments. This is a more adult version of a porridge because now your baby is becoming more and more used to texture.

½ cup brown rice
½ leek
½ inch fresh ginger
3 scallions
1 tablespoon canola oil
1 cod fillet
4 cups water
¼ cup or a handful of kombu seaweed
1 tablespoon miso paste

1 In a food processor, grind the brown rice for a few seconds until the pieces are no longer whole (but not a fine powder—you want to keep the small shapes).

2 Wash and chop the leeks and scallions.

3 Peel the ginger and chop into very small pieces.

4 In a pan, heat the oil and sauté the cod for 3 to 4 minutes.

5 Transfer the cod to a dish, mash it with a fork, and set aside.

6 In the same pan, heat the ginger, leek, and scallions until they soften, about 5 to 7 minutes.

7 Add the rice and sauté for about 3 minutes.

8 Add the kombu, miso paste, cod, and water, and cover. Bring to a boil, then simmer until the porridge is thick and creamy, about 20 to 30 minutes.

9 Return the cod to the cooking pan with the vegetables and rice, and mix well together.

10 Serve warm in bowls.

 vegetables

Butternut Squash "Risotto"

2 to 4 servings

I call this dish "risotto" because I find that butternut squash, when cooked and mashed lightly, looks a lot like cooked rice. It is simple to make, yet full of flavor and beta-carotene.

> **6 cups dashi stock (page 44)**
> **½ cup cubed butternut squash**
> **1 cup rice**
> **1 teaspoon ground hemp seeds**
> **1 tablespoon yogurt (optional)**
> **1 teaspoon chopped chives (optional)**

1 In a medium pot, bring the stock to a boil. Add the squash and cook until it is tender when pierced with a fork, approximately 10 to 12 minutes.

2 Add the rice, cover the pot, and cook until the rice is very soft, approximately 20 minutes.

3 Remove from the heat and add the hemp seeds.

4 Mash the squash with a fork so that small pieces are left, looking like a rice mash.

5 Serve by itself or with a dollop of yogurt and chives on top.

Almond Gnocchi
with Sage Brown Butter   *4 servings*

This recipe may seem a bit more complicated than others, but it is not as difficult as it sounds, and it is a nice alternative to a classic potato gnocchi. This is a great way to include almonds in your child's diet, and the delicate flavor of sage complements the gnocchi.

4 Yukon Gold potatoes
½ cup ground almonds
1 teaspoon, plus 2 tablespoons salt
1 egg
¾ cup spelt flour
¼ stick butter
2 fresh sage leaves
1 teaspoon nutmeg

1 Preheat the oven to 350°F.

2 Wash the potatoes and wrap them in foil. Bake them for 60 to 90 minutes.

3 Cut the sage leaves into small pieces. Set them aside.

4 Remove potatoes from the oven and let them cool. Remove potatoes from foil and peel them; mash using a potato grater or a fork (don't mash them with a spoon or whip the potatoes—they will become thick like glue).

5 Combine the mashed potatoes with the flour, ground almonds, 1 teaspoon salt, and egg, and mix well into a ball.

6 Flour the countertop or cutting board, cut the ball of dough into 4 sections, and roll out each section. Cut into small pieces the size of your thumb.

7 Boil a pot full of water and add 2 tablespoons of salt. Drop in the gnocchi and boil for a few minutes until they pop up to the surface of the water.

8 Meanwhile, in a pan, melt the butter, sage, and nutmeg and let cook on medium heat until the butter begins to bubble and turn a dark color. Do not let it burn (butter quickly burns, so be careful). Turn off heat and set aside.

9 Drain the gnocchi and immediately add them to the pan with the brown butter and mix.

10 Toss and serve warm.

Babaganoush: Roasted Eggplant Puree with Pita Wedges   *4 servings*

The best babaganoush I had was in Istanbul. They grilled the eggplant on low heat for an hour, and then they peeled off the burned skin, mashing up the tender flesh with garlic. Most of us won't have the time to grill with a young baby in tow, so this is a quick version, which is also delicious. This recipe is without the raw garlic usually found in traditional babaganoush because it would be too harsh for babies.

> 2 eggplants
> 1 teaspoon cumin
> 2 tablespoons olive oil
> 1 tablespoon tahini
> 1 teaspoon lemon juice
> 1 teaspoon salt
> 2 pita breads, cut into pieces

1 Turn the oven to broil.

2 Wash the eggplants and poke several holes in them with a fork. Put them on a baking sheet and broil for about 40 minutes, rotating every 10 minutes, or until they feel very tender when touched with a fork.

3 Remove from the oven and peel off the skin, which should be completely black.

4 Put the flesh in a bowl and mash with a fork. Mix in the cumin, olive oil, tahini, lemon juice, and salt.

5 Cut the pitas into quarters and toast them lightly for a few minutes.

6 Serve them on a plate with the babaganoush—you can spread it evenly on the pita for the baby or yourself.

Stewed Eggplant with Sesame   *4 servings*

Cooking eggplant in a broth until it's soft is a great way to enjoy the supple texture of eggplants. It becomes almost soupy and can be enjoyed with the cooking liquid, which has lots of flavor.

> 2 eggplants
> 1 kombu seaweed
> 1 tablespoon soy sauce
> 1 tablespoon mirin
> 2 tablespoons sesame seeds
> 1 teaspoon hulled hemp seeds

1 Wash the eggplants and cut them into medium-sized pieces. Put them in a bowl of water (3 to 4 cups) in the sink and soak for 5 minutes (this will allow the dark juices in the eggplant to come out). Drain.

2 In a pot, add the eggplant, seaweed, soy sauce, mirin, and enough water to cover. Cover with a lid and cook on medium heat until the eggplants have softened completely, approximately 20 minutes.

3 Meanwhile, toast the sesame seeds in a dry pan for 2 to 3 minutes.

4 When the eggplant is cooked, add the sesame seeds, hemp, and mix well.

5 Serve with rice.

Cauliflower with Dates   *4 servings*

This recipe is inspired by the restaurant Jaleo in Washington, DC. The combination of sweet and savory is unexpected and refreshing.

½ head of cauliflower
4 dried pitted dates
1 tablespoon olive oil
1 tablespoon pine nuts
1 teaspoon nutmeg
2 tablespoons chicken stock
1 teaspoon ground walnuts
salt, to taste

1   Cut the cauliflower into small pieces, keeping just the florets and discarding the stems. In a large pot, boil 4 cups of water with 1 tablespoon of salt. Add cauliflower and cook for 7 to 10 minutes.

2   Drain and put the cauliflower on a paper towel.

3   Cut the dates into small pieces. In a pan, heat the oil, add the pine nuts and dates, and cook for 2 minutes.

4   Add the cauliflower, nutmeg, chicken stock, salt, and walnuts and cover, cooking until the cauliflower is tender when pierced with a fork, approximately 7 to 10 minutes.

5   Serve hot or at room temperature.

Spinach with Soy and Sesame   *4 servings as a side dish*

This is a light spinach dish that can be prepared in a few minutes and is a great side dish to fish or meat dishes.

1 pound fresh spinach
1 tablespoon soy sauce
1 tablespoon mirin
1 teaspoon sesame oil
2 tablespoons sesame seeds

1   Bring to boil a pot of water with 1 tablespoon salt. Wash the spinach and cut it into small pieces. Put the spinach in the boiling water for 1 minute, and then take it out and drench it in a bowl of ice water.

2   In a medium pot, heat the soy sauce, mirin, and sesame oil for 3 minutes.

3   Meanwhile, in a dry pan, dry roast the sesame seeds for 2 to 3 minutes on medium heat or until they are golden and aromatic.

4   In a large bowl, toss together the spinach, sesame oil mixture, and sesame seeds.

5   Serve warm or at room temperature.

Miso Pasta with Beets and Oregano

4 servings

Oregano is an herb that contains high amounts of Omega-3 fatty acids. It is not very strong in flavor, and you can integrate it into many recipes, especially pasta. Here is a pasta dish made with miso soybean paste and red beets.

2 red beets
2 tablespoons miso paste
1 tablespoon ground flaxseeds
1 teaspoon dried oregano
2 tablespoons olive oil
¼ cup grated Parmesan cheese
4 cups elbow macaroni pasta
1 tablespoon chopped chives
salt and pepper, to taste

1 Preheat the oven to 350°F.

2 Bake the beets for 45 to 60 minutes, until soft.

3 Cut them in half, peel the skin off the beets, scoop out the insides, and puree in a food processor.

4 Add the miso, flaxseeds, oregano, olive oil, and Parmesan cheese to the beets.

5 Bring a pot of water to a boil and cook the pasta with salt, following the instructions on the package.

6 Before draining, take out 4 to 5 tablespoons of the cooking liquid and mix it into the bowl of miso mixture.

7 Drain the pasta, and then toss together in a bowl with the miso mixture.

8 Sprinkle with chives and serve immediately.

Nutty Kale

4 servings

Kale is often considered a bitter green, but when served with nuts and raisins like in this recipe, it becomes a great sweet/savory dish.

1 pound fresh kale
1 teaspoon crushed hazelnuts
1 teaspoon crushed almonds
1 teaspoon crushed walnuts
1 teaspoon hulled hemp seeds
1 tablespoon unsalted pumpkin seeds
1 tablespoon raisins

1 Wash the kale and cut out the hard stems in the center of the leaves and discard. Cut the kale leaves into thin julienne strips, and then cut again into very small, bite-sized pieces.

2 In a pot, bring water to a boil and add kale. Lower the heat and keep cooking until the kale softens, about 7 to 10 minutes.

3 When the kale is soft (take one out and bite into it), take it out of the boiling water and dunk it in ice water; drain and transfer it to a mixing bowl.

4 In a pan, heat the butter, and then pour it on the kale. Add the nuts, seeds, and raisins and toss.

5 Serve at room temperature with rice porridge.

Roasted Yam Veggie Balls

4 to 6 servings as a side dish or a snack

This is a great finger-food snack. As I mentioned earlier, at around 9 to 10 months my son refused to eat anything except finger foods— foods he could touch and pick up himself—so I had to come up with a number of nutritious bite-sized meals.

> **2 yams**
> **1 Red Delicious apple**
> **½ cup ricotta cheese**
> **2 tablespoons ground flaxseed**

1 Preheat the oven to 375°F.

2 Wash and cover the yams and apple with foil and roast them for 1 hour until they are completely cooked and soft.

3 Take them out of the oven; peel them and discard the outer skin of the yams and apple; and put them into a bowl. Mash them with a fork and add ricotta cheese and flaxseeds.

4 Roll into small balls with your hands.

5 Serve at room temperature.

Potato Patties

4 servings as a side dish or as a finger-food snack

> **2 large Idaho potatoes**
> **¼ cup whole wheat flour**
> **1 tablespoon ground flaxseeds**
> **¼ cup water**
> **salt, to taste**

1 Preheat the oven to 375°F.

2 Wash the potatoes and place them on a baking sheet. Roast for 1 hour.

3 Meanwhile, put flour and ground flaxseeds in a bowl and make a well in the center. Pour the water into the middle and slowly mix using your hands, incorporating the mixture in the outer part of the bowl a little at a time. Knead the mix inside the bowl until it becomes a dough.

4 When the potatoes are done, scoop out the flesh and integrate it into the dough, which should become fluffier.

5 Make small balls, and then flatten them with the palm of your hand. Heat a non-stick pan and cook patties on medium heat until golden.

6 Sprinkle with salt and serve warm. Makes 8 to 10 patties.

Mashed Potatoes with Seaweed and Miso

2 to 4 servings as a side dish

This is a great way to pack extra nutrition into a standard mashed potato dish—just sprinkle in some seaweed seasoning (found at your Whole Foods or at a health-food store)—it is made of dried seaweed with sea salt. It has a very mild flavor and an easy go-to spice to add an extra boost to your dish.

2 Idaho potatoes
1 tablespoon kelp seasoning
1 tablespoon miso paste
1 tablespoon butter
¼ cup yogurt

1 Preheat the oven to 375°F.

2 Wash potatoes and place them on a baking sheet. Roast for 50 to 60 minutes until they are completely cooked and softened.

3 Take them out of the oven and scoop the flesh into a bowl. Mash it with a fork.

4 Mix in the rest of the ingredients, and mix with a fork.

5 Serve warm.

Miso Snap Peas

4 servings as a side dish

Adding miso into cooked vegetables is a very traditional Japanese cooking method to add flavor to a boiled green. The vegetables are usually cooked *al dente*, meaning not too soft and overcooked.

3 cups snap peas
1 tablespoon miso paste
1 tablespoon water
1 teaspoon sesame oil

1 Bring to boil a pot of water with 1 tablespoon of salt. Boil the snap peas for 4 to 5 minutes.

2 Drain, and then dunk them in a bowl of ice water (to stop the cooking process and keep the bright green color).

3 Drain again and cut into small pieces.

4 In a small cup, mix the miso paste, water, and oil until smooth.

5 In a bowl, toss peas together with the miso mixture and serve.

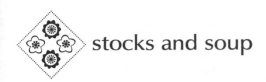

stocks and soup

Chicken Stock

4 to 6 servings

Making your own chicken stock might seem like a hassle, but chicken stock is actually quite easy to make and to store, and the delicate flavors enhance any dish. It is true there are now very good store-bought organic, low-sodium stocks; however, I tend to make my own stock whenever possible, especially when I have an extra piece of chicken leg, because I know exactly how much salt and other ingredients are in the stock. There are many ways to make a stock, but this initial stock for babies is made by boiling the chicken, which makes for a mild flavor without extra fat.

1 leek
1 carrot
1 onion
2 chicken thighs
1 bay leaf
1 teaspoon dried thyme
8 cups cold water
1 teaspoon salt (optional)

1   Roughly chop the vegetables and set them aside.

2   In a large pot, add the cold water, vegetables, chicken thighs, bay leaf, and thyme. Bring to a boil; simmer covered until the chicken falls apart when touched with a fork, approximately 60 to 90 minutes.

3   Remove the chicken bits; place them in a small bowl, discarding the bones and ligaments. Strain the liquid through a mesh strainer into a bowl, making sure to remove all the bits of vegetables and herbs. You can discard the vegetables or puree them and serve separately from the clear stock.

4   Add salt, if desired (it is important not to salt the stock while cooking because the liquid could become too salty as it reduces and boils).

5   Store the stock in an airtight container in the refrigerator for up to 3 days or freeze for up to 1 month. You can use the chicken meat with the stock or separately—just mash it up a bit with a fork before serving.

Fish Stock

4 to 6 servings

Contrary to good-quality chicken stock, which is readily available in most stores, good fish stock is more difficult to find. In the previous chapter, I introduced a katsuo fish stock (page 44), which is super easy to make and full of flavor. This fish stock is made from fish bones and can be a bit more time consuming, but the result is a rich, full-bodied stock that makes it worth the effort. Different kinds of fish can be used for the stock, and the main thing is to use fresh fish bones, whether procured from your fish market just as bones (ask the fishmonger for leftover bones after if he has filleted some fish) or by using the whole fish as in the recipe below. You can also fillet the fish yourself (the "correct" way to make the stock), but who has time for that with a baby in the house?

½ **leek**
1 **carrot**
½ **onion**
1 **fillet of butter sole**
   (or any kind of flat fish)
1 **bay leaf**
1 **teaspoon dried thyme**
1 **teaspoon salt (optional)**
8 **cups cold water**

1 Chop the leek, carrot, and onion into small pieces.

2 In a large pot, add the cold water, the sole, vegetables, and herbs; bring the mixture to a boil. Lower the heat and cover the pot, letting it simmer until the sole begins to fall apart, approximately 15 to 20 minutes.

3 Strain the liquid through a mesh strainer into a bowl, making sure that all of the bits from the sole and vegetables are strained out, and the liquid is clear. You can mash the vegetables and serve with the soup, or serve the clear stock on its own.

4 Store the stock in an airtight container in the refrigerator for up to 3 days or freeze for up to 1 month.

Shiitake Mushroom Dashi Stock

4 to 6 servings

This is a vegetarian stock that is one of the foundations of Asian cuisine. Shiitake mushrooms, especially when dried, have a powerful aroma and flavor and can enhance many dishes. Usually, the mushrooms are strained and discarded, but I think that the mushrooms themselves add an interesting texture to a meal, so I have integrated them into this recipe.

5 **large shiitake mushrooms**
8 **cups water**

1 In a large pot, bring the water to a boil. Add the mushrooms; lower the heat and simmer for 10 to 15 minutes.

2 Let cool, and remove the mushrooms.

3 Cut off the hard stems and chop the top part of the mushrooms into small pieces. Return the pieces to the stock.

4 Store the stock in an airtight container in the refrigerator for up to 3 days or freeze for up to 1 month.

Tofu Miso Soup
2 to 4 servings

Miso soup is a staple in Japanese cuisine and is easy to make as long as you have the right ingredients on hand. It is also a soup that children love, and you can be as creative as you like, varying combinations to include meats, vegetables, and herbs. Miso paste can now be bought at most Whole Foods stores, as well as specialty Asian grocery stores. It can also be ordered through Amazon. Miso soup is traditionally made using dried instant dashi stock, but because this usually contains MSG I don't use it for any recipes for babies and toddlers.

- 4 cups cold water
- 1 large kombu seaweed
- 4½ teaspoons miso paste
- 1 tablespoon dried kelp seaweed for soup
- ½ cup tofu
- chopped scallions (optional)

1 In a medium-sized pot, add water and the large kombu seaweed and the dried kelp seaweed. Bring to a boil, and then simmer on low heat for 15 minutes.

2 Add the miso paste and mix it with a spoon until the paste is completely dissolved.

3 Rinse the tofu under cold running water, and cut it into small, bite-sized pieces. Gently add it to the soup and heat for 2 more minutes.

4 Sprinkle in the scallions, if using, and serve in individual bowls. Make sure you taste the tofu for temperature before serving to your baby because it retains heat longer than the soup.

Chicken Wonton Soup
2 to 4 servings

This soup is one of my son's all-time favorites, and I make it for him on the weekends. The slippery texture of the wontons in a mild soup is a perfect lunch paired with chunky bread or a bowl of rice. You can use shrimp, fish, or other proteins in this wonton recipe. It may seem complicated, but making wontons is quite simple—mix up the protein and fill up a little sack that shrinks when cooked in the broth. You can make a bunch of them over a weekend for lunch and freeze the rest for later use.

- 2 scallions, green part only
- ½ pound ground chicken
- 1 teaspoon ground flaxseeds
- 1 teaspoon, plus 1 tablespoon soy sauce
- 28 to 30 wonton wrappers
- 2 cups chicken stock

1 Cut the scallions into small pieces.

2 In a bowl, mix the scallions, ground chicken, flaxseeds, and 1 teaspoon soy sauce. Shape the mixture into 4 to 6 balls using the palm of the hand. Wrap each ball with a wonton wrapper and set aside.

3 In a pot, bring the chicken stock and 1 tablespoon soy sauce to a boil. Lower the heat and add the chicken wontons, simmering on medium heat for 12 to 15 minutes.

4 Serve warm with rice porridge on the side. Makes 28 to 30 wontons.

 shiso

Shiso Leaves

Shiso leaves, a mild and beautifully scented Japanese herb that is reminiscent of mint leaves, is actually higher in DHA Omega-3 than flaxseeds. It also contains potassium, calcium, iron, manganese, vitamins C, A, K, B1, and B2, and folic acid. My grandmother used to grow them in her garden, and the scent of the leaves always reminds me of her, even though I was only 2 years old when she passed away. You can purchase dry shiso leaves online or at your local grocers. You can also purchase the fresh leaves, or order the seeds and grow them in your garden.

Frozen Shiso Leaves

Freezing precut shiso leaves is the best way to keep them preserved and ready for quick use. Sprinkle them onto rice or protein dishes, and they will thaw quickly.

Bunch of shiso leaves

1 Chop up the leaves carefully in small pieces. Put them inside in an airtight container and freeze.

Shiso Paste   *2 to 4 servings*

You can use this spread in a similar way to pesto—in a sandwich, in salads, or as a seasoning for meats and fish for feeding your baby. It's very flavorful and gives a good DHA boost to any dish.

Bunch of shiso leaves
5 to 10 tablespoons water

1 In a food processor, add the leaves and water and pulse until the paste is smooth and thick.

2 Store the paste in an airtight container for 3 to 5 days in the refrigerator and for up to 2 months in the freezer.

Shiso Pesto Sauce   *2 to 4 servings*

This is a great alternative to the traditional pesto sauce made uniquely with basil. I like to add the shiso leaves for extra DHA. I also like to add other greens for variety, like arugula or mache lettuce.

Bunch of shiso leaves
Bunch of basil leaves
¼ cup pine nuts
3 to 5 tablespoons water
3 tablespoons olive oil
salt and pepper, to taste

1 Put everything into a food processor and pulse until smooth.

2 Store in an airtight container and mix with pasta, fish, or meat.

 fish and seafood

Mackerel

When it comes to fish, mackerel is among the highest in Omega-3 fatty acid content. Some say that the oil from salmon contains more Omega-3, but the actual flesh of the mackerel is considered to have more fatty acid content than salmon. Mackerel has a rich dense flavor, and it is delicious grilled, braised, or cooked in stock.

Baby Mashed Mackerel

2 servings

This is a simple way to cook mackerel, an oily fish with a powerful flavor for a baby. The stock from the seaweed and the mushrooms will temper the flavor, while helping to stew the flesh.

4 fresh mackerel fillets (you can ask your fishmonger to clean whole mackerel and fillet them for you)
2 cups water
1 sheet kombu seaweed
2 dry shiitake mushrooms
1 tablespoon soy sauce

1 In a pot, add all of the ingredients together and bring to a boil. Cover and simmer for 5 to 7 minutes.

2 Take the pot off the heat, remove the kombu and mushrooms, and, with a fork, mash up the fish in its stock.

3 Serve on its own or accompanied by rice porridge.

Salmon

Salmon is one of the richest sources of Omega-3 fatty acid per serving (4,023 mg in a cup). It is a great source of protein, as well as vitamins A and C, folate, calcium, magnesium, and potassium. Contrary to mackerel, salmon is less oily and more neutral in flavor, hence easier for you to cook and for your kids to eat on a daily basis. You can integrate salmon in a multitude of dishes, and you will find many recipes in this book.

Salmon with Daikon Radish

2 to 4 servings

This is a traditional way to cook fish in Japan—to stew it with dashi and daikon radish. The twist is the flaxseeds, but it does not modify the classic flavor because flaxseeds are neutral in taste.

> ½ daikon radish
> 1 cup water
> 1 tablespoon soy sauce
> 2 tablespoons dashi (page 44)
> 1 tablespoon mirin
> 2 salmon fillets
> 1 tablespoon ground flaxseeds

1 Peel the daikon radish twice, and cut it into small pieces.

2 In a small pan, add the water, soy sauce, dashi, and mirin, and heat on medium heat.

3 Add daikon pieces and let cook until tender when pierced with a fork, approximately 15 minutes.

4 Then add the salmon fillets and cook for 5 to 7 minutes.

5 Remove from the heat and sprinkle with flaxseeds.

6 Mash up the fish with a spoon and serve with rice or on its own.

Halibut with Red Pepper, Celery, and Carrots   *2 to 4 servings*

Halibut is another fish that is rich in Omega-3 fatty acids, and you can easily find it in most supermarkets.

> 1 red pepper
> 1 celery rib
> 1 carrot
> 1 cup Dashi Stock (page 44)
> ¼ cup or a handful of dried kombu seaweed
> 2 halibut fillets
> 1 teaspoon ground pumpkin seed kernels

1 Chop the pepper, celery, and carrot into small pieces.

2 In a medium pot, add dashi stock and seaweed, and bring to a boil.

3 Add the chopped vegetables to the stock and cook until tender when pierced with a fork, approximately 7 to 10 minutes.

4 Cut the halibut fillets into small chunks and add them to the stock and veggies. Cook for 5 to 7 minutes.

5 Remove from heat and add the ground pumpkin seed kernels.

6 Serve with rice porridge, either mashed up with a fork or as is.

Salmon and Egg

2 to 4 servings

This is a double DHA whammy, with both salmon and eggs for an Omega-3-packed meal. The combination of salmon and eggs creates a nice blend of texture and flavor.

- 1 tablespoon scallions
- 1 teaspoon canola oil
- 1 salmon fillet
- 4 eggs
- 2 tablespoons seaweed dashi stock or store-bought dashi sauce
- 1 teaspoon ground flaxseeds

1 Chop the scallions into very small pieces and set aside.

2 In a pan, heat the oil on medium heat and cook the salmon for 5 minutes.

3 Transfer the salmon to a plate, shred it into pieces, and set aside.

4 Beat the eggs in a bowl, then add the dashi, flaxseeds, and cooked salmon. Pour the egg and salmon mixture into the pan used earlier to cook the salmon and either scramble the mixture or cook until the eggs are set and firm to make an omelet.

5 Serve warm or at room temperature.

Cauliflower Mash with Salmon

4 servings as a side dish

Cauliflower, when cooked well and mashed, is similar to mashed potatoes. When you stir in some cooked salmon and yogurt (rather than cream), it is a great blend of mild flavors. You can also enjoy the cauliflower mash with Parmesan cheese.

- 1 head of cauliflower
- 1 fillet wild-caught salmon
- 2 tablespoons yogurt
- 1 teaspoon nutmeg
- salt and pepper, to taste
- 1 tablespoon grated Parmesan cheese (optional)

1 Preheat the oven to 375°F.

2 Wash the cauliflower and cut it into small florets. Bring a pot of water to a boil. Add the cauliflower and cook for 7 to 10 minutes; drain when they are tender and can be easily pierced with a knife or fork.

3 Meanwhile, place the salmon on a baking dish covered with foil and bake for 5 to 7 minutes.

4 Remove from the oven and place it in a mixing bowl. Discard the skin and any bones, and mash it with a fork.

5 Mash the cauliflower with a fork, and then mix it with the salmon.

6 Add the yogurt, nutmeg, salt, and pepper and serve, with the grated Parmesan cheese, if using.

Halibut Macaroni Gratinee   *4 servings*

I love making gratinees, and I grew up on a whole variety of them as a child. This dish is very much like a baked mac 'n' cheese enhanced with the Omega-3-rich halibut.

> 4 cups elbow macaroni pasta
> 2 tablespoons olive oil
> 2 halibut fillets
> ½ onion
> 1 tablespoon butter
> 1 tablespoon flour
> 1 cup yogurt
> 1 teaspoon nutmeg
> salt and pepper, to taste
> 3 tablespoons Mozzarella cheese
> 3 tablespoons panko bread crumbs

1   Preheat the oven to 375°F.

2   Bring to a boil a pot of water with 1 table-spoon of salt, and cook the macaroni according to package instructions.

3   Drain the macaroni and put into a bowl. Toss with 1 tablespoon of olive oil, and set aside.

4   Cover a baking sheet with foil and bake the halibut fillets for 4 to 6 minutes, or until the fillets are opaque, being careful not to overcook.

5   Meanwhile, mince the onion. Heat the remaining 1 tablespoon of olive oil and butter in a pan and cook the onions on low heat until they are translucent, about 5 minutes.

6   Add flour and cook for 3 minutes.

7   Whisking constantly, add the yogurt, then the nutmeg, salt, and pepper, and cook for 3 to 5 more minutes until the mixture becomes creamy. Add the fish, mashing it with a fork.

8   Stir the sauce and fish into the pasta and pour the mixture into a baking dish.

9   Sprinkle cheese and bread crumbs over the top and bake for 10 to 12 minutes.

10 Let cool for 10 minutes before serving.

Creamy Orzo with Shredded Crabmeat   *4 servings*

Crabmeat is a source of protein and contains good amounts of Omega-3 fatty acids, vitamin A, folate, calcium, magnesium, and potassium. It is a delicate food and goes well with creamy sauces, as well as eggs.

> ½ onion
> 1 tablespoon butter
> 1 tablespoon flour
> ½ cup yogurt
> 2 cups chicken stock
> 1 pound cooked crabmeat
> 4 cups cooked orzo
> 1 teaspoon walnut oil

1   Mince the onion finely. In a pan, heat the butter and cook the onions on low heat until they are translucent, 5 to 7 minutes.

2   Add flour and cook for 2 minutes.

3   Add yogurt and stock and stir until the mixture thickens, about 5 minutes.

4   Add crabmeat, then the orzo and toss.

5   Drizzle with walnut oil.

6   Serve warm.

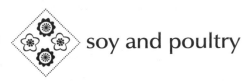 soy and poultry

Soybeans

The benefits of soybeans as a superfood are extensive. Not only are they packed with Omega-3 fatty acids, they are considered a "complete protein," equal to animal foods, but minus the saturated fats. They have high levels of vitamins A, C, K, and B12, iron, folate, calcium, magnesium, potassium, and fiber, and they are extremely versatile. They come as frozen edamame beans in their pods, dried soybeans, made into tofu, or sprouted for bean sprouts. You will see a variety of ways to cook soybeans in this book. Here is one simple way to include all that soybeans have to offer by making them into a powder that you can sprinkle on many dishes.

Ground Dried Soybeans

In Japan, these dried soybeans are eaten as snacks, and they are also used for holiday events to ward off bad spirits (*oni*). They have a nutty flavor and, when roasted, can taste almost like peanuts. I purchase unsalted dried soybeans at Whole Foods, in the dry nuts section.

2 cups dried unsalted soybeans

1 Preheat the oven to 350°F.

2 On a nonstick baking sheet, spread the soybeans and roast for 5 to 7 minutes until slightly golden.

3 Remove from the oven and let cool for 15 minutes.

4 Put the soybeans into a food processor and pulse until they become a fine powder.

5 Store it in an airtight container in the refrigerator (can keep for 1 to 2 weeks). Sprinkle the powder over purees and various dishes.

Baked Spinach Tofu

4 servings

This spinach tofu is similar to a tofu burger. It is simple to make and can be varied to include different vegetables and proteins, like kale, cheese, or fish. The soft texture is great, and you can bake it into any fun shapes and molds.

1 cup fresh, uncooked spinach
2 cups of tofu
1 egg
1 tablespoon soy sauce
1 teaspoon wheat germ
1 tablespoon canola oil

1   Preheat the oven to 375°F.

2   Fill a medium pot with water and bring it to a boil.

3   Meanwhile, chop the spinach into small pieces.

4   Open the package of tofu, drain it, and rinse it with water. Cut the tofu in half. Boil the pieces for 2 minutes; remove them from the pot and save the boiled water.

5   Drop the spinach into the boiling water for 2 to 3 minutes and drain.

6   In a bowl, mix the tofu, spinach, egg, soy sauce, and wheat germ until everything is integrated; it will be mushy.

7   Line a baking dish (a small loaf pan 8x4x2½ inches or a small square dish 8x8x1½ inches) with parchment paper and oil it with the canola oil. Put the mixture on the parchment paper and bake for 15 to 20 minutes, or until set and firm, in a water bath (put the baking dish into a larger baking dish filled with hot water).

8   Serve warm or at room temperature.

Tofu Steak

4 servings

This is one of the simplest ways to prepare tofu. For cooking tofu on the pan, as done in this recipe, make sure you buy firm tofu curd rather than silken so that the tofu does not fall apart.

2 cups firm or extra firm tofu
salt and pepper, to taste
1 teaspoon garlic powder
1 tablespoon cornstarch
1 tablespoon canola oil
1 tablespoon soy sauce
1 tablespoon mirin

1   Remove the tofu from the package and drain it (wrap it up in a paper towel or cheesecloth and place in a strainer for 25 to 30 minutes). When well drained, cut the tofu into quarters and season it with salt, pepper, garlic powder, and cornstarch.

2   Heat the oil in a pan and cook the tofu for 3 to 4 minutes on each side until golden.

3   In a small bowl, mix together the mirin and soy sauce.

4   Place the cooked tofu on a serving dish and pour the mirin mixture over the top.

5   Serve warm, accompanied by rice or potatoes.

Sesame Chicken with Tofu and Seaweed

This is a nice and quick sauté method that won't dry out the chicken because the stock and the tofu give it a gravy-like sauce.

2 thin strips of chicken tenders
1 cup Dashi Stock (page 44)
¼ cup chopped soft tofu
1 teaspoon dried seaweed powder
1 teaspoon canola oil
½ teaspoon sesame oil
1 teaspoon ground sesame seeds

1 Cut the chicken tenders into small pieces. In a pan, heat the two oils on medium heat.

2 Sauté the chicken until golden, and then add the stock and tofu and simmer for 10 minutes.

3 Sprinkle the seaweed powder and ground sesame seeds and remove from heat.

4 Serve with rice porridge.

Chicken Savory Flan   *4 servings*

In Japan, this dish is called *Chawanmushi,* meaning "steamed bowl," because a bowl is filled with an egg mixture and steam cooked until set. When I was a child it was one of my favorite dishes, and it continues to be my all-time favorite. It has a wonderful texture, close to a custard, with a savory stock full of flavor.

I use bone-in chicken thighs in this recipe, which I cut into small pieces. I find that the thighs have more flavor and retain the moisture for this dish.

4 eggs
½ cup dashi stock or chicken stock
2 tablespoons soy sauce
½ carrot
1 teaspoon sesame oil
2 chicken thighs with bone in, cut into small pieces
1 teaspoon chopped chives
2 scallions

1 Preheat the oven to 375°F.

2 In a bowl, whip together the eggs and the dashi or chicken stock. Add soy sauce.

3 Cut the carrots in small pieces.

4 In a pan, heat the sesame oil and add the carrots, chicken, and chives and sauté for 5 to 7 minutes, until the chicken is well cooked.

5 Pour the egg mixture evenly into four ovenproof bowls. Then divide the carrot, chicken, and scallions into the bowls.

6 Place the bowls in a deep baking dish and fill the dish with hot water (this method is called a *bain marie*). Bake for 12 to 15 minutes until the eggs are set.

7 Let cool for 5 to 7 minutes.

8 Serve warm, making sure it is not too hot for your child.

Udon Sauté with Chicken *4 servings*

Noodle dishes are always a favorite of little ones. Udon noodles are great both in a broth and as a sautéed noodle dish. The high starch quality of the noodles gives a gravy-like thickness to the sauce that the noodles are being sautéed in. For variety, you can use other protein ingredients in place of chicken, like beef, lamb, or fish.

    4 cups cooked udon noodles
    2 tablespoons miso paste
    1 cup water
    ½ carrot
    ¼ cup frozen spinach, thawed
    1 tablespoon canola oil
    4 chicken tender fillets

1 Dice the noodles into small pieces. Wash and cut the carrot into similar size pieces, and then do the same with the spinach.

2 In a pan, heat the oil, and then add the chicken and sauté until golden, 5 to 7 minutes.

3 Add carrots and cook for 5 more minutes.

4 Add spinach and then miso paste, and cook for 3 minutes.

5 Add the noodles and water and stir until the liquid thickens a little, about 5 minutes.

6 Remove from heat and serve warm.

Turkey Meatballs *4 servings*

My son adores meatballs, whether they are made with ground turkey, beef, or lamb. You will find many versions of meatballs in this book because I think they are a perfect way to integrate ingredients and flavors from many cultures, from Asia to the Middle East.

    1 pound ground turkey
    1 egg
    ½ onion
    1 tablespoon soy sauce
    1 teaspoon mirin
    3 tablespoons ground flaxseeds
    1 tablespoon ground wheat germ
    1 teaspoon ketchup
    1 teaspoon Worcestershire sauce
    1 tablespoon canola oil

1 Mince the onions into very fine pieces.

2 In a second bowl, combine ground turkey, egg, minced onions, and the rest of the ingredients. Mix well by hand.

3 Form small balls using a 1 tablespoon measuring spoon.

4 In a pan, heat the oil and cook the meatballs on medium heat for 5 to 7 minutes or until they are dark golden. You can also check by poking a fork into the meatballs and checking the color of the juice.

5 Serve with rice porridge.

 desserts

Snacks and Treats

I know many mothers who avoid sweets entirely for their children, and I do understand their position. Personally, I feel that sweets are one of life's pleasures, and I want to impart the joys of eating all kinds of good, healthy foods in moderation. I try to give my son occasional sweet treats that are both beneficial and delicious, with protein, vitamins, and minerals. In this book, you will find many desserts and snacks inspired from different regions of the world.

Moroccan Date "Truffles"   *4 servings*

I love desserts emanating from the Middle East, like these "truffles" from Morocco. The sweets in this region are based on dried fruits, packed with vitamins, and contain very little artificial sugar. They are perfect for your little one.

> **2 cups pitted dates**
> **½ cup ground walnuts**
> **2 tablespoons water**
> **1 teaspoon vanilla**
> **2 tablespoons apple juice**
> **1 tablespoon roasted sesame seeds**
> **1 cup dried coconut**

1 Cut the dates in half (removing the pits if there are any remaining), and then dice them into small pieces. Put the pieces into a bowl and combine with walnuts, water, apple juice, and vanilla. Mix well.

2 Make small, bite-sized balls.

3 In a pan, dry roast the sesame seeds on low heat for about 3 to 4 minutes until they are golden.

4 In a plate, combine coconut and sesame seeds; roll the balls in the mixture until well coated.

5 Store truffles in an airtight container in the refrigerator for up to 7 days. This recipe makes about 2 dozen truffles.

Rhubarb and Apple Crumble *4 servings*

Rhubarb is a tart vegetable that is often considered and cooked as a fruit. It contains vitamins A and K, folate, calcium, magnesium, and potassium, and is a great way to introduce tart flavors to your child.

> 2 rhubarb stalks (red part only; be sure to remove the leaves)
> 2 apples
> 1 cup cut-up strawberries
> 3 tablespoons apple juice
> 1 teaspoon ground cinnamon
> ½ stick softened butter
> 1 cup old fashioned oats
> ½ cup oat flour
> ¼ cup brown sugar

1 Preheat the oven to 375°F.

2 Wash and cut the rhubarb into small pieces. Peel and core the apples, and cut them into similar pieces.

3 Toss the fruit together with the apple juice and cinnamon. Pour mixture into a large baking dish (a round baking dish 8x2 inches, or a square dish 8x8x2 inches).

4 In a bowl, mix the butter and brown sugar with a hand mixer until fluffy.

5 Incorporate the oat flour, mixing for 2 to 3 minutes, then add the oats; the mix should become mealy in texture.

6 Sprinkle this oat mixture on top of the apple and rhubarb mixture in the baking dish and bake for 30 to 40 minutes, or until the top of the oat crumble becomes golden.

7 Let cool and serve.

Almond No Butter Cookies

20 to 25 cookies

This is another recipe inspired by pastries from the Malgreb region of North Africa. There is practically no butter used in their pastries. There is also very little use of dairy or white sugar. The sweetness comes from the fruits, and the texture of the pastries is dry and crunchy because of the lack of butter.

> FILLING:
> 1 cup ground almonds
> ¼ cup brown sugar
> 2 eggs
> 1 teaspoon almond extract
> 1 teaspoon ground cinnamon
>
> COOKIE PASTRY:
> 2 cups whole wheat flour
> 1 teaspoon salt
> 2 tablespoons canola oil
> 1 cup water
> 1 teaspoon almond extract
> ¼ cup confectioner's sugar for dusting

1 Preheat the oven to 350°F.

2 For the filling, mix all ingredients in a bowl and set aside.

3 For the pastry, mix together the flour and salt. Make a well in the center and add the oil, water, and almond extract. Using your fingers, mix in the flour from the outer part of the bowl into the well to make a dough.

4 Knead the dough for 10 minutes until soft.

5 Transfer the dough onto a floured surface and roll it out until it is ⅛-inch thick. Using a knife, cut it into 20 to 25 squares.

6 Take a half tablespoon of filling and roll it into a log shape with your hands. Repeat until all the fillings are shaped.

7 Place one filling "log" on top of each piece of dough and wrap it, dabbing the edges with water. Press together the edges to seal. Place them on an oiled baking sheet and prick each with a fork.

8 Bake for 20 minutes.

9 Let cool on a rack or a plate and dust with confectioner's sugar and serve.

Roasted Apples, Raisins, and Kelp Compote   *2 to 4 servings*

You might ask yourself, kelp in a dessert? You will be surprised; seaweed is used in many dessert drinks and dishes in Southeast Asia, like Thailand and Vietnam. It gives a silky texture that is fun for your child to explore.

2 apples
¼ cup water
½ cup raisins
2 tablespoons hijiki kelp

1 Preheat the oven to 375°F.

2 Wash and wrap apples in foil. Roast them in the oven until they have softened completely, approximately 40 to 50 minutes.

3 Meanwhile, soak the raisins and hijiki in the water. Toss them together, and then let them sit and soak in the liquid for about 10 minutes, hydrating the raisins and kelp.

4 When the apples are done, take them out of the oven and peel them. Put the flesh into a food processor with the raisins, kelp, and the soaking liquid and puree until smooth.

5 Serve cold or room temperature with yogurt or cottage cheese.

Bulgur Spelt Apple and Fig Bread

6 to 8 servings

I love spelt flour. It gives a deeper, nuttier flavor than refined white flour and packs more nutrition into the recipe. I also love the rough texture of bulgur. For my son, bulgur is a difficult texture when I try to serve it to him as a salad or plain. But he loves it in this bread.

1 cup bulgur
¾ cup boiling water
1 cup whole wheat flour
1 cup spelt flour
1 tablespoon baking powder
1 teaspoon salt
¼ cup brown sugar
1 cup dried figs
1½ cups milk
2 eggs
⅓ cup applesauce
½ cup chopped walnuts

1 Preheat oven to 350°F.

2 In a bowl, mix together the bulgur and water and let it soak for 30 minutes. Fluff the grains with a fork and set them aside.

3 Grease two small loaf pans (8x4x2½ inches) or one large loaf pan (9x5x3 inches) and dust it with flour.

4 In a bowl, stir in both flours, baking powder, salt, and brown sugar.

5 In another bowl, whisk together the milk, eggs, and applesauce until smooth. Stir in the figs, bulgur, and walnuts.

6 Add to the dry ingredients.

7 Pour into the greased pan and bake for 1 hour.

Persimmon Compote

4 servings as a snack or dessert

Persimmon fruit is an Asian fruit that is cultivated in the fall. They are extremely high in phytonutrients and antioxidants, as well as vitamins A, C, B, and B6, folic acid, potassium, and manganese. In flavor and texture, there is nothing quite like it because it is both crunchy and slippery, and it tastes like an amalgam of prune, ripe plum, and mango. You can find it at most Whole Foods stores in the fall.

2 persimmons
¼ cup water
1 teaspoon ground flaxseeds

1 Peel and cut the persimmons into small pieces. In a pot, combine persimmons and water and cook on medium heat until the fruit has completely softened, approximately 15 minutes.

2 Remove from the heat. Sprinkle in flaxseeds and stir.

3 Serve with yogurt, tofu, or cottage cheese.

Whole Wheat Bread Pudding *4 servings*

Bread puddings are a great way to make a warm baked dish without really baking—no flour, no mixing up the dough—just cut up leftover bread, stir in some extras, and pop it into the oven. In France, this is a dish I make almost every week for breakfast, using baguette crusts from our dinner the previous night that I don't want to go to waste.

> 4 slices raisin cinnamon whole wheat
>   bread, toasted
> 2 eggs
> 1 cup milk
> ½ cup cream
> 1 tablespoon almond extract
> ½ cup raisins
> ½ cup chopped walnuts
> ¼ cup honey
> 1 tablespoon dark brown sugar
> 2 tablespoons Greek yogurt per serving

1 Preheat oven to 350°F.

2 Break up the toast into small pieces.

3 In a bowl, combine all of the ingredients except for the brown sugar and yogurt.

4 Pour into a baking dish, and then sprinkle with the brown sugar.

5 Bake for 55 to 60 minutes, until the custard has set and turned a golden caramel color.

6 Serve warm with a dollop of whipped Greek yogurt.

Peanut Butter and Jelly Bread Pudding *4 servings*

The combination of peanut butter and jelly is a classic, and this bread pudding is a perfect way to bring those familiar flavors into a dessert.

> 4 slices toasted whole wheat bread
> 2 eggs
> 1 cup milk
> ½ cup cream
> 1 tablespoon vanilla extract
> 1 teaspoon ground hemp
> ¼ cup peanut butter
> 2 tablespoons brown sugar
> 1 tablespoon agave nectar
> ¼ cup lingonberry or black raspberry jam
> 2 tablespoons Greek yogurt per serving

1 Preheat oven to 350°F.

2 Break up the toast into small pieces. In a bowl, combine all of the ingredients except for the jam and yogurt.

3 Pour into a baking dish, and then sprinkle with the jam.

4 Bake for 55 to 60 minutes, until the custard has set and turned a golden caramel color.

5 Serve warm with a dollop of whipped Greek yogurt.

Quinoa Almond Pudding *6 to 8 servings*

This is a delicious and healthy dessert featuring vitamin-packed quinoa. It is best served warm or at room temperature.

> 3 eggs
> 3 tablespoons brown sugar
> ¼ cup yogurt
> 1 cup applesauce
> 1 tablespoon almond extract
> ½ cup ground almonds
> 3 cups cooked quinoa
> ¼ cup raisins

1 Preheat the oven to 375°F.

2 Separate the egg whites from the egg yolks. In a bowl, mix the egg yolk with the brown sugar, yogurt, applesauce, almond extract, and ground almonds. Stir in the quinoa and mix well.

3 In another bowl, beat the egg whites until they are fluffy.

4 Gently fold the egg whites into the quinoa mixture.

5 Pour into a baking dish (either a square 8x8x1½ inches, or a rectangular 11x7x2 inches) and bake for 45 to 55 minutes until it becomes golden.

Banana Coconut Tapioca with Sesame Seeds *4 servings*

Tapioca is a fantastic way to introduce a new and different texture to your child. It's plump and bouncy, and has a gelatin-like feel, but it's made of tapioca flour, which is very neutral and can be integrated into sweet or savory dishes. This is a very typical Vietnamese dessert that is not too sweet, but really hits the nice comfort-food spot.

> 1 banana
> 2 cups coconut milk
> 1 tablespoon brown sugar
> ¾ cup tapioca
> 2 tablespoons sesame seeds, roasted
> 1 tablespoon chia seeds

1 Peel and cut the banana into small pieces.

2 In a pan, add the coconut milk, brown sugar, banana, and tapioca and cook on medium heat for 10 to 15 minutes.

3 When the tapioca turns pearl-like and plump, remove from the heat and let cool for 5 minutes.

4 Sprinkle with sesame and chia seeds and serve.

Crunchy Walnut Pinwheels

6 to 8 servings

This is a great snack that is easy to make with ready-made phyllo pastry sheets and keep for a week in an airtight container.

> 3 tablespoons olive oil
> ¼ cup finely ground walnuts
> ¼ cup old fashioned rolled oats
> 1 teaspoon cinnamon
> 5 tablespoons agave nectar
> 3 tablespoons water
> 6 sheets of phyllo pastry
> 2 tablespoons honey

1 Preheat the oven to 375°F.

2 Put the olive oil in a small bowl and have ready a pastry brush or a small spoon. In a bowl, mix together the walnuts, oats, cinnamon, agave nectar, and water.

3. Lay out one phyllo pastry sheet on a clean surface and brush it with a bit of olive oil. Repeat with two more sheets, layering one on top of the other. Then spread the third sheet with the walnut and cinnamon mixture. Cover with another layer, and brush it with oil. Repeat with the two last layers, and then roll the entire pastry like a jelly roll, rolling from the long side to the other side.

4. Brush the entire pastry with oil, and place it on a greased baking pan. Bake for 20 to 30 minutes; take it out of the oven and immediately drizzle with honey.

5. Let the roll cool for 10 minutes and cut it into ¼-inch slices.

6. Serve by itself or with a dollop of yogurt. Makes 10 to 12 pinwheels

Coconut Mango Millet Bake

6 to 8 servings

This dish is crumbly and dry in texture, and while some kids may love it, others may prefer something with added moisture. You can always add a cup of apple juice to the recipe, before or after baking for added moisture, and you can also always add in yogurt as a topping as you serve it.

> 4 cups milk
> 1 cup millet
> 1 cup shredded coconut
> 2 cups frozen mango
> 1 cup chopped dried mango
> 1 tablespoon vanilla extract
> ¼ cup agave nectar
> 1 cup mango juice
> 1 tablespoon brown sugar

1. Preheat the oven to 375°F.

2. In a pan, heat the milk until warm, approximately 3 to 4 minutes.

3. Add the next six ingredients and stir to combine.

4. Pour into a greased baking dish (a square pan 8x8x2 inches, or a rectangular pan 11x7x2 inches) and bake for 1 hour.

5. In a bowl, mix together the mango juice and brown sugar. Pour over the pudding just after taking it out of the oven.

6. Serve warm or at room temperature.

Barley Pudding with Banana, Apricots, and Cashews *6 to 8 servings*

Barley has a pearly texture and a nutty flavor that combines well with fruits. This is really as simple as you can have it—mix everything together and bake for an hour. You can add other kinds of fruits, dry or fresh, and, for special treats, add in some white or chocolate chips.

> 2 cups cooked barley
> 2 cups yogurt
> ½ cup chopped apricots
> 1 banana, mashed
> ¼ cup cashews
> 2 eggs
> 1 to 2 tablespoons yogurt per serving

1. Preheat the oven to 375°F.

2. In a bowl, mix together all of the ingredients.

3. Pour into a greased baking dish (a square pan 8x8x2 inches, or a rectangular pan 11x7x2 inches) and bake for 1 hour.

4. Serve with a dollop of yogurt.

Chocolate Sesame Cupcakes

6 to 8 servings

These cupcakes have ground sesame, which give them a dense texture and a nutty consistency. If your child is allergic to sesame, you can replace the sesame with ground almonds or ground wheat germ.

¾ cup cocoa powder
1 cup whole wheat flour
½ cup ground sesame (or ground walnuts)
2 tablespoons ground flaxseeds
1½ teaspoons baking soda
1 teaspoon baking powder
1 teaspoon salt
2 eggs
¾ cup warm water
¾ cup buttermilk
3 tablespoons canola oil
1½ cups brown sugar
1 teaspoon vanilla extract
1 tablespoon white sesame for decoration

1 Preheat oven to 375°F.

2 Prepare muffin tray with cupcake liners.

3 Sift together the cocoa powder, flour, flaxseeds, sesame, baking soda, baking powder, and salt.

4 In another bowl, mix together the eggs, warm water, buttermilk, oil, brown sugar, and vanilla until well blended and smooth.

5 Slowly add the flour mixture into the egg mixture and mix well.

6 Fill each muffin cup ⅔ full with the batter, then sprinkle each with a bit of sesame.

7 Bake for 20 to 25 minutes, and let cool.

five

12 to 18 months

Food Diversity and the Emergence of Busy, Picky Eaters

Your beautiful baby is now a toddler—it was a strange feeling for me to find that my little baby was becoming a young boy already.

Becoming a 1-year-old is a huge developmental step. Your toddler is moving, maybe even talking and walking. And she is now ready for an expanded array of foods and can eat with the grown-ups. This makes it easier to prepare one meal for the entire family rather than cooking different batches of food like a line cook. In this section, you will find recipes that can be served as a family meal and enjoyed by everyone. For adults, you may want to add more salt, spices, or flavorings in some of the dishes, which are, in principle, generally mild and meant for a toddler's taste buds.

What to Expect

This is also the time when your toddler might develop fussiness or pickiness in foods. For my son, it happened, literally, from one day to the next. All of a sudden, right before he turned 12 months, he decided that tomato sauce was not for him, even though he had been happily eating pasta with tomato sauce for months. Then he decided that he did not like cooked carrots, and he would only eat raw carrots. Then he decided that he did not like carrots at all.

This period was indeed a challenging time for me and my son. I had to have several options and alternatives available during a meal so that I could get him to eat *something*. I have been told at times that this is not the right way, that I should insist on a particular meal, and if he won't eat it, let him go hungry—but I didn't have the heart to take this route. So I always had something that he would accept—a cup of yogurt, cottage cheese, etc.—just in case.

According to specialists,[*] issues of picky eating are related to how your child's taste buds function. The five different taste buds (sweet, salty, bitter, sour, and umami) have different levels of sensitivity, with one of those taste buds typically extra sensitive to a particular flavor. This is often the major factor in the emergence of pickiness and why some kids don't like certain strong flavors in some vegetables or meats. The important thing is to keep trying the food with your child, perhaps by varying the temperature or texture of the food, or combining it with other foods that your child likes.

One feeding tip recommended by research is the "Magic 10." Researcher Lucy Cooke of University College of London says that, while many parents give up on a particular food after one or two tries, "nothing happens until they have tried it at least 10 times."[†] This is a very similar attitude to the French, who say that a child can't be determined to dislike a particular food until they have tried it at least a dozen times.

It is important to keep in mind the idea of balance in your child's diet, and your child should be getting at least 1 tablespoon of protein, 1 tablespoon of fruit or vegetables, and 1 tablespoon of carbohydrates at each meal at 12 months. It is also essential to keep an open mind about how your child consumes the variety. Many kids eat erratically, and on some days, they may only seem to eat protein, while for a particular meal they may only be open to eating carbohydrates. In the end, they usually balance out the needs, so there is no need to push the matter and make eating a forceful situation.

[*] Dr. Lisa Stern, pediatrician and Bonnie Modugno, certified nutritionist.
[†] Robin Nixon, "How to Handle Kids' Picky Eating," www.livescience, 24 November 2010.

Your child has a better chance of overcoming this difficult "picky eating" period if she has been exposed to a variety of flavors, giving her a good foundation to her palate. With the diversity of flavors, textures, and smells that your child has been provided with through the recipes in the previous chapter, your child will soon regain acceptance to all kinds of foods.[*]

How Much Should My Child Be Eating?

Your child should still be drinking breast milk or formula, but many pediatricians recommend switching to cow's milk rather than formula at this stage. They also recommend that your child be consuming only about 16 ounces to 24 ounces a day in order to limit liquid calories from milk products. Many also recommend that up to 4 ounces of water or juice be consumed each day.

Feeding Guide: 12 to 24 Months:[†]
Dairy: 2 cups a day (yogurt, milk, and natural cheeses)
Grains and Cereals: 3 ounces per day
Fruit: 1 cup per day
Vegetables: 1 cup per day
Proteins: 2 ounces per day

Sample One-Day Menu:[‡]
BREAKFAST:
½ cup iron-fortified breakfast cereal or 1 cooked egg (not more than 3 eggs per week)
¼ cup whole milk (with cereal)
4 to 6 ounces juice
Add to cereal one of the following: ½ banana, sliced or 2 to 3 large sliced strawberries

---

[*] "Cooke recommends using the time from 4 months to 2 years old to expose children to as many different foods as possible. That way, when the pickiness of toddlerhood sets in, they are retracting from a larger repertoire," Robin Nixon, "How to Handle Kids' Picky Eating," November 24, 2010.

[†] www.babycenter.com.

[‡] American Academy of Pediatrics, "The Complete and Authoritative Guide: Caring for Your Baby and Young Child," Ibid., p. 285.

SNACK:

    1 slice toast or whole wheat muffin

    1 to 2 tablespoons cream cheese or peanut butter

    1 cup whole milk

LUNCH:

    ½ sandwich: tuna, egg salad, peanut butter, or cold cuts

    ½ cup cooked green vegetables

SNACK:

    1 to 2 ounces cubed cheese or 2 to 3 tablespoons pitted and
       diced dates

    1 cup whole milk

DINNER:

    2 to 3 ounces cooked meat, ground or diced

    ½ cup cooked yellow or orange vegetables

    ½ cup pasta, rice, or potato

    ½ cup whole milk

In many countries in the world, there is no limit to the amount of milk that a child takes in a day. In Holland, for example, where the population is the tallest in the world, there is absolutely no limit to milk consumption, and children, as well as adults, drink milk all day long. But many children are lactose intolerant, which means you will need to find other calcium sources for your child. If your child is lactose intolerant, there are many great options—almond milk, rice milk, or soy milk. My son tends to not love milk, so it is a struggle to get him to drink even the minimum amount, but I try to make sure he gets the minimum required amount every day. If your toddler has a difficult time drinking cow's milk, try using interesting cups or straws and try blending different flavors in the milk, like pureed fresh strawberries or blueberries. You can also add more calcium to his diet by integrating milk, yogurt, or cottage cheese into his dishes.

This is the perpetual question: how much do you feed your toddler? As always, this varies according to each child. Some experts say ¾ cup to 1 cup of porridge or food per meal is enough for a 1-year-old toddler, while others say 4 to 6 tablespoons will suffice. For me, these measurements have never worked. Some days, my son will eat an unbelievable amount of noodles or rice, and other days, I can barely get two spoonfuls in before he gets fussy. The truth is, particularly at this age, they are eager to move about, and it is difficult to get them to focus on eating. My advice is to try, and try again, and don't get too obsessed with the "norms" in feeding quantities that are out there to which you compare the eating habits of your child. Let her get up and take a break if need be, and then try again. Let her be fussy and picky, and be tolerant when she doesn't feel like eating too much. And most of all, don't let fear or anxiety take over—your child will feel it, and you don't want that to be a part of the eating experience for your child. Your child will eat when her body tells her to. As long as you make an effort to vary the kind of foods you give her and you are patient with your child, it will all go well. Again, think of it as a sensory experience for your child, and look at feeding as a developmental tool.

Introduce New Flavors

Even if your child is picky, from 12 to 24 months of age is actually the time to introduce the broadest range of foods, colors, textures, and flavors. Your child is ready for it, and it is the decisive year when what your child eats will shape her eating habits for the rest of her life.[*] Your baby has more taste buds at birth and during the first years of her life than she ever will have again; they will eventually disappear as she grows into adulthood. The more flavors she is exposed to in the first year, the more open she will be to new flavors.[†] I learned from my mother, who never gave us the same dinner twice in a month or even several months. She pored over her 20-volume encyclopedia of recipes every day to try to cook new and interesting dishes for me and my brother. While cooking

---

[*] "A baby has around 10,000 taste buds, far more than adults. They are not just on the tongue, but also on the sides, back, and roof of the mouth. Eventually, these extra taste buds disappear," "Fascinating Baby Brains: 11 Facts Every Parent Should Know About Their Baby's Brain," Robin Nixon, Live Science, June 14, 2011.

[†] "Cooke recommends using the window between 2 months to 2 years old to expose children to as many different foods as possible. That way, when the pickiness of toddlerhood sets in, they are retracting from a larger repertoire," "How to Handle Kids' Picky Eating," Ibid.

varied dishes takes effort and energy, it is a rewarding and enriching experience to try new foods with your family, as well as nourishing.

In this section, you will find more beef and other protein dishes. When choosing beef, remember that grass-fed beef has more Omega-3, and wild-caught salmon is definitely a better choice because it not only has more Omega-3 content, but it also has fewer antibiotics and other pesticides than are given to farm-raised salmon. As for fish in general, I tend to stick to salmon, herring, halibut, and anchovies as well as some seafood—crab, shrimp, scallops, and squid—and stay away from the mercury risks found in large fish like swordfish and tuna.

Foods Your Child Can Enjoy at 12 Months
Blueberries
Citrus fruits
Cow's milk
Egg, whole
Honey
Strawberries
Blackberries
Tomatoes

 soup

Chicken with Ginger Rice Soup

4 servings

Ginger has many nutritional benefits. It is good for circulation, the respiratory system, as well as for fighting diseases, and it contains important vitamins and minerals like magnesium, iron, potassium, manganese, vitamins C, E, and B6. I love the flavor of ginger, and while it gives off some heat, children tend to love it in soups, noodles, and in pastries. The difference in using fresh or dried ginger is in the flavor, and some recipes are better with fresh, while others, especially for baked goods, are better with dried grated ginger.

1 tablespoon canola oil
1 teaspoon sesame oil
4 chicken thighs, washed and drained
1 tablespoon of chopped fresh ginger
1 cup white rice
6 cups organic prepared chicken stock
1 teaspoon soy sauce
2 tablespoons chopped scallions
1 egg
1 tablespoon sesame seeds

1 In a large pot, heat the two oils on medium heat. Add the chicken and cook on both sides until brown, about 4 minutes on each side.

2 Add the ginger and the rice and cook until the rice becomes transparent.

3 Add the stock and the soy sauce and bring to a boil for 2 minutes. Lower the heat and let simmer for 45 minutes on very low heat, covering the pot with a lid.

4 Add the chopped scallions.

5 Separately, in a small bowl, crack the egg and whip it briskly with a fork; then pour it into the soup. The egg will separate and disintegrate into the soup. Cook for 3 more minutes.

6 Serve with a sprinkle of sesame seeds.

Quinoa Soup with Cod   *4 servings*

Quinoa is a great carbohydrate to include in soups for substance and protein. When added to a stock, it keeps its shape and does not dissolve into the liquid, as many carbohydrates do, so it also adds great texture.

> **1 tablespoon pine nuts**
> **1 red pepper**
> **1 green pepper**
> **½ onion**
> **1 avocado**
> **1 tablespoon olive oil**
> **salt and pepper, to taste**
> **4 cod fillets**
> **1 garlic clove, crushed**
> **2 cups cooked quinoa**
> **5 cups vegetable stock or dashi stock**

1 Place the pine nuts on a foil-lined baking sheet and toast them for 2 to 3 minutes in the toaster oven. Set aside.

2 Wash and cut the peppers, onion, and avocado into small bite-sized pieces.

3 In a pan, heat the olive oil on medium heat. Salt and pepper the fillets, mash them lightly with a fork, and place them in the pan. Cook for 5 to 7 minutes or until opaque in color and transfer them to a plate.

4 In the same pan, cook the onions until they become translucent, 5 to 7 minutes.

5 Add the garlic and the peppers and cook for 3 to 4 minutes.

6 Finally, add the avocado, quinoa, fish, and the stock and cook for another 5 minutes.

7 To serve, sprinkle each bowl of soup with pine nuts and add salt and pepper to taste.

Smooth Garbanzo Bean Soup

4 servings

Garbanzo beans, or chickpeas, are a great legume packed with protein, fiber, folate, and iron. This is a wonderful garbanzo soup from Spain. The classic version includes lots of cured meats, sausages and beef, which can be a bit much for the little tummies, so this is a light version with the same great flavor.

I recommend using dried beans for this recipe. It is an extra step to soak the dried beans overnight, but it really only takes a minute to pour the beans into a bowl of water and leave it in the refrigerator. To reduce the cooking time, you could use canned beans, which have the same nutrients and require no advance prep, but be aware that there are many BPA plastic lining issues with canned goods.* If canned goods are specified as being BPA free and organic, it is fine to use them to save the time needed for soaking.

> **4 cups dry garbanzo beans (soaked overnight in a bowl of water)**
> **1 onion**
> **1 carrot**
> **1 celery rib**

---

* Bisphenol A (BPA) is a chemical compound used to make many plastics. BPA and its presence in plastic bottles, containers, and other materials has become a subject of great concern because it exerts weak hormone-like properties which could cause negative effects, especially in children. Starting in 2008, several governments questioned its safety, prompting some retailers to withdraw polycarbonate products. A 2010 report from the United States Food and Drug Administration (FDA) raised further concerns regarding exposure of fetuses, infants, and young children

2 tablespoons olive oil
1 tablespoon tomato paste
1 pound pork shank or ½ pound pancetta
8 cups chicken stock
2 tablespoons cumin
2 tablespoons thyme
1 bay leaf
2 tablespoons walnut oil

1 Drain the beans. Dice the onions, carrot, and celery into small pieces.

2 In a large pot, heat the olive oil. Add the onions and cook until translucent, 3 to 4 minutes. Add the carrots and celery and cook for 5 minutes.

3 Add the tomato paste and cook for 2 minutes.

4 Add the shank or the pancetta and cook for 5 minutes.

5 Add the chicken stock, cumin, thyme, and bay leaf, and bring to a boil. Simmer, covered, for 2 to 3 hours or until the beans are tender and the shank meat falls apart.

6 With a hand mixer, blend the soup in the pot until smooth.

7 Serve with a drizzle of walnut oil. If you're using canned beans, the cooking time would be reduced to half, to 1 hour to 1½ hours.

Potato, Leek, and Kale Soup with Brown Rice
4 servings

2 potatoes
1 onion
1 leek
Handful of kale
2 tablespoons olive oil
4 cups chicken stock
2 cups cooked brown rice
1 tablespoon chopped chives
4 tablespoons sour cream

1 Peel and cut the potatoes into small chunks. Wash, peel, and cut the onion, leek, and kale into small pieces, discarding the hard stems of the kale.

2 In a soup pot, heat the oil on medium heat. Add the onion and cook for 4 to 5 minutes, until it becomes soft and translucent.

3 Add the leek and kale and sauté for 3 to 4 minutes until they soften.

4 Add the potatoes and chicken stock, and bring to a boil. Simmer for 20 to 30 minutes.

5 With a hand mixer, blend/puree the soup until it becomes smooth and frothy.

6 Divide the rice into four soup bowls. Pour the soup on top, and add salt and pepper; sprinkle some finely minced chives.

7 Serve with a dollop of sour cream.

(U.S. Food and Drug Administration. Update on Bisphenol A for Use in Food Contact Applications: January 2010; 15 January 2010 [cited 15 January 2010]). "Consumer groups recommend that people wishing to lower their exposure to bisphenol A avoid canned food and polycarbonate plastic containers (which shares resin identification code 7 with many other plastics) unless the packaging indicates the plastic is bisphenol A-free," Ashley Ahearn. War of the Sciences; September 19, 2008 (cited 2 February 2012).

Lentil Soup with Pancetta and Oregano

4 servings

This lentil soup has more flavor than the lentils in the 8-month chapter thanks to the pancetta and Parmesan ear/crust, which is the outer crust of a real Parmesan cheese. You can either ask your cheese shop to give you the crust, which is usually discarded, or save the crusts from the Parmesan cheese that you use. Serve with a crusty, multigrain bread and a small green salad. You can also make this soup with turkey bacon.

1 onion
2 carrots
2 celery ribs
4 to 6 slices pancetta or turkey bacon
1 tablespoon olive oil
salt and pepper, to taste
2 cups dried lentils
6 cups water
Ear/crust of Parmesan cheese
1 tablespoon cumin
1 teaspoon thyme

1 Peel and chop the onion, carrot, and celery into small pieces. Cut the pancetta into small pieces.

2 In a pan, heat the olive oil. Add the pancetta, sprinkle with salt and pepper, and cook for 5 to 7 minutes until the pieces become golden, tossing with a wooden spoon to make sure all of the sides are cooked.

3 Add the onion and cook on low/medium heat until it becomes translucent, about 5 minutes.

4 Add the celery and carrot and sauté for another 3 minutes.

5 Add the lentils, water, cheese, and the spices, and cover. Bring to a boil, and then simmer until the lentils become soft, approximately 60 to 90 minutes. I tend to prefer the lentils very soft and almost mushy, so I cook it for at least 90 minutes, if not longer.

6 Drizzle with olive oil, and sprinkle on some grated Parmesan cheese. Serve with bread.

Coconut Curry Pumpkin Carrot Soup from Zanzibar

4 servings

This recipe is my version of the kind of spicy soups and sauces cooked in coconut milk from Zanzibar and the other cities on the coast of Kenya. They are Indian spices, but they're cooked with an African flair, and the aroma will infuse your entire house. This soup is creamy, yet light, and sweet from the pumpkin and carrots. With the spices that give it depth, it will quickly become a classic in your family.

4 carrots
1 onion
1 tablespoon canola oil
1 tablespoon cumin
1 tablespoon curcuma
1½ teaspoons ground ginger
1 teaspoon ground coriander
1 teaspoon ground cardamom
salt and pepper, to taste
1 pound of pumpkin cut into chunks
2 cups coconut milk
8 cups chicken stock

1 Wash and peel the carrots, and then cut them into small chunks. Cut the onion into small slices.

2 In a pan, heat the oil and add the onion and cook on medium heat until it becomes translucent, about 5 to 7 minutes.

3 Add the spices and cook for 2 to 3 minutes.

4 Add the pumpkin and carrots and sauté for 5 minutes.

5 Add the coconut milk, chicken stock, and the rest of the ingredients and bring to a boil. Simmer and cook for 60 to 90 minutes, until the pumpkin and carrots become soft.

6 Remove from the heat, and, using a hand mixer, blend/puree the soup until it becomes smooth and frothy.

7 Serve warm.

Buckwheat Noodle Soup with Seaweed and Halibut   *4 servings*

Buckwheat is rich in magnesium and flavonoids, which extend the effects of vitamin C in the body. It also has phytonutrients with powerful antioxidants that help to protect against diseases. Buckwheat is not a cereal grain, but a flower seed; it has a deep nutty flavor.

14 ounces buckwheat noodles
4 cups water
2 tablespoons dashi fish stock, dried (if using liquid fish stock, use 4 cups of fish stock instead of water)
2 tablespoons dried kelp
2 halibut fillets
1 tablespoon chopped scallions

1 In a pot of boiling water, cook the noodles according to package instructions and drain. The noodles may stick together a bit; sprinkle water on them to help spread them apart.

2 In another pot, add the water with stock, kelp, and chunks of halibut and cook on medium heat until the halibut is completely cooked and flakes apart, about 10 to 15 minutes.

3 In a small bowl, put a small portion of the noodles and pour the stock mixture on top.

4 Serve with a sprinkle of chopped scallions.

Mediterranean Fish Soup   *4 servings*

In the city of Marseille in the south of France, the fish-stew bouillabaisse is a local delicacy—a rich broth with tomatoes and garlic, loaded with seafood.

½ **pound cod**
½ **pound mussels**
½ **pound shrimp**
½ **fennel bulb**
1 **carrot**
1 **onion**
2 **fresh tomatoes**
2 **tablespoons olive oil**
½ **teaspoon saffron**
3 **cups water**
salt and pepper, to taste

1 Cut the cod into small pieces. Wash the mussels well and put them into a bowl with salt; cover the bowl with a plate and refrigerate for 30 minutes. Peel and devein the shrimp.

2 Chop the fennel, carrot, and onion into small pieces.

3 Dunk tomatoes in hot water for a few seconds, then peel off the skin. Cut the tomatoes into small pieces.

4 In a pot, heat the oil on medium heat. Add the onion and cook until it becomes translucent.

5 Add the fennel and carrots, cook for 3 minutes; then add the tomatoes, saffron, water, and salt and pepper. Bring to a boil and let simmer for 20 minutes.

6 Add the fish and mussels, and cook for 3 to 5 minutes, or until the mussel shells open up, discarding mussels that do not open up in the cooking process.

7 Add the shrimp for 2 minutes, and remove from the heat. The shrimp will continue to cook in the remaining heat of the liquid.

8 Let cool and serve with chunky bread.

vegetables, fruits, and salads

Warm Goat Cheese Salad with Orange Citrus Dressing

4 servings

You may be thinking, *my baby, eating a goat cheese salad*? It may sound like a very adult meal, but kids do love warm goat cheese, especially when it's coated in a crunchy outer layer. The key is not to make the dressing too tangy. This salad calls for baby greens, but you can try any kind of fresh greens to see what your child likes best. Just keep trying—she will eventually get in tuned with it.

    1 egg white
    3 tablespoons panko bread crumbs
    3 tablespoons canola oil
    8 slices of goat cheese
    1 tablespoon olive oil
    1½ teaspoons white wine vinegar
    1½ tablespoons orange juice
    1 teaspoon orange zest
    1 teaspoon thyme
    1 teaspoon oregano
    salt and pepper, to taste
    ½ pound/1 bag of baby greens

1 Whip up the egg white in a small bowl. Put the bread crumbs on a plate. Heat canola oil in a pan on low to medium heat.

2 Dip a slice of goat cheese into the egg white, and then roll it in the bread crumbs, making sure it is well coated.

3 Put the cheese into the pan and cook until the crust is golden, 2 to 4 minutes; flip it over to the other side for 2 to 4 minutes. Repeat with all of the slices.

4 In a bowl, mix together all of the ingredients for the dressing and quickly toss with the baby greens. Divide the greens among four plates, and arrange the cheese, putting two slices on each plate.

5 Serve.

Roasted Beets with Goat Cheese

2 to 4 servings as a side dish

Beets and goat cheese is a wonderful pairing of sweet and tangy flavors. It is colorful and challenging to the palate due to the slippery feel of the beets and the sticky texture of the goat cheese.

2 beets
4 tablespoons soft goat cheese
2 tablespoons Pine Nut Puree (page 104)

1 Preheat the oven to 375°F.

2 Wash the beets, wrap them in foil, and roast them in the oven for 60 minutes until they are soft when poked with a fork.

3 Remove the foil and peel off the skins. Cut the beets into small, bite-sized pieces and put onto a plate.

4 Spoon goat cheese over the beets. Drizzle on pine nut puree.

5 Serve at room temperature.

Roasted Vegetables with Yogurt Dressing

4 servings

Roasting vegetables slowly is a simple way to enhance and intensify the flavors of the vegetables. Combined with the goat cheese flaxseed dressing, this dish includes protein, calcium, folic acid, Omega-3, and carbohydrates.

1 red pepper
1 zucchini
1 eggplant
2 tablespoons olive oil
1 tablespoon cut fresh basil
1 teaspoon salt
1 teaspoon thyme
3 tablespoons goat cheese
1 teaspoon lemon juice
2 teaspoons yogurt
1 tablespoon ground flaxseed

1 Preheat the oven to 300°F.

2 Wash and cut the pepper, zucchini, and eggplant into small pieces. Toss with olive oil, basil, salt, and thyme. Roast in the oven for 30 to 40 minutes or until the vegetables are tender.

3 Meanwhile, in a bowl, mix the cheese, lemon juice, and yogurt, blending well.

4 When the vegetables are done, remove them from the oven and place them on a serving plate.

5 Drizzle the goat cheese mixture on top, sprinkle with ground flaxseeds, and serve.

Herb Roasted French Fries

4 servings

These roasted potatoes are healthier versions of classic French fries, which are cooked in oil. They are simple and free of the oil or the mess involved in frying potatoes.

4 potatoes or yams
1 tablespoon sea salt
½ teaspoon paprika
1 tablespoon dried oregano
1 teaspoon ground cumin
1 teaspoon ground hemp seeds

1 Preheat the oven to 375°F.

2 Peel and cut the potatoes into thin batons. Soak in cold water for 5 minutes.

3 Drain, pat dry, and toss in a bowl with all of the ingredients except for the hemp seeds.

4 Roast in the oven for 15 minutes, and then toss them around and roast for 15 more minutes.

5 Remove potatoes from the oven, and cool for 5 minutes.

6 Sprinkle with hemp seeds and serve.

Persimmons and Carrots with Tofu

4 servings

This might seem like a strange mix—a vegetable, a fruit, and tofu. It is actually a very fresh and surprising combination of textures and flavors for a nice light salad. It is nicely balanced as well, with good amounts of beta-carotene and protein.

1 package silky tofu, drained
2 tablespoons ground sesame seeds
1½ teaspoons sugar
1 tablespoon light soy sauce
2 carrots
2 persimmons

1 In a bowl, mash the tofu.

2 Mix in the sesame, sugar, and soy sauce and set aside.

3 Peel and cut the carrots in thin strips. Peel and cut the persimmons into eighths.

4 Toss the carrots and persimmons with the tofu mixture and serve.

Braised Pumpkin with Cinnamon and Cloves   *4 to 6 servings as a side dish*

Cloves are a nice source of Omega-3 fatty acid, but you can't consume it on its own. You can integrate it into your dishes for a deep flavor. This is a great side dish packed with beta-carotene and vitamin C.

1 pound pumpkin cut into medium chunky pieces
1 cinnamon stick
2 cups vegetable stock
1 tablespoon honey
2 cloves
1 teaspoon nutmeg
Zest of ½ lemon
1 tablespoon chopped cilantro

1 Preheat the oven to 375°F.

2 Mix all of the ingredients together and pour them into a large greased baking dish (square 8x8x2 inches, or a round 9x2 inches). Cover with foil and bake for 40 to 50 minutes or until the flesh of the pumpkin is tender when pierced with a fork.

3 Remove the foil cover and bake for 10 more minutes.

4 Take out of the oven and let cool for 5 to 7 minutes. Remove the cloves.

5 Sprinkle with cilantro. Serve warm.

Fresh Figs with Prosciutto, Pistachio, and Ricotta Cheese

4 servings

Figs are full of protein, vitamins A and K, folate, calcium, and potassium. But this fruit is even more wonderful because of its incredible texture—it's soft and crunchy at the same time—and it's amazingly beautiful. The dark purple or blue exterior opens up to a crimson flesh with a white lining.

> 4 slices organic prosciutto (without nitrates)
> 4 fresh figs
> 4 tablespoons of fresh ricotta cheese (or fresh goat cheese)
> 2 tablespoons olive oil
> 2 tablespoons honey
> 4 tablespoons crushed pistachio nuts
> 1½ teaspoons chopped fresh mint

1 Take out four small plates. On each plate, place one slice of prosciutto and top it with a fig that has been cut open on top.

2 Put the cheese in the middle of the figs and drizzle with olive oil and honey. Sprinkle pistachio nuts and a tiny bit of mint.

3 Serve immediately with some bread.

Green Mache Salad

4 servings

This recipe calls for fresh mache, and the crunchy yet subtle flavor of the greens is a nice introduction to salad for your child. Mache, also called lamb's lettuce, consists of very tender and fragile dark green leaves originating from France. You can buy it in most supermarkets now, next to the arugula and other greens. It has a mild flavor, and many kids like it raw or warm, cooked quickly with olive oil. I like to use raspberry vinegar, as it gives a wonderful scent to the dish. If you can't find it, you can always use white wine vinegar.

> ½ pound mache greens
> 1 Fuji apple
> 1 tablespoon olive oil
> 1½ teaspoons raspberry vinegar
> 3 tablespoons finely ground walnuts
> 1 teaspoon thyme
> 1 teaspoon oregano
> salt and pepper, to taste

1 Wash the mache gently but carefully. Mache grows in sandy earth, so there is usually a lot of residual sand between the leaves. Dry in a paper towel and set aside.

2 Peel and cut the apple into small chunks.

3 In a bowl, mix the oil, vinegar, and herbs with a whisk.

4 Gently toss everything together in a salad bowl, being careful not to bruise the mache leaves.

5 Serve with crackers, bread, or as a side to meats and fish.

purees, compotes, sauces, and spreads

Pureed Blackberries
2 to 4 servings

Blackberries have less acid than strawberries and raspberries, which you may want to wait to introduce to your baby until she is at least 12 months old. It is also a wonderful superfood, containing Omega-3 fatty acids, vitamin C, and other vitamins. You can serve this with porridge, mixed together for a milder flavor than straight blackberries. The tiny seeds inside the berries make for an interesting texture.

1 cup fresh blackberries
2 tablespoons water

1 Wash blackberries carefully. Steam in a steamer for 5 for 7 minutes.

2 Puree with water and let cool.

3 Serve with yogurt, porridge, or mashed banana.

Blueberry Puree
2 to 4 servings

Blueberries are considered to be the most potent of all berries in terms of antioxidant content, and similar to blackberries, they are considered a superfood, packed with phytonutrients.

1 cup organic blueberries (fresh or frozen)

1 Wash blueberries under running water. Put them in a food processor and puree until smooth.

2 In a small pot, cook the pureed berries on medium heat for 5 to 7 minutes, and then remove from heat.

3 Let cool and serve a little portion at a time (2 teaspoons) by itself or with rice porridge. The berries are intense in flavor and could be heavier on the digestive system than the other fruits that your baby has previously tried. When the baby becomes accustomed, serve them with yogurt, tofu, or other neutral and complementary purees.

Blueberry Flaxseed Banana Mash

2 servings

Blueberries are the ultimate superfood. A brainfood packed with phytonutrients—antioxidants—as well as Omega-3 fatty acids, potassium, calcium, and vitamins C, K, E, and A. Your baby can eat them in their raw form, which is the best way for your baby to absorb all of the nutrients that these berries provide.

> **2 tablespoons raw blueberries**
> **1 teaspoon almond butter**
> **½ banana**
> **1 teaspoon ground flaxseeds**

1 In a small bowl, mash the banana with a fork.

2 Add the blueberries and mash together.

3 Add the almond butter and the flaxseeds and mix well.

4 Serve immediately.

Cherry Puree

2 to 4 servings

Cherries are a wonderful stone fruit, packed with calcium, magnesium, potassium, vitamins C, K, and A, fiber, Omega-3 fatty acids, and a good load of antioxidants. They could be a bit strong for an infant's tummy, so I recommend cooking them before trying to serve them raw.

> **1 cup pitted cherries (fresh or frozen)**

1 Wash cherries under running water. Put them in a food processor and puree until smooth.

2 In a small pot, cook the pureed cherries on medium heat for 5 to 7 minutes.

3 Remove them from the heat and let cool.

4 Serve a small portion at a time (2 teaspoons) by itself or with rice porridge, tofu, or cottage cheese.

Pine Nut Puree

4 to 6 servings

Pine nuts are a classic element in Mediterranean cuisine, and they are loaded with vitamins A, E, and K, folate, calcium, magnesium, potassium, protein, and Omega-3 fatty acid. This is a wonderful condiment that adds great flavor to many dishes.

> **1 cup pine nuts**
> **¼ cup walnuts**
> **¼ cup water**
> **1 tablespoon olive oil**
> **1 teaspoon salt**

1 In a pan, dry roast the pine nuts and walnuts for 2 minutes until they are golden. Let cool.

2 In a food processor, combine the pine nuts, water, olive oil, and salt. Puree until smooth.

3 Store in an airtight container in the refrigerator for up to 1 week.

Fresh Pesto Sauce with Cashews and Spinach

4 to 6 servings

Classic pesto calls for pine nuts and uses only basil leaves. This cashew version is what I learned to make in West Africa, where I couldn't buy pine nuts. In fact, most packaged pesto sauce actually uses cashew nuts rather than pine nuts because it is cheaper and has a similar flavor. I also add spinach—which you can't taste here—since it boosts the iron, folic acid, and Omega-3 content and gives the pesto a thicker consistency.

2 bunches fresh basil
½ garlic clove
½ cup cashew nuts
¼ cup olive oil
½ cup frozen spinach, thawed

1 Roughly cut up the basil and the spinach.

2 Smash the garlic and peel it.

3 In a food processor, puree the basil, garlic, and nuts. Slowly add the olive oil.

4 Serve with pasta, or use as a spread for sandwiches.

Tofu Flaxseed Avocado Spread/Dip/Sauce   *4 to 6 servings*

This is a very versatile sauce that can be used as a dip or a spread. It's rich in DHA Omega-3 fatty acid, protein, and folate. It is delicious on chicken, in sandwiches or pasta, or as a dip for raw vegetables.

1 package silken soft tofu
1 avocado
1 tablespoon ground flaxseeds
1 tablespoon lemon juice
2 tablespoons canola mayonnaise
salt and pepper, to taste

1 Drain the water from the tofu by putting it on a paper towel and placing it in a strainer for 15 minutes.

2 In a bowl, mash the tofu and the avocado together.

3 Mix in the rest of the ingredients and refrigerate for 10 minutes.

4 Serve with chicken, veggies, or with a tomato sandwich.

Cucumber and Fennel Raita

4 servings as a condiment

Raita is an Indian condiment that is usually served with curries and grilled tandoori dishes. You can serve this as a side dish, as a sauce on grilled meats and fish. It is usually only made with cucumbers, but I have added fennel because it gives a nice aroma and texture to the raita. Fennel, on top of being a beautiful, aromatic vegetable, is packed with folate, calcium, and potassium.

½ cucumber
¼ fennel bulb
½ cup Greek yogurt
1 teaspoon lemon juice
salt and pepper, to taste

1 Wash and remove the dark green skin of the cucumber, as well as the core that contains the seeds. Julienne it in thin, long slices. Cut the fennel in the same thin slices.

2 In a bowl, toss the vegetables with yogurt, lemon juice, and salt and pepper.

3 Refrigerate for 15 to 30 minutes.

4 Serve as a dip or a spread.

Tofu Tahini Basil Spread   *4 to 6 servings*

Tahini is a Mediterranean spread made from toasted sesame seeds and gives depth to this spread, which is rich in folate, protein, and vitamin C.

> 1 package silken soft tofu
> 2 tablespoons tahini
> 2 tablespoons chopped fresh basil
> 2 tablespoons olive oil
> salt and pepper, to taste

1 Drain the water from the tofu by putting it on a paper towel and placing it in a strainer for 15 minutes.

2 In a bowl, combine all of the ingredients and mix well.

3 Refrigerate for 10 minutes.

4 Serve with meats, vegetables, or on toast.

Edamame Tapenade and Dip

4 servings as a dip/condiment

This edamame tapenade is perfect for adding fresh tangy taste and a crunchy texture to any dish, with an added folic acid, vitamin C, and Omega-3 component. It is also delicious simply on toast or as a dip for carrots, celery, or other vegetables.

> 2 cups frozen edamame, thawed
> 1 mint leaf
> 3 cilantro stems
> 2 tablespoons olive oil
> 1 teaspoon lime juice
> 1 teaspoon salt

1 In a food processor, puree the edamame, mint, and cilantro. Slowly add the oil and lime juice.

2 Sprinkle with salt and serve with raw vegetables like carrots, celery, and cucumbers, or use as a spread on sandwiches.

Chicken Sandwich with Edamame Tapenade   *2 sandwiches*

This is just one kind of sandwich you could combine with the edamame tapenade. You can use any kind of protein or simply add some avocado and cheese for a vegetarian version.

> 4 slices whole grain bread
> 4 tablespoons Edamame Tapenade (page 106)
> 4 slices roast chicken
> 2 tablespoons cream cheese

1 Toast the bread slices for a few minutes until golden.

2 Spread the bread with edamame tapenade and cream cheese; add the chicken slices. Cut into thin strips.

3 Serve with sliced apples.

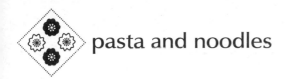

pasta and noodles

Pasta with Everything Sauce
4 servings

This recipe is inspired by my dear friend, Cynthia, who told me about her favorite sauce. She sautés any kind of vegetable with tomato sauce and then purees it. She serves it with cheese and pasta, and her children love it. It is a great way to integrate all kinds of vegetables into a simple dish.

4 cups mini ziti pasta
½ onion
1 carrot
1 leek
½ cup cut broccoli florets
½ cup cut cauliflower florets
3 fresh tomatoes
1 tablespoon olive oil
1 crushed garlic clove
1 tablespoon ground flaxseeds
4 tablespoons grated Parmesan cheese
1 teaspoon thyme

1 Bring a large pot of water to a boil. Add 1 tablespoon salt and cook the ziti according to package instructions. Drain when done.

2 Cut the onion, carrot, leek, broccoli, and cauliflower into small pieces and set aside.

3 Fill a medium pot with water and bring it to a boil.

4 In the meantime, cut an x into the bottom of the tomatoes and remove the top hard stem. Get a bowl of ice water ready.

5 Dip the tomatoes into the boiling water for 1 minute, and then dunk them in ice water, so that their skin will slip off. Peel off the skin and cut the tomatoes into small pieces.

6 In a pan, heat the olive oil. Add crushed garlic and cook for 1 minute; then remove the garlic from the pan.

7 Add the onions and cook 4 to 5 minutes.

8 Add the carrots and cook 3 minutes.

9 Add the leek, broccoli, thyme, and cauliflower and cook for 5 minutes.

10 Finally, add the tomatoes and cook covered for 5 to 7 minutes.

11 Add salt and pepper to taste and stir in the ground flaxseeds.

12 Pour the sauce over the ziti and serve warm with Parmesan cheese.

Pasta with Brussels Sprouts *4 servings*

Brussels sprouts are an incredible superfood with high amounts of vitamins K, C, and Bs, folate, Omega-3 fatty acids, protein, iron, calcium, and potassium. It is a cruciferous vegetable, like cabbage and kale. It should not be overcooked because it will lose its nutrients and begin to lose the crunchy texture.

> 4 cups mini shell pasta or other kind of mini pasta
> 1 tablespoon olive oil
> ½ cup diced pancetta
> 1 clove garlic (crushed and chopped)
> 1 cup Brussels sprouts (washed and cut into quarters)
> 1 teaspoon thyme
> 1 teaspoon oregano
> 1 cup chicken stock
> 3 tablespoons grated Parmesan cheese
> salt and pepper, to taste
> 1 teaspoon hulled hemp seeds

1 In a pot, boil water for the pasta and add salt. Cook the pasta according to package instructions. Drain when done.

2 In a medium-sized pot, heat oil and sauté the pancetta for 5 minutes.

3 Add garlic, Brussels sprouts, thyme, and oregano, and sauté for another 5 minutes.

4 Drain the pasta; drizzle with olive oil and toss.

5 Add the chicken stock to the Brussels sprouts and cover. Continue to cook on medium heat until the sprouts are tender when pierced with a fork, approximately 5 minutes.

6 In a large bowl, combine the pasta and the Brussels sprouts sauce. Toss with the Parmesan cheese and hemp seeds.

7 Serve immediately.

Fusilli with Boursin Cheese, Chives, and Cream *4 servings*

This is a super simple recipe that you can make as quickly as you can boil the pasta. Boursin cheese is a very mild, creamy cheese with herbs and is great as a base of sauces for meats and pasta.

> Bunch of chives
> 4 cups uncooked fusilli pasta
> ½ package boursin cheese
> ¼ cup cream
> ¼ cup milk
> 1 tablespoon ground flaxseeds
> 1 tablespoon wheat germ
> salt and pepper, to taste

1 In a large pot, bring water with salt to a boil.

2 Meanwhile, wash and dice the chives into small pieces.

3 Boil the pasta following the instructions on the package, usually 7 to 12 minutes.

4 Drain the pasta and then return it to the same pot with the rest of the ingredients. Mix well. The heat of the pasta will melt the cheese and infuse the aroma of the chives into the cream sauce.

5 Serve immediately.

Ziti with Salmon, Tomatoes, Spinach, and Ricotta

4 servings

This dish packs in folic acid, protein, vitamin C, calcium, carbohydrates, and DHA Omega-3. If you can't find kamut pasta, which is very high in complex carbohydrates and protein, you can use whole grain pasta, which is also high in complex carbohydrates and is easier to find in most supermarkets.

4 cups uncooked kamut or whole grain ziti
½ onion
1 tablespoon canola oil
2 tomatoes
1 fillet of fresh, wild-caught salmon
½ cup fresh spinach
¼ cup ricotta
3 tablespoons cream
salt and pepper, to taste

1 In a pot, bring water with salt to a boil; then add ziti. Cook the ziti, following the instructions on the package. Drain when done.

2 Meanwhile, finely mince the onion and put it in a pan with the oil. Cook on low heat until the onions are transparent, but still pale.

3 While the onions are cooking, cut and wash the tomatoes (peel, seed, and cut into small pieces) and add to the pan. Cook for 5 minutes.

4 Cut the salmon into small pieces, and add to the pan (a sharp, wet knife helps slice through raw fish with ease). Cook for 3 more minutes.

5 Chop the spinach into small pieces and add to the pan. Increase the heat to high; add the ricotta and cook for 3 to 4 more minutes.

6 Stir the sauce and remove it from the heat; then add the cream.

7 Drain the ziti, and add it to the pan with the sauce, and toss.

8 Add salt and pepper to taste.

3 Cheese Brainfood Mac and Cheese

4 servings

This is a brainfood version of the classic mac 'n' cheese because it contains vegetables and whole grains, as well as flaxseeds and wheat germ. It is very simple to make and very similar in flavor to the classic mac 'n' cheese, but it features the added benefits of protein, added vitamins, and DHA Omega-3 fatty acid.

> 4 cups buckwheat or whole wheat elbow macaroni
> 1 tablespoon canola oil
> 2 tablespoons grated carrots
> 2 tablespoons frozen spinach, thawed
> 2 tablespoons chopped red pepper
> 2 cups organic shredded cheddar cheese
> ½ cup shredded Pecorino Romano cheese
> ½ cup Parmesan cheese
> ½ cup cream
> 1 tablespoon ground flaxseeds

1 In a large pot with salt, cook the macaroni following the instructions on the package.

2 Meanwhile, heat a pan with oil and add the carrots, spinach, and red pepper; cook for 5 to 6 minutes until they soften, and remove from the heat.

3 Add the rest of the ingredients to the pan and toss to mix well.

4 When the macaroni is cooked, drain and then add it to the vegetables and cheese mixture, stirring until all of the elements are combined.

5 Serve immediately.

Bean Noodles with Chicken, Mushrooms, Chives, Chia Seeds, and Lemon Zest

4 servings

These noodles are made with soybean curd, which usually gives them more protein than rice noodles or other kinds of noodles. The lemon zest and mint give it a fresh light flavor.

> 10 dry shiitake mushrooms
> 1 tablespoon canola oil
> 2 chicken thighs
> 16 ounces bean noodles
> 5 to 7 chives
> 3 tablespoons soy sauce
> ½ lemon
> 1 tablespoon chia seeds

1 Soak the mushrooms in a bowl of warm water and set aside.

2 In a pan, heat the oil. Add the chicken thighs and cook on medium heat for 20 minutes, flipping over so the thighs become golden brown on all sides.

3 Meanwhile, fill a large pot with water and bring to a boil. Add the bean noodles and cook until tender, 5 to 7 minutes.

4 Drain the noodles and run under cold water 1 minute and set aside.

5 Chop up the chives.

6 Remove the mushrooms from the water (don't discard the water—it will be used in the sauce); cut them up and discard the stems; chop them into small pieces.

7 Add the mushrooms to the chicken; add the soy sauce, juice, and zest of ½ lemon and cook for 5 minutes.

8 Remove the chicken from the sauce and shred it into small pieces; return it to the sauce.

9 Add the noodles and mix well.

10 Sprinkle the chives and chia seeds and serve.

....

Sautéed Noodles with Chicken, Shiitake Mushrooms, Green Beans, and Zucchini

4 servings

This is a great recipe because as long as you have a package of good dry noodles and mushrooms, you can make this dish with just about any meat, veggies, or leftovers you may have in your fridge. For a long time, this was the only way my son would eat zucchini and green beans—mixed in with the noodles. The stock from the dried mushrooms gives this dish depth and a mild sweetness, when combined with mirin.

5 large dried shiitake mushrooms
1 zucchini
2 large scallions
½ cup green beans
2 chicken thighs
16 ounces dry egg noodles
1 tablespoon canola oil
3 tablespoons soy sauce
3 tablespoons mirin
1 tablespoon nuoc nam fish sauce
2 tablespoons ground peanuts (optional)
1 tablespoon chopped fresh cilantro
4 small lime wedges

1 In a small bowl, soak the mushrooms in a cup of water while you prepare the other ingredients. Bring to boil a pot of water with 1 tablespoon salt.

2 Meanwhile, wash and chop the zucchini into small pieces, as well as the scallions and green beans.

3 Remove the skin and fat from the chicken and cut the meat into small chunks. Boil the noodles and the green beans until tender, 4 to 6 minutes.

4 Drain, run under cold water for 1 minute, and toss the noodles and separate so that they don't stick together. Set aside.

5 In a pan, heat the oil and cook the chicken on medium heat for 5 to 7 minutes, tossing to make sure all sides are cooked.

6 Add the zucchini and cook for 3 to 5 more minutes until it softens.

7 Take out the mushrooms, reserving the liquid. Cut off and discard the hard stems, if any, and cut the mushrooms into small pieces. Add them to the pan with the mushroom liquid.

8 Add the scallions, soy sauce, mirin, and fish sauce; cover and let it simmer for 10 to 15 minutes, until everything has become tender.

9 Finally, add the cooked noodles and green beans and toss carefully in the sauce, making sure that the sauce coats the noodles well.

10 You can sprinkle ground peanuts and chopped cilantro (optional) and serve with a lime wedge.

 sushi

Sushi Rice

4 servings

Sushi rice is something that kids love in Japan. It is flavored rice—a bit sweet, a bit tangy—and goes well with so many dishes beyond raw fish. Sprinkle with sesame seeds and chia seeds, and there is your "brainfood" sushi rice. You can serve this with all kinds of meats, stir-fries, and vegetables. The following are recipes for kids—this makes for a great finger food—and except for the caviar sushi, are all made with cooked fish. You can make variations of this sushi rice by blending in dried or baked fish, such as salmon or tuna, or chopped or shredded vegetables, such as green peas, edamame, spinach, or broccoli.

> 4 cups freshly cooked rice
> 2 tablespoons rice vinegar
> 1 teaspoon sugar
> 1 teaspoon salt
> 1 teaspoon sesame seeds
> 1 teaspoon chia seeds

1 In a bowl, combine the cooked rice, preferably warm, with the vinegar, sugar, sesame seeds, chia seeds, and salt.

2 Fold together with a large spatula or a pastry spatula, being careful not to break the rice (this will make the rice sticky and not fluffy).

3 Sprinkle with your favorite topping.

FACING: *Soft Udon Noodles with Sardines and Chives, page 197.*

ABOVE: *Garbanzo Bean Cookies, page 136; Fresh Figs with Mascarpone, Honey, and Pistachio Nuts, page 248.* FACING: *Hawaiian Halibut with Macadamia Nut and Flaxseed Crust, page 226; Sautéed Spinach with Chia and Sesame Seeds, page 154.*

ABOVE: *Roasted Beets with Goat Cheese, page 100.*
FACING: *Chicken and Egg Domburi, page 126.*

ABOVE: *Goat Cheese Balls with Red Pepper, Crushed Walnuts, and Chives, page 208.*
FACING: *Miso Soup with Clams, Kale, and Young Potatoes, page 144.*

ABOVE: *Beef with Scallions and Hemp Seeds, page 128.* FACING: *Bean Noodles with Chicken, Mushrooms, Chives, Chia Seeds, and Lemon Zest, page 110.*

ABOVE: *Stewed Eggplant with Sesame, page 62.*
FACING: *Pureed Carrots, page 34; Pureed Green Peas, page 24; Pureed Potatoes, page 22.*

ABOVE: *Chocolate Sesame Cupcakes, page 86.*
FACING: *Buckwheat Noodle Soup with Kelp/Seaweed and Salmon, page 149.*

ABOVE: *Baked Salmon Wontons, page 121; Roasted Yam Veggie Balls, page 65; Sushi Rice with Salmon and Chopped Edamame, page 112.* FACING: *Creamy Orzo with Shredded Crabmeat, page 74.*

Baby Crab and Avocado Sushi

2 servings

This is a great cooked sushi that is easy to prepare. You don't have to worry about the freshness of the fish because the crab is cooked. Avocado, interestingly, tastes and feels like raw tuna when eaten with soy sauce.

> ½ avocado
> ½ cucumber
> 4 dry nori seaweed leaves (the kind used for sushi)
> 1 cup sushi rice
> ¼ pound cooked crab meat

1   Peel the avocado and cucumber and slice them thinly.

2   On a bamboo sushi roller, place one seaweed leaf, and then spread ½ cup sushi rice with a spatula until it covers the entire seaweed leaf.

3   Put the roller perpendicular to where you are standing. Take a handful of crabmeat and place it near the edge. Carefully place 2 to 3 slices of avocado and cucumber. You don't want to overfill the inside of the sushi because it will become hard to roll.

4   With firm pressure, roll the bamboo roller until the entire roll folds in.

5   Remove from the roller and cut into small pieces. Repeat with the other cup of rice and ingredients.

6   Serve with a small bowl of soy sauce on the side.

Smoked Salmon Chirashi-Zushi

2 to 4 servings

Chirashi-zushi means "scattered sushi," and is, in a way, deconstructed sushi. It is not shaped into balls or rolls by hand. Instead, the topping is always served loosely on top of the sushi rice, so this allows for a diversity of ingredients. Chirashi-zushi looks like a tart, with beautiful fish laid on top, and diced radish, shiso leaves, and ginger for accompaniments. It is a casual and simple way to eat sushi, and home-cooked sushi is often served this way. This recipe calls for only smoked salmon because it is cooked and easy to purchase, but you can top this with any kind of cooked fish. For a fun presentation, you can mold the rice with a square or round mold before placing it on a serving plate.

> 2 cups sushi rice
> 2 slices smoked wild-caught salmon
> 1 teaspoon sesame seeds
> 1 tablespoon shredded basil leaves
> 1 tablespoon shredded mint leaves
> 1 teaspoon lemon zest

1   In a square mold, place the rice and press down slightly to create a bit of firmness in the rice.

2   Cover the rice completely with the salmon.

3   Sprinkle with sesame seeds, basil, mint, and lemon zest.

4   Remove the mold and serve at room temperature. (You can serve this without soy sauce because the smoked salmon is salty enough for a toddler.)

FACING: *Coconut Curry Pumpkin Soup, page 96.*

Mini Caviar Sushi

2 to 4 servings

Caviar? Yes, caviar! I loved all kinds of caviar growing up. In Japan, there are so many varieties of seasonal caviars. In the United States and elsewhere, fresh caviar is difficult to find, but there are more and more fishmongers selling salmon roe and tobiko flying fish caviars, which are all very good and not too expensive. If you can't get these caviars, ask your local fishmonger or supermarket for caviar in jars. They will also be good, although a bit more salty than the fresh ones. Caviar is a potent source of Omega-3 fatty acid (a whopping 1,086 mg per cup) and also contains protein, vitamins A and D, calcium, magnesium, and potassium.

½ cucumber
2 cups sushi rice with 1 teaspoon chia
   seeds
Red flying fish (tobiko) caviar
Black flying fish caviar
Salmon roe

1 Peel, seed, and chop the cucumber into small pieces. Set aside.

2 Moisten your hands with water. Take a tablespoon of rice and roll it into a ball with the palm of your hands. Repeat until all of the rice has been rolled into mini balls.

3 On two small plates, spread the 2 tobiko caviars. Roll ⅓ of the rice rolls into the red caviar, the other ⅓ into the black caviar, until they are covered. Set onto a large serving plate.

4 Place the other 1/3 of the rice balls on the plate, and with a small spoon, top them with the salmon caviar (salmon roe is thicker and more plump, so it will simply rest on top of the rice balls).

5 Sprinkle the entire plate with cucumber pieces.

6 Serve with or without soy sauce.

Egg Custard Sushi

2 to 4 servings

This is my take on the classic "tamago nigiri sushi"—egg custard sushi. While my mother is an expert at making these multi-layered custards, I am not, and, to be honest, I don't often have the patience. So I do this simple version, which works just as well, and leaves me more time to work on play-dough with my son.

> 1 teaspoon canola oil
> 2 eggs
> 1 teaspoon sugar
> Pinch of salt
> 1 tablespoon chopped chives
> 2 cups sushi rice

1   In a nonstick pan, heat the oil on low to medium heat and make sure the entire pan has been well oiled.

2   Meanwhile, crack the eggs into a bowl and mix well with sugar, salt, and chives.

3   Add the eggs to the pan and cover the entire pan with the thin layer of the egg mixture. After 2 to 3 minutes, or when the egg mixture begins to turn pale and cooked, fold opposite sides of the mixture into the middle, so that you are left with a thin rectangle. Flip it to the other side for 2 to 3 minutes.

4   There are several presentation options. One is to cut the egg custard into strips and place them as toppings on the sushi rice served in a shirashi-zushi way. The other is to roll the sushi rice into small balls and place slices of egg custard on top.

Shrimp Sushi Packages

2 to 4 servings

This is a fun way to present and eat sushi, and your child can help wrap and decorate the packages.

> 4 cooked shrimp
> ½ avocado
> 2 cups sushi rice
> 2 teaspoons soy sauce
> 2 Egg Custards (previous recipe)
> Fresh chive stems
> Fresh cilantro
> Fresh mint

1   Peel and chop the shrimp into very small pieces, and repeat for the avocados. In a bowl, combine the rice, soy sauce, chopped shrimp, and avocado. Set aside.

2   Modify the egg custard recipes such that you cook the eggs without folding them in, taking them out as flat crepes. Let them cool.

3   When the egg crepes are fully cooled, cut them into small squares. Top them with a tablespoon of the rice mixture.

4   Wrap it up on the top and tie it with a chive stem, cilantro, or mint. You can make different kinds of "packages" and tie them up in a variety of ways.

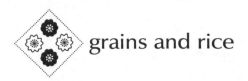

grains and rice

Quinoa

4 to 6 servings

Quinoa is a great carbohydrate because it also contains protein. It is a seed that is a staple in Latin America, and it's packed with folate, calcium, magnesium, iron, and other nutrients. It has a nutty flavor and an interesting texture that is both crunchy and soft. Although it is not a grain, it is very similar to couscous or bulgur in texture. It is neutral enough to combine it with almost anything, and it can be prepared as a savory dish or in sweet desserts, like puddings and flan.

> 4 cups water
> 2 cups quinoa
> 1 teaspoon walnut oil

1 In a pot, bring the water to a boil. Add the quinoa and reduce the heat to low. Cook until tender and fluffy, approximately 20 to 22 minutes.

2 Take off the heat. Drizzle walnut oil, toss, and serve.

3 Cheese Kamut Arugula Bread

4 to 6 servings

Of all of the grains, kamut contains the largest amount of protein. It has a very subtle nutty flavor, and it gives a bit more density than normal white flour. This recipe uses pancake mix because it already includes the baking powder/soda.

> 2 cups Kamut pancake mix
> 2 eggs
> 2 tablespoons canola oil
> ½ cup sour cream
> 1½ cups milk
> ¼ cup grated Parmesan cheese
> ¼ cup grated Asiago cheese
> ¼ cup grated cheddar cheese
> 1 cup fresh arugula, chopped
> 3 tablespoons chia seeds

1 Preheat the oven to 375°F.

2 Put pancake mix in a bowl. Make a well in the center and add eggs, oil, sour cream, and milk; mix well.

3 Add the chesses and mix.

4 Add the arugula and chia seeds and mix.

5 Pour the batter into an oiled baking pan and bake for 50 to 60 minutes, or until the center is dry when poked with a long toothpick or knife.

6 Let cool and serve with a drizzle of olive oil.

Salmon Rice Pilaf

4 servings

Rice pilaf is a rice dish cooked in stock and traditionally finished off in the oven. This is the simpler stove-top version.

1 onion
1 carrot
2 tablespoons canola oil
2 salmon fillets
1 cup rice
3 cups dashi stock (or chicken stock)
¼ cup peas

1 Peel and finely chop the onions. Rinse, peel, and cut the carrot into small pieces.

2 In a pan, heat 1 tablespoon oil on medium heat. Salt and pepper the fillets, and then gently put them in the pan; cook for 5 to 7 minutes or until opaque.

3 Transfer the fillets to a plate and use a fork to break them into small, flaky pieces.

4 In the same pan, heat the remaining tablespoon of oil; add onions and cook until they become translucent, approximately 5 minutes.

5 Then add the rice and cook until the grains also become translucent, approximately 5 minutes.

6 Add the stock, carrots, and peas and bring the mixture to a boil. Cover and simmer for 20 minutes.

7 When the rice and vegetables are done, add the fish and mix well.

8 Serve warm.

Vegetable Rice Pilaf

4 servings

This is similar to a risotto, except you don't have to stand over it and stir for 20 minutes while it cooks in the stock. You can cover the pan and let it cook on its own. The texture is, of course, not as runny as a risotto, but it's delicious just the same.

1 onion
1 carrot
1 cup green beans
½ red pepper
2 tablespoons olive oil
1 cup rice
3 cups chicken stock
¼ cup grated Parmesan cheese
1 teaspoon chia seeds
salt and pepper, to taste

1 Wash and dice the onions, carrot, green beans, and red pepper into small pieces.

2 In a pan, heat the oil on medium heat. Add the onion and sauté until pale and translucent, 5 to 7 minutes.

3 Then add the carrots and cook for 3 minutes; add the green beans and cook for 3 minutes; then add the red pepper and cook for 1 minute.

4 Add the rice and cook until it becomes translucent like the onions, 3 to 4 minutes.

5 Then add the chicken stock and bring the mixture to a boil. Reduce the heat and cover, allowing it to simmer for 20 minutes.

6 When done, fluff the rice with a fork and mix in the cheese and the seeds.

7 Add salt and pepper to taste.

 **fish and seafood**

Mackerel with Ginger, Mirin, Cilantro, and Soy *2 to 4 servings*

Mackerel is the richest source of Omega-3 fatty acid, and its dark and dense flesh renders a strong flavor. It is good grilled, broiled, or roasted, but this super simple recipe with soy and ginger brings out the richness of the fish.

> 1 inch of fresh ginger
> 3 tablespoons mirin
> 3 tablespoons soy sauce
> 1 cup water
> 2 large or 4 small whole mackerel, gutted and cleaned
> Handful of fresh cilantro leaves without the stems

1 In a large pot, combine all of the ingredients except the fish and bring to a boil.

2 Add the fish and cook until the flesh is flaky when prodded with a fork, approximately 5 to 7 minutes.

3 Serve with the sauce or by itself, with rice or baked potatoes. Garnish with fresh cilantro leaves. Carefully remove bones before serving.

Trout with Fennel, Apricots, Almonds, and Couscous

4 servings

This is a twist to the classic French trout with almond sauce with the sweet and tart tang of the dried apricots. This dish is both interesting and beautiful, and trout is a great source of Omega-3 fatty acid, as well as protein, vitamin A, folate, calcium, magnesium, potassium, and phosphorus. Just be careful that you remove all of the tiny bones in the fish—there are many.

1½ cups whole grain couscous
½ fennel bulb
1 onion
4 to 6 dried apricots
1 tablespoon olive oil
2 cups vegetable stock
4 medium/large trout, cleaned
¼ cup slivered almonds
salt and pepper, to taste
1 teaspoon butter

1 For the couscous, bring to a boil 2¾ cups water with ¼ teaspoon salt and butter. Add the couscous, stir, and take off the heat. Cover and allow the water to be absorbed by the couscous for 7 to 10 minutes. Fluff the grains with a fork.

2 Wash and cut the fennel and onion into thin julienne strips. Cut the apricots into similar thin strips.

3 In a pan, heat the olive oil and add the fennel and onions, cooking on medium heat until they soften, approximately 5 to 8 minutes.

4 Add the stock, trout, almonds, and apricots and cover, cooking for 6 to 8 minutes, or until the trout is fully cooked. Check for doneness by poking the flesh; if it is firm

and dry, it is done. If any part of the flesh feels like jelly or clings to the knife, it is still uncooked.

5 To serve, put the couscous on a large platter and place the trout and the vegetables on top. Serve the sauce in a bowl on the side.

Tofu, Salmon, and Baby Spinach

4 servings

This is a stir-fry dish that can be varied with different types of fish or other kinds of protein.

1 package firm tofu
4 salmon fillets
4 cups fresh baby spinach
2 teaspoons sesame oil
½ cup chicken stock
1 tablespoon soy sauce
1 tablespoon canola oil
1 tablespoon sesame seeds

1 Drain the tofu in a strainer for at least 30 minutes, and then cut it into bite-sized pieces.

2 Cut the salmon into small pieces.

3 Wash and drain the spinach, and then give it a rough chop.

4 In a pan, heat the sesame oil on medium heat. Add the tofu and cook for 3 to 4 minutes.

5 Add the salmon and cook for 3 minutes, and then give it a toss.

6 Add the spinach, the chicken stock, and soy sauce, and cook until the spinach has wilted, approximately another 3 to 4 minutes.

7 Serve with rice.

Black Cod and Rice

4 servings

This is a simple dish that takes a few minutes to prepare. Miso, the fermented soy bean paste, enhances fish, poultry, and vegetables, and contains not only Omega-3, but also provides a "complete" protein, comparable to proteins found in meat and eggs.

> 2 tablespoons of miso paste
> 1 tablespoon water
> 4 fillets of black cod
> 2 tablespoons of sesame oil
> 1 teaspoon of sesame seeds
> 1 teaspoon of ground flaxseeds
> Rice

1 Preheat the oven to 375°F.

2 In a small bowl, mix the miso paste and water together until well integrated and smooth. Miso paste, depending on the brand, can be a bit thick, so this allows you to water it down a bit in order to coat the fish.

3 Line a baking pan with aluminum foil. Place the cod (skin side down or darker side down) on the foil and spread the miso paste evenly on top.

4 Then drizzle the sesame oil over the fish, topping it with the seeds. Bake for 7 to 10 minutes.

5 Serve on a bed of rice.

Portuguese Fish Stew with Salmon (Cozido)

4 servings

Cozido means stewed, and it is a term used for any dish that has fish or seafood with vegetables. The flavor of the stock is derived from the fish and the vegetables, so it is mild and light. You can enjoy it with a drizzle of olive oil and even a bit of lemon juice.

> ½ head of white cabbage
> 1 carrot
> 1 leek
> 1 celery rib
> 1 sweet potato
> salt and pepper, to taste
> 2 large salmon steaks
> 2 tablespoons olive oil
> 6 cups vegetable stock

1 Wash and cut the cabbage, carrot, leek, and celery into large chunks. Peel and cut the sweet potato into large chunks.

2 Salt and pepper the salmon on both sides.

3 In a large pot, heat the olive oil on medium heat.

4 Add the salmon steaks and cook for 3 to 4 minutes; flip to the other side and cook 3 to 4 more minutes. Transfer the salmon to a plate and set aside.

5 Add the vegetables to the pot and stir-fry for 3 to 4 minutes, and then add stock.

6 Cook for 10 to 15 minutes or until the vegetables are tender; then return the salmon to the pan for 2 minutes.

7 Serve immediately with some multigrain bread and a drizzle of olive oil.

Crunchy Fish Fritters

4 to 6 servings as a snack or finger food

I learned to make these fritters in West Africa—Guinea-Bissau. As a former Portuguese colony, Guinea-Bissau is heavily influenced by classic Portuguese cuisine, and this is a very typical dish.

> 2 medium potatoes
> 2 codfish fillets or salmon fillets
> 2 tablespoons chopped chives
> ¼ cup crushed walnuts
> 1 egg, whipped in a small bowl
> salt and pepper, to taste
> ¼ cup oil for light frying

1 Preheat oven to 375°F.

2 Wash and peel the potatoes, and then soak them in cold water to remove the starch. Bring a pot of water to a boil, add potatoes, and cook for 10 to 15 minutes or until they are very tender. Drain and set aside.

3 Bake the fish for 5 minutes in the oven. Take it out and mash it with a fork in a bowl.

4 In a separate bowl, mash the potatoes, and then add the fish and the chopped chives, walnuts, egg, salt and pepper, and mix well.

5 Use the palm of your hand to roll this mixture into small balls (about a tablespoon for each ball), about 20 to 24 balls, depending on the size.

6 Heat the oil in the pan and cook the fritters for 2 to 3 minutes without touching the balls at first, turning them around until they are golden. Add more oil if needed.

7 When done to golden color, place them on a plate covered with paper towels to drain excess oil.

8 Let cool for 5 to 7 minutes and serve.

Baked Salmon Wontons

4 servings as a snack or finger food

Wonton wrappers make great snacks for kids, especially when baked, because baking turns the wrappers into a crunchy bundle. This recipe uses salmon, but these wrappers can be filled with other kinds of fish, chicken, or ground beef.

> 1 salmon fillet
> 1 tablespoon sesame oil
> 2 teaspoons soy sauce
> 1 egg
> 12 wonton wrappers

1 Preheat the oven to 375°F.

2 Cut the salmon into very small pieces. In a bowl, toss the salmon with the sesame oil and soy sauce.

3 In a small bowl, whip up the egg.

4 Place a spoonful of the salmon mixture inside each wrapper, and, with the tip of your finger, dab egg mixture onto the edge of the wrapper. Close the wrapper into a triangle, and then close up the left and right corners; then close the upper fold, like an envelope.

5 Place on a greased baking tray and bake for 15 to 20 minutes or until golden.

6 Let cool and serve.

Takoyaki Broccoli Crepes

4 servings as a snack or finger food

Takoyaki means grilled octopus, but this finger food, much like a fritter, is a very classic street food served during festivals and special events in Japan. The classic version requires a special grilling pan that makes round fritter balls. Since the grilling pan is difficult to purchase, I've created this crepe version, which can be made in any frying pan. If octopus is difficult to get in your area, you can use 3½ ounces cooked shrimp in place of octopus.

> 1 cup multigrain flour
> ¼ cup chopped cooked broccoli
> 1 egg
> 2 cups water
> 1 cup chopped octopus or shrimp
> 2 cups chopped cabbage
> 3 tablespoons chopped scallions
> 2 tablespoons canola oil
> 1 tablespoon ground flaxseeds
> 3 tablespoons bonito flakes
> 3 tablespoons shredded nori
> 1 tablespoon Worcestershire sauce
> 1 tablespoon ketchup

1 In a bowl, mix together the flour, egg, and water, and then refrigerate for 1 hour.

2 Boil the octopus or shrimp for 5 to 7 minutes, and then cut them into small pieces.

3 Chop the cabbage and scallions into fine pieces.

4 In a pan, heat half of the oil and spread evenly to coat the pan. With a ladle, pour in the batter, and then top it with a few pieces of the octopus or shrimp, scallions, and cabbage. Cook on low-medium heat for 4 to 6 minutes. Flip to the other side and cook for another 3 to 5 minutes.

5 Serve with bonito flakes, shredded nori seaweed, and flaxseeds on top.

6 Mix together the Worcestershire sauce and ketchup in a small bowl and serve on the side.

Provence Inspired Mussels with Thyme, Fennel, and Cherry Tomatoes

4 servings

Don't be afraid to introduce seafood to your baby (unless, or course, she is potentially allergic—she is potentially allergic if either one of the parents is known to be allergic, or allergy is in the family). The textures in seafood—shrimp, mussels, scallops, and clams—are all wonderful, slippery, and exciting to the new palate. This dish, mussels infused with the scent of fennel and provincial herbs, is a perfect weekend meal. It's great with roasted potatoes or multigrain bread to soak up the flavorful sauce.

> 2 pounds fresh mussels
> 2 tablespoons olive oil
> 2 roughly crushed garlic cloves
> ¼ fennel bulb
> ½ pound fresh cherry tomatoes
> Bunch of fresh thyme
> 1 teaspoon dried rosemary
> (For adults, you can sprinkle a tablespoon of Pastis liqueur before serving.)

1 Wash and clean the mussels carefully.

2 Fill a large bowl with salt water and add the mussels; cover and refrigerate for 30 minutes (this allows sand to be eliminated from the mussels).

3 In a large pot, heat the olive oil. Add the garlic and fennel, and cook for 2 minutes; then add tomatoes. Cook for 5 minutes.

4 Add the mussels, thyme, and rosemary, and cook for 4 to 6 minutes, or until all of the mussels have opened up (discard any mussel that does not open up).

5 Toss so that the mussels are mixed with the tomatoes and herbs.

6 Serve warm with multigrain bread or roasted potatoes.

Simple Shrimp Cakes   *4 servings*

These shrimp cakes are a nice way to make a crunchy main dish or a snack with this protein source that's rich in DHA. My son loves these cakes, so I make extra batches for a meal, then leave the leftovers for his lunch box the following day.

   5 tablespoons wheat germ
   2 cups cooked shrimp (shelled and
      deveined)
   2 tablespoons chopped fresh chives
   1 tablespoon soy sauce
   1 tablespoon mirin
   2 eggs
   1 cup whole wheat bread crumbs
   1 tablespoon canola oil
   3 to 4 tablespoons peanut oil for cooking

1 Spread the wheat germ evenly on a plate.

2 In a food processor, blend the shrimp, chives, soy sauce, mirin, eggs, bread crumbs, and oil.

3 Scoop the mixture out of the processor and shape it into small patties. Dredge the patties in the wheat germ on the plate, making sure all sides are covered.

4 Heat a pan with the peanut oil and cook the patties for 3 to 4 minutes on each side until golden.

5 Let cool on a plate lined with a paper towel.

6 Serve the shrimp cakes with a bit of soy sauce or on their own.

Coconut Shrimp   *4 servings*

Cooking shrimp in coconut milk is a very South-Indian or South-East Asian way. The sweetness of the milk blends well with the saltiness of the shrimp, and this dish is a very simple Thai approach.

   1 pound shrimp
   2 cups coconut milk
   1 tablespoon nuoc nam fish sauce
   1 stalk of lemongrass
   1 tablespoon chopped cilantro

1 Peel the shrimp and put the shells in a small pan with ¼ cup water. Devein the shrimp and refrigerate them.

2 Cover the pan with the shrimp shells and bring it to a boil; remove from heat and set aside.

3 In another pan, add the coconut milk, fish sauce, and lemongrass and bring to a boil. Bring down the heat and simmer until the sauce thickens, approximately 15 to 20 minutes. Add the shrimp shell liquid.

4 Add the shrimp and cook, turning them around in the sauce with a wooden spoon, until the shrimp turns pink, approximately 3 to 5 minutes—but do not overcook.

5 Take off heat and sprinkle cilantro leaves, and serve with rice.

 chicken

Tofu, Kale, and Chicken Burgers

4 servings

These are tender tofu burgers that are a great alternative to beef burgers. They're good with ketchup, but also with a dash of soy sauce and sesame oil instead. Chicken is a lean source of protein; combining it with kale and chia seeds gives this dish a good amount of folate, iron, Omega-3 fatty acid, and potassium. I often add ground hemp to burger recipes, which is very easily found in Whole Foods—they are simply ground up hemp seeds which look like wheat germ. It adds extra Omega-3 fatty acids and folate into any dish.

> 2 cups firm tofu
> ¼ cup frozen kale, thawed
> ¼ pound ground chicken
> 1 teaspoon ground hemp
> 1 egg
> ½ cup ground walnuts
> ¼ cup wheat germ
> 1 teaspoon chia seeds
> 2 tablespoons soy sauce
> 1 teaspoon ketchup
> salt and pepper, to taste
> 2 tablespoons canola oil

1 Drain the tofu in a strainer for at least 30 minutes to make sure all of the water is removed.

2 Drain the kale also for 10 minutes, then squeeze out the water with your hand. Chop the kale into similar small–sized pieces.

3 In a bowl, mix everything very well by hand, except the tofu. The mixture should become sticky.

4 Add the tofu, a little at a time, integrating it by hand bit-by-bit into the chicken mixture. Mix well.

5 Scoop out about two tablespoons of the mixture at a time and make balls, then patties in the palms of your hands (about 20 patties); sprinkle with salt and pepper on each side.

6 In a pan, heat oil on medium heat, and then cook the patties on low to medium heat about 6 to 8 minutes on one side without touching, then

carefully flipping them onto the other side for 6 to 8 minutes until they are golden and crispy on the outside.

7 Serve warm with rice or with a hamburger bun.

Tangy Filipino Adobo Chicken

6 to 8 servings

Adobo is a Spanish word for sauce. The Filipino version refers to dishes cooked in vinegar. It is simple and renders an unexpected tangy, salty, and deep flavor. This recipe serves 6 to 8 people. I usually make a large batch and freeze leftovers for the following week.

> 2 tablespoons canola oil
> 1 whole chicken cut into eighths (or depending on your preference, you can do 8 pieces of chicken breasts or 8 pieces of chicken thighs)
> 3 garlic cloves, chopped
> 1 cup soy sauce
> 1 cup rice vinegar (or white wine vinegar)
> 1 bay leaf
> 2 cups water
> 1 teaspoon honey
> 1 teaspoon thyme
> 1 cup snow peas
> 1 potato, peeled and chopped

1 In a pan, heat oil on medium heat. Add the chicken, skin side down, and cook for 4 to 5 minutes until golden; flip to the other side.

2 Add garlic and cook for 3 to 4 minutes.

3 Add the rest of the ingredients and cook for 30 to 40 minutes, or until the chicken is very tender.

4 Add the snow peas and potatoes.

5 Serve with rice.

Cinnamon Chicken with Anise Star, Cloves, and Caramelized Onions

4 servings

This chicken dish is inspired by a Chinese tradition of cooking meats with star anise. Usually this is done with pork, but I prefer it with chicken. The recipe gives an unusual depth to chicken, with cloves and a touch of honey.

> 8 chicken thighs
> 2 onions
> 1 tablespoon canola oil
> 1 tablespoon brown sugar
> 1 tablespoon ground cinnamon
> 1 tablespoon honey
> 4 star anise
> 4 cloves
> ½ cup tomato sauce
> 4 cups chicken stock

1 Remove the skin from the chicken and trim away excess fat.

2 Peel the onion and cut into thin slices. In a pan, heat oil on medium heat; add the onions and brown sugar. Cook for 7 to 9 minutes until completely soft and translucent.

3 Add the chicken thighs and cook for 5 minutes on one side until golden; flip to the other side for 5 minutes.

4 Add the rest of the ingredients and bring to a boil. Cover and simmer for 60 to 90 minutes or until the meat falls off the bone; remove from heat.

5 Serve with rice.

Chicken and Egg Domburi   *4 servings*

Domburi means "bowl" in Japanese, and it refers to one-dish meals with different meats or vegetables cooked in a simmered sauce or gravy and poured over warm rice. It is a go-to meal for me because no matter how picky my son may be, he will always eat a domburi.

> 1 onion
> 4 chicken thighs
> 1 scallion
> 5 tablespoons soy sauce
> 3 tablespoons mirin
> 5 tablespoons water
> 1 tablespoon cooking sake
> 4 eggs
> 4 cups cooked brown or white rice

1   Cut the onion in half and then into thin slices. Cut the chicken into small chunks, discarding the skin. Chop the scallion into small pieces.

2   Spread the onions in a pan and add the soy sauce, mirin, water, and sake. Cook on low to medium heat for 5 to 7 minutes, or until the onion begins to soften.

3   Add the chicken and cook for 5 to 7 minutes, covered.

4   In a small bowl, whip the eggs into a foamy mix; add the scallions and pour over the chicken in the pan. Cook for 2 to 3 minutes, covered, and remove from the heat while it is still soft and not completely cooked—the remaining heat will cook the eggs through.

5   Pour the entire mixture into four bowls filled with the rice.

6   Serve immediately.

Ginger Chicken Teriyaki   *4 servings*

Teriyaki sauce is a favorite with many kids in Japan because of its sweet and savory sauce. The best way to do this is on a grill, but you can always cook it in a pan or even in the oven.

> 1 tablespoon canola oil
> 8 chicken thighs
> 1/3 cup soy sauce
> 1/3 cup mirin
> 2 cups water
> 1 tablespoon sesame seeds
> 1 tablespoon chopped ginger
> 1 tablespoon chia seeds

1   In a large grilling pan or frying pan, heat the oil on medium heat. Put the thighs skin side down in the pan and cook for 5 to 7 minutes or until the skin turns golden. Flip to the other side and cook for another 5 to 7 minutes.

2   Add the rest of the ingredients, except the chia seeds; cover the pan and cook on low heat for 30 to 40 minutes—you can cook it longer if you prefer that the chicken is so well cooked that it falls off the bone.

3   When done, remove from heat and sprinkle with chia seeds.

4   Serve with brown or white rice.

Chicken and Red Rice   *4 servings*

This bright red and green rice dish is one of my son's favorite dishes and a Japanese classic for children—the equivalent of American mac 'n' cheese. You can play around with the presentation and make small faces on the plate.

1 tablespoon canola oil
1 onion, cut into small pieces
2 chicken thighs, cut into small pieces
4 cups cooked rice
2 to 3 tablespoons ketchup
¼ cup frozen sweet peas, thawed
Two slices of orange peel and two cherry
    tomatoes (optional: for decoration to
    make a face)

1 In a large pan, heat the oil on medium heat. Add the chopped onions and cook until they are transparent, but pale in color. Transfer the onions to a plate.

2 In the same pan, add a bit more oil and cook the chicken on all sides until golden brown, about 7 to 10 minutes.

3 Return the onions to the pan. Add the cooked rice and the ketchup and stir until the rice takes on an even red color.

4 Add the peas and cook for 2 more minutes.

5 Serve immediately, putting it as a large round mound on a flat plate and making a decoration on top.

beef, pork, and other proteins

Beef with Scallions and Hemp Seeds
4 servings

This is a twist on a classic Japanese dish, Negima, scallions wrapped in thin slices of beef. Hemp seeds and canola oil increase the Omega-3 quotient, and the peppers add beautiful colors to this dish.

> 2 thick New York strip or rib eye beef steaks (well marbled)
> Bunch of green scallions
> 1 tablespoon canola oil
> 1 tablespoon sesame oil
> 3 tablespoons soy sauce
> 2 tablespoons mirin
> ¼ cup water
> 1 tablespoon ground hemp seeds

1 Wrap the beef steaks in plastic wrap and freeze for 1 hour until they become stiff. Freezing the meat allows you to cut it into thin slices more easily than if it were not. (Although the chefs at Le Cordon Bleu would frown at this technique, we do this often in Asia for recipes.) With a sharp knife, carefully slice the steaks into very thin pieces.

2 Wash the scallions and cut off the ends, keeping only the green parts; cut these into quarters. This should give you good size stems.

3 Take the thin strips of beef, which should have softened and thawed a bit after being cut, and place one strip on a clean surface. Put three or four scallion stems inside, and then roll into something that looks like a cigar roll. Place on a plate. Repeat until all of the beef slices have been filled and rolled.

4 In a pan, heat the canola and sesame oils. Cook the beef rolls carefully, on medium heat for 3 to 4 minutes; carefully turn them over to the other side for another 3 to 4 minutes.

5 Add the soy sauce, mirin, and water. Cover the pan and cook for another 5 minutes.

6 Remove from heat, sprinkle with hemp seeds, and serve with rice.

Couscous with Beef, Onions, and Raisins
4 servings

Moroccan cuisine blends sweet and savory in combinations that always surprise me. This is a take on classic Moroccan fare—couscous with beef and raisins. My son loves this combination of beef with sweet onions and raisins, and he always seems to finish his plate, even in his pickiest moments.

> 3 tablespoons golden raisins
> 1½ cups water
> 1 teaspoon salt
> 1 cup couscous
> 2 tablespoons olive oil
> 1 tablespoon butter
> 2 New York strip steaks, cut into small pieces
> 3 onions, thinly sliced
> 1 teaspoon ground cinnamon
> 1 teaspoon ground ginger
> 1 teaspoon orange juice
> 1 tablespoon honey
> 1 tablespoon chopped cilantro

1 In a small bowl, soak the raisins in ½ cup water for 15 minutes. Set aside.

2 In a pot, bring 1½ cups of water to a boil with the salt, and then add the couscous. Stir and remove from the heat, cover, and let stand for 10 minutes. Fluff the grains with a fork; replace the cover; and set aside while you prepare the sauce.

3 In a pan, heat the oil and the butter on low to medium heat. Add the beef strips and cook for 5 minutes. Transfer to a plate and set aside.

4 In the same pan, add the onions and cook until they are transparent and soft, about 10 minutes, being careful not to burn them.

5 Add the cinnamon, ginger, honey, and raisins with the water, and cook for 5 to 7 minutes.

6 Add the beef and cook for 3 to 4 more minutes. Remove from heat.

7 Place the couscous on a serving plate and top with the beef.

8 Pour the liquid from the pan into a separate serving bowl, and pour the liquid sauce on top of the couscous as you serve (otherwise, the couscous gets soggy).

9 Sprinkle with cilantro and serve warm.

Fried Tofu with Soy   *4 servings*

I don't fry a lot of foods, but sometimes I think the crunchy texture is fun and interesting for the little ones, and toddlers need adequate fat in their diet. This tofu is soft and crunchy, with a salty-sweet sauce, and with red peppers for vibrant color.

> 2 (12 ounce) packs soft silken tofu
> 4 tablespoons cornstarch
> 4 cups canola oil for frying
> 1 cup dashi stock or chicken stock
> 2 tablespoons soy sauce
> 2 tablespoons mirin
> 1 tablespoon finely diced red pepper
> 1 tablespoon grated fresh ginger
> Few shiso leaves or mint leaves

1 Drain the tofu in a strainer for at least 30 minutes. Cut each tofu piece into four pieces.

2 Spread the cornstarch on a plate and pat the tofu with it on all sides, coating it well.

3 Heat the oil on medium to high heat for 5 to 6 minutes. Fry the tofu until the pieces become golden, 3 to 4 minutes. Place them on a plate covered with paper towels.

4 In a small pan, heat the stock, soy, and mirin, and bring to a boil.

5 Put the tofu in 4 small serving bowls. Pour the sauce over, then garnish with red pepper, ginger, and the leaves.

Mini Lettuce Wraps with
Coconut Pork and Sardines   *4 servings*

With these South-Asian-inspired lettuce wraps, your child can make her own rolls at the table. It can be messy, but a lot of fun—an interesting approach to finger foods. Sardines are a great source of DHA, but they are not very common in the U.S. In Portugal, sardines are a national staple, and they are my favorite food when I visit the Algarve coast. There, the sardines are grilled outside with some sea salt and are either enjoyed straight off the grill or in a marinade with olive oil, potatoes, garlic, and a sprig of rosemary.

1 head of red leaf lettuce
1 teaspoon canola oil
½ pound ground pork
4 whole sardines
1 cup coconut milk
1 tablespoon nuoc nam fish sauce
½ inch fresh ginger
1 teaspoon honey
1 lemongrass stalk, finely chopped

1 Preheat the oven to 375°F.

2 Wash the lettuce and separate the leaves. Pat dry and set aside.

3 In a pan, heat the oil. Add the pork and cook for 5 to 7 minutes.

4 Meanwhile, roast the sardines in the oven for 4 to 5 minutes.

5 Remove the cooked flesh of the sardines from the bones and add it to the pan with the pork—be very careful to remove all the bones and check to make sure there are no small pieces left in the flesh.

6 Add the rest of the ingredients and cook for 15 to 20 minutes, then add the coconut milk and cook until the sauce thickens and clings to the pork, about 20 minutes on low heat.

7 Remove from the heat and let cool.

8 Serve on a plate, next to a plate of the washed lettuce. Place a tablespoonful of the pork mixture in a lettuce leaf, roll up, and enjoy.

snacks and desserts

Grilled Mochi Rice Cakes with Sweet Soy Dip

4 servings

These are not the dried crackers you may find in the snack aisle in the supermarket. Asian rice cakes are sticky rice pounded into a paste and dried into small cubes. They look like white pale Lego blocks before being cooked. They are a great snack, and now you can get them in brown rice cakes as well. You find them either in the Asian section of a Whole Foods market or at an Asian grocery store. More and more health food stores are also carrying them.

> 4 dried rice cakes
> 1 tablespoon sugar
> 2 tablespoons soy sauce

1 Heat a stove-top griller on medium high heat. Place the rice cakes directly on top and cook for 4 to 6 minutes until they puff and become golden. Flip them to the other side and cook for another 4 to 6 minutes.

2 Meanwhile, in a bowl, mix together the sugar and soy sauce.

3 Take the rice cakes off when done, and let them cool for 5 minutes. The outside of the cakes will be crunchy, and the inside will be gooey, and it will smell wonderful.

4 Serve with the dip on the side.

Oven Roasted Root Veggie Chips

4 servings as a snack

As an alternative to potato chips, these "chips" are great snacks.

> 1 yam
> 1 sweet potato
> 1 Idaho potato
> 2 carrots
> 1 red beet (optional)
> 1 teaspoon sea salt
> 1 tablespoon Parmesan cheese
> 1 tablespoon canola oil or olive oil
> 1 tablespoon ground flaxseeds

1 Preheat the oven to 350°F.

2 Peel the vegetables, and slice them thinly.

3 Put the slices on a baking sheet lined with parchment paper. Sprinkle with olive oil and salt. Roast in the oven for 15 to 20 minutes or until crisp, tossing them from time to time.

4 Sprinkle with Parmesan cheese and flaxseeds before serving.

Roasted Crunchy Rice Balls   *4 servings*

These rice balls are great for a quick lunch, as well as for picnics and meals on the go. You can mix herbs, meats, or veggies in the rice as well, in order to vary the texture.

> 4 cups cooked rice (white or brown)
> 1 tablespoon ground flaxseeds
> 1 tablespoon sesame seeds
> 2 tablespoons soy sauce
> 1 teaspoon brown sugar
> 1 tablespoon mirin
> 1 tablespoon water

> Dried seaweed sheets (dark thin flaky seaweed that is sold in large sheets. These are the kinds that are used to roll sushi in most restaurants. It can be bought in the Asian section at Whole Foods.)

1 Preheat the oven to 350°F.

2 In a bowl, combine the rice with the flaxseeds and sesame seeds, and mix. Then, using the palm of your hand, roll the rice into tight, small balls, squeezing with a bit of pressure to make compact rice balls. The size can vary, but they should be small bite-sized balls (1 cup should make around 4 to 6 balls).

3 In a small bowl, mix the soy sauce, mirin, water, and sugar. Set aside.

4 Line a baking sheet with parchment paper and place the rice balls on top. Bake for 5 to 6 minutes, then brush the soy mixture lightly on top.

5 Bake for another 2 minutes, then take the balls out of the oven and let cool for a few minutes.

6 Serve with nori pieces wrapped around them like mini sushi balls.

Spelt Crepe with Honey, Flax, and Walnuts   *4 to 6 servings*

Crepes are great for kids—they are versatile and can be made as a snack, dessert, or a savory meal. It is perfect for a brunch, and, in France, they do a savory crepe first, perhaps with ham and cheese, followed by a sweet crepe with sugar or jam. It is also a fun project to make crepes with your child and fill them together, and even decorate them with sprinkles or dried fruits.

1 cup spelt flour
1 teaspoon salt
1 cup milk
2 tablespoons butter, melted
2 eggs
3 tablespoons honey
1 tablespoon water
¼ cup ground walnuts
1 tablespoon ground flaxseeds

1 In a bowl, mix together the flour and salt. Add the milk little by little, whisking constantly to avoid lumps. Add butter and eggs, and beat until smooth.

2 In a smaller bowl, combine the honey, water, walnuts, and flaxseeds.

3 Heat a pan on medium heat. Soak a paper towel in canola oil, and then dab the paper on the pan to coat it well with oil. (Repeat after cooking each crepe.)

4 Pour one ladle (about ¼ cup) of batter onto the pan and cook for about 2 minutes, or until the bottom side is golden. Flip and cook for another 2 minutes.

5 Spread 1 tablespoon of the walnut mixture thinly over the crepe.

6 Fold into thirds to close.

7 Serve warm.

Garbanzo Bean Crepes with Blackberry Compote   *4 to 6 servings*

Garbanzo bean flour is a great alternative to normal white flour because it is all about the protein, and it has a mild flavor that goes well in a sweet recipe. Black raspberry contains a good dose of Omega-3 fatty acid, and, while it may be bitter when eaten raw, this compote sweetens the fruit with natural agave nectar, which is full of vitamins and minerals.

2 tablespoons honey
1 cup blackberries
1 tablespoon cornstarch
3 tablespoons water
1 cup garbanzo bean flour
1 teaspoon salt
1 cup milk
2 tablespoons butter, melted
2 eggs
1 tablespoon confectioners' sugar

1 In a small pan, mix honey and blackberries and cook on low heat for 5 to 7 minutes.

2 In a cup, mix together the cornstarch and water, and add into the pot with the berries. Cook for 3 to 5 more minutes, remove from the heat and set aside.

3 In a bowl, mix together the garbanzo bean flour and salt. Add the milk little by little, whisking constantly to avoid lumps. Add butter and egg and beat until smooth.

4 Heat a pan on medium heat. Soak a paper towel in canola oil, and then dab the paper on the pan to coat it well with oil. (Repeat after cooking each crepe.)

5 Pour one ladle (about ¼ cup) of batter onto the pan and cook for about 2 minutes, or until the bottom side is golden. Flip and cook for another 2 minutes.

6 Transfer the crepe onto a plate and repeat with the remaining batter. Fill each crepe with the blackberry compote.

7 Close the crepe and sprinkle with a bit of confectioners' sugar and serve.

Whole Wheat Rose Crepes with Lychee Cream

4 servings

This recipe is inspired by the French pastry chef Pierre Herme, who is famous for his delicate macaroons. His rose macaroons with lychee offer such a beautiful flavor combination, but macaroons are not the easiest to make on a whim. These crepes integrate the same flavors but in a simple crepe that you can whip up for a snack. Rosewater/essence is now available in many grocery stores, and it is a wonderful flavor alternative to vanilla or almond. Many Middle Eastern desserts are made with this essence as well as the gorgeous orange blossom essence, which is a bit more difficult to find in stores.

    1 cup whole wheat flour
    1 teaspoon salt
    1 cup milk
    2 tablespoons butter, melted
    2 eggs
    1 teaspoon rose flower essence
    ½ cup canned lychees, with its syrup
    1 cup whipping cream
    2 tablespoons confectioners' sugar
    4 to 6 whole lychees, for presentation

1 In a bowl, mix together the flour and salt. Add the milk little by little, whisking constantly to avoid lumps. Add the butter, eggs, and the essence, and beat until smooth.

2 For the filling, puree the lychee with its syrup in a blender until completely blended.

3 Then in a bowl, whip the cream until the peaks stiffen; then add the sugar and whip a little longer.

4 Gently fold in the lychee puree and cover with plastic. Refrigerate while you prepare the crepes.

5 Heat a frying pan. Soak a paper towel in canola oil, and then dab the paper on the pan to coat it well with oil. (Repeat after cooking each crepe.)

6 Pour one ladle (about ¼ cup) of batter onto the pan and cook for about 2 minutes, or until the bottom side is golden. Flip and cook for another 2 minutes.

7 Transfer to a plate. Repeat until all of the crepes are cooked.

8 Place each crepe on a plate. Fill the middle with the lychee cream, and gently fold in both sides like an envelope. Put a dollop of cream on top, and place a whole lychee on it.

9 Serve immediately.

Orange, Chia Seed, and Mint Fruit Salad with Orange Blossom Syrup

4 servings

This is a refreshing fruit salad served in many countries in the Maghreb region—Morocco, Tunisia, Algeria—perfect for warm summer afternoons as a snack or after a rustic meal like a couscous with beef. This recipe integrates crunchy chia seeds for a dose of DHA Omega-3. If you can't find orange blossom extract, you can use the zest of one orange with a cup of warm water mixed with 1 tablespoon sugar.

    2 navel oranges
    3 to 5 mint sprigs
    1 teaspoon orange blossom extract
    Juice of ½ orange
    1 tablespoon honey
    1 tablespoon chia seeds

1 Cut the peels off the oranges and cut them into thin slices. Lay them on 4 separate plates.

2 Wash and cut the mint leaves into thin strips and lay them on top of the oranges.

3 In a bowl, mix together the extract, orange juice, honey, and chia seeds until well blended.

4 Pour onto the oranges, break up the orange segments and serve.

Caramel Pancakes (Dora-Yaki)

16 to 18 mini pancakes, 6 to 8 servings

These Japanese pancakes are denser and more moist than the light French crepes, and they are usually served with a sweet paste made of stewed azuki beans.

> 2 eggs
> ½ cup brown sugar
> 1 teaspoon mirin
> 2 tablespoons water
> 1 tablespoon honey
> 1 cup whole wheat flour, sifted
> 1 tablespoon ground hemp seeds
> 1 teaspoon baking powder
> 1 teaspoon baking soda
> ½ cup cream
> 1 tablespoon confectioners' sugar

1 In a bowl, beat together the eggs and sugar until foamy. Add the mirin, water, and honey, and mix. Gradually add the sifted flour and hemp, and whisk until well blended.

2 Heat a pan on medium heat and oil it well with a paper towel that has been dabbed with canola oil; repeat this after each pancake.

3 Pour ½ ladle of batter into an oblong shape and cook for 2 to 4 minutes, until the batter begins to bubble in the center, and the bottom is golden. Flip and cook for 2 to 4 minutes more.

4 Transfer to a plate and cover with a paper towel to avoid drying out while you cook the rest of the batter. Repeat with the remaining pancakes.

5 In a bowl, whip the cream until it thickens, and add the sugar, whipping it a few seconds more.

6 When the pancakes have cooled completely, fill them with a teaspoon of cream. Fold up slightly so that the folds touch.

Variation: Banana and Cream Filling

> 1 banana
> 2 tablespoons shaved chocolate

1 Instead of using azuki bean paste, place a few slices of banana into the pancake, and then add the cream and close into a fold.

2 Sprinkle chocolate shavings on top and serve.

Garbanzo Bean Cookies   *6 to 8 servings*

OK, so you're thinking, beans in cookies? Sounds strange, but you will be very surprised that all you taste in these cookies is a nutty flavor. They are so good, and they are full of protein and complex carbohydrates. I got the idea from my dear friend Belle, who was inspired by energy bars.

½ cup brown sugar
¼ cup olive oil
1 egg
2 cups garbanzo beans
1 cup whole wheat or quinoa flour
½ cup oat bran
2 tablespoons ground flaxseeds
1 teaspoon cinnamon
1 teaspoon baking soda
¼ cup dried cranberries
¼ cup dark chocolate chips (optional)
¼ cup chopped dried dates
¼ cup almonds or walnuts

1 Preheat the oven to 350°F.

2 In a food processor, pulse the sugar, oil, egg, and beans together. Then put the mixture in a large bowl.

3 In a separate bowl, mix together the dry ingredients.

4 Then, using your hands, combine the dry ingredients with the wet mixture until it takes on a firm dough-like consistency.

5 Line a baking sheet with parchment paper, and, with a small spoon, scoop up the dough and drop small balls onto the baking sheet.

6 With a moist finger, press down the dough a bit with the tip of your finger and bake for 10 to 12 minutes or until golden.

7 Let the cookies cool on a rack and serve.

Frozen Grape Treats

Serves 4 to 6 as a snack

There was a period when my son only wanted ice and frozen bits of fruit to gnaw on. You can do this with many fruits, and grapes are a very simple treat—just pop them in the freezer!

2 cups of organic grapes, washed

1 Cut the grapes in quarters and put the pieces in a plastic container. Freeze them for 2 hours.

2 Take out the desired quantity, and serve a few at a time as frozen treats.

Zucchini Bread   *Serves 4 to 6*

Zucchini, when baked, is sweet, and my friends are often very surprised to hear that they are eating a vegetable bread because it tastes closer to a fruit bread.

3 cups whole wheat flour
1½ teaspoons salt
2 teaspoons cinnamon
1 teaspoon baking soda
1 cup brown sugar
1 cup vegetable oil
4 eggs, beaten
½ cup water
2 cups grated zucchini
1 teaspoon lemon zest
1 teaspoon vanilla
¼ cup ground flaxseed
1 cup walnuts

1 Preheat the oven to 350°F.

2 In a bowl, mix flour and salt, and then add in cinnamon, baking soda, flaxseed, and sugar.

3 In another bowl, mix the oil, vanilla, eggs, water, zucchini, and lemon zest.

4 Combine the dry ingredients into the wet mixture and mix with your hands. Fold in the nuts.

5 Pour the mixture into 2 oiled loaf pans. Bake for 45 minutes to 1 hour.

No Butter, No Sugar Banana Nut Bread

Serves 4 to 6

I love banana bread, but I don't always love so much sugar and butter in the baked goods I make for my son. This bread gets its sweetness from the pineapples and the bananas, and its moisture from the canola oil.

1½ cups whole wheat flour
¼ teaspoon salt
1 teaspoon baking soda
1 teaspoon cinnamon
¾ cups organic pureed pineapple (from a jar)
¾ cup canola oil
2 ripe bananas, mashed
1½ cups walnuts
1 tablespoon ground flaxseeds

1 Preheat the oven to 350°F.

2 In a bowl, combine the flour and salt, and then add the baking soda and cinnamon.

3 In a separate bowl, mix the pineapple, oil, and bananas.

4 Combine the dry mixture with the wet mixture until blended. Fold in the walnuts and flaxseeds.

5 Pour the batter into two oiled loaf pans. Bake for 50 to 55 minutes.

No Butter Oatmeal Cookies

Serves 6 to 8

I think oatmeal cookies are a great snack for the little ones, and I have multiple versions of the oatmeal cookie idea. There is no butter in these cookies and barely-there brown sugar. Cookies without butter come out with differences in texture and flavor than those with butter because the fat content is different. But they are crunchy and delicious.

¼ cup brown sugar
1 teaspoon vanilla extract
1 egg
¾ cup organic applesauce
½ teaspoon salt
1 cup whole wheat flour
1 teaspoon baking soda
1 tablespoon ground flaxseed
3 cups rolled oats
2 cups of dried cranberries/almonds/ raisins/bing cherries

1 Preheat the oven to 350°F.

2 In a bowl, mix the sugar, vanilla, egg, and applesauce.

3 In another bowl, mix the salt with the flour, and then add the baking soda and flaxseeds.

4 Add flour mixture to the applesauce mixture, and mix well. Fold in the oats, and then the dried fruits/nuts.

5 On a baking sheet lined with parchment paper, drop the mixture by small spoonfuls and flatten the cookies with your fingers (the dough will not flatten while baking because there is no butter).

6 Bake for only 7 to 9 minutes or until golden brown.

Belle's Steel Cut Oatmeal with Azuki Beans
2 servings

My dear friend Belle serves oatmeal with azuki bean paste for her beautiful girl Ava, who loves it. This is a delicious breakfast, especially for cold winter mornings. It's full of great nutrition, with fiber, complex carbohydrates, protein, iron, and folic acid, and a sprinkle of ground hemp adds DHA Omega-3. Steel cut oatmeal takes longer to cook than quick oats, but it has more fiber and freezes better than the instant kind. It is worth making a big batch at one time and freezing the rest in small portions.

2 cups cooked steel cut oatmeal
1 cup milk
1 tablespoon ground hemp
2 tablespoons cooked azuki bean paste

1 In a pan, heat the oatmeal with the milk for a few minutes until warm. Remove from the heat, sprinkle hemp, and add the paste on top.

2 Mix and serve.

Banana and Fig Bread Pudding
4 to 6 servings

Bread pudding is a quick and satisfying dessert because it takes very little time and effort. For kids, it is a comfort food, and I usually make this on the weekends with the leftover chunks of bread that I had put in the freezer.

4 slices whole wheat bread, toasted
2 eggs
1 cup milk
½ cup cream
1 tablespoon vanilla extract
1 teaspoon ground hemp
1 banana, cut into pieces
10 or 12 dried figs, cut into small pieces
2 tablespoons honey
1 tablespoon dark brown sugar
2 tablespoons Greek yogurt per serving

1 Break up the toast into small pieces. In a bowl, mix together all of the ingredients, except the yogurt, and pour into a baking dish.

2 Bake for 55 to 60 minutes, until the custard has hardened and turned a golden caramel color.

3 Serve warm with a dollop of whipped Greek yogurt.

Fresh Fruit Pakoras

4 to 6 servings

Pakoras are Indian fritters, usually made with chickpea batter and fried. But they can also be phyllo-pastry-wrapped meat or vegetable patties. In this recipe, I have simply replaced the savory filling with fresh fruit. You can use any kind of fruit (dried or fresh) and also add nuts.

> ½ cup strawberries
> ½ banana
> 1 kiwi
> 4 phyllo pastry sheets
> 1 tablespoon confectioners' sugar
> 1 tablespoon chia seeds
> 1 teaspoon cinnamon
> 4 tablespoons canola oil
> 2 tablespoons honey

1 Preheat oven to 375°F.

2 Wash and cut all of the fruit into small pieces. Mix together in a bowl with the sugar, seeds, and cinnamon and set aside.

3 Cut each phyllo sheet into four equal size squares.

4 Place one quarter-sheet of phyllo on a clean surface and brush it lightly with the olive oil. Place a second quarter-sheet on top. Spread the fruit mixture in the center of the second sheet.

5 Place a third quarter-sheet on top of the fruit mixture and brush with olive oil, then place the last sheet on top.

6 Fold each corner of the phyllo to the center. Then cut the folded sheet diagonally into four triangles.

7 Bake for 10 to 15 minutes, until the phyllo pastry is golden.

8 Take out of the oven and drizzle with honey. Makes about 20 pakoras.

No Butter Tunisian Almond Cookies

6 to 8 servings

These almond cookies are flaky and crumbly, and they are a protein-rich snack. You can add dried nuts, and on special occasions, add chocolate chips.

> 7 cups almonds
> 4 eggs
> ⅔ cup sugar
> ½ teaspoon vanilla extract
> 3½ tablespoons baking powder
> 1 teaspoon ground cinnamon
> 1 tablespoon ground flaxseeds
> 1 cup confectioners' sugar

1 Preheat the oven to 350°F.

2 Place the almonds on a baking sheet and roast in the oven for 5 minutes.

3 Take out the almonds and let them cool for a few minutes; put them in a food processor and coarsely chop for a few seconds (it does not have to be powder).

4 In a bowl, mix together the eggs and sugar. Then add the vanilla, baking powder, cinnamon, and flaxseeds.

5 Integrate the chopped almonds and knead together by hand. Roll the dough into small balls and flatten them a bit.

6 Dust both sides with confectioners' sugar and bake on a greased baking sheet for 7 to 10 minutes.

six

19 to 24 months
Daring World Flavors

Your child is now probably a walking, talking, and running little person, full of energy and always on the go.

Feeding your toddler becomes more and more of a challenge as he realizes how much fun it is to be up and about. Sitting becomes a chore for your child—for driving, for the stroller, and for eating. At the same time, the picky, fussy stage emerges in many children. So brace yourself for many interesting experiences in cooking, feeding, and teaching your child what food is all about. For me, this was what I called a "going-back-to-basics" period because it forced me to think about each food's essential qualities and how to make it as palatable, interesting, and fun as possible for my child to enjoy.

In order to keep my child's attention during meals, I talked about the origin of that particular food, how it grew, and where it came from. I would do short "demonstrations"—show the uncooked form of a pea, for example, and compare it with the cooked mashed kind. I would also present the meals in mini plates and trays and present an interesting look to the meal, or place the meals in handmade "plates" of lettuce, banana leaf, or other kinds of edible or organic items. Other times I would make special shapes and figures with food. Serving children food in mini bowls, cups, or plates is so much fun for them, and it's a good way to entertain them without bringing toys to the table.

And of course, I would spend time making new dishes for my son, which he often refused to try. No matter how frustrating it became at times, I kept at it, and after what seemed like a very long time, he came back around and began to try new foods, including raw vegetables and even smelly cheeses that I never thought he would ever touch. The key is to be patient and to be gently persistent, without being overbearing. Research has shown that children's food preferences from ages 2 to 4 are major indicators of their preferences later in life. It is worth the effort to try to include a wide variety of flavors and textures so that your child is open to as many different sources of nutrients and vitamins as possible.

For example, my son refused to eat green beans for a very long time. I tried every single way of cooking the beans to see if he would eat them—baked, boiled, sautéed, even fried. And then one day, for no apparent reason, he picked up a string bean and began eating it. And he has been eating them ever since, in all kinds of ways. It is a mystery for me, but this is the way it is for most things—he may resist initially, but eventually, he comes around to trying it, especially if I make it often enough and if he sees me eating it. So my advice is—*don't give up.*

How Much Food Should My Child Be Eating?

Milk is still a big part of your child's diet, and it is important to keep providing him with at least 16 ounces of milk per day and up to 32 ounces. This becomes more and more of a challenge as you transition from a sippy cup to a regular cup. To be honest, I kept the sippy cup for a long time just to make sure my son kept drinking his daily dose of milk. Then I tried flavored milk with fresh fruits, and then eventually, he began to drink milk in his regular toddler cup. But this was a long process. The reason I share this with you is because for me, it seemed like everyone else was having such an easy time with milk, as well as with feeding. But it is not true. We all struggle to find the right way for our child. The best way, for me, was to be as observant of my child as I could be, being attentive, patient, and careful about not pushing.

Feeding Guide:[*]

- Bread, Cereal, Rice or Pasta: 6 servings per day (serving size: ½ slice whole wheat bread, ¼ cup pasta)

- Fruit: 3 servings per day (serving size: ¼ cup cooked, ½ cup raw)

- Vegetables: 2 servings per day (serving size: ¼ cup cooked, ½ cup raw)

- Milk, Yogurt, Cheese: 4 servings per day (serving size: ½ cup yogurt, ¾ ounce cheese)

- Meat, Poultry, Fish, or Beans: 2 servings per day (serving size: 1 tablespoon, 1 egg, 1 cup cooked beans)

Trying World Flavors

Because this period is still the formative time for your child's taste buds, it is important to keep introducing new flavors, textures, and combinations of foods to stimulate the palate and the senses. Even though it may not always be apparent, you are creating the foundation for his preferences. The more variety you introduce, not only will your child receive more nutrients from diverse foods, the more open he will be to new and different flavors and foods throughout his life. So I encourage you to be daring, bold, and keep trying new ingredients and foods, even if your child seems resistant to them at first.

[*] http://www.babycenter.com/0_age-by-age-guide-to-feeding-your-toddler_1736045.bc.

 **soup**

Miso Soup with Clams, Kale, and Young Potatoes   *4 servings*

Miso soup can be made in an endless combination of ways. This soup with clams is special because of the rich broth, which is enhanced by the clam liquid. With kale, it is a complete meal in one.

1 pound fresh littleneck clams
1 cup young fingerling potatoes
6 cups cold water
1 large kombu seaweed
2 tablespoons miso paste
2 cups frozen kale, thawed
1 tablespoon chopped scallions

1 Scrub the clams, and place them in a bowl; cover it with a kitchen towel, and refrigerate them while you prepare the soup.

2 Wash the potatoes, and cut them into quarters. In a large pot, bring to a boil the potatoes with enough water to cover them. Simmer for 10 to 15 minutes until the potatoes are soft when pierced with a knife. Drain.

3 In another pot, combine the cold water and seaweed and bring it to a boil. Cover and simmer for 10 minutes.

4 Add the miso paste, kale, and potatoes, and cook for 5 minutes.

5 Add the clams and cook until all of the shells open up. Discard any clams that have not opened up after 4 to 5 minutes.

6 Sprinkle with scallions and serve warm.

Butternut Squash Soup with Amaretti, Wheat Germ, and Walnut Crumble

4 to 6 servings

Butternut squash is sweet and full of flavor, and it can be used in a variety of ways. Packed with beta-carotene, the squash is perfect for a beautiful soup with a sweet touch of walnut and amaretti. The combination of amaretti cookies and squash/pumpkin is often used in Italian dishes as a filling for ravioli. In this dish, I use the same concept, but I adapt it to a light soup that is easy for kids to enjoy. The heavy cream at the end is optional; you can serve this as a straight squash soup or as a creamy version.

1 onion
1 tablespoon canola oil
4 cups cubed butternut squash
8 cups chicken stock
2 tablespoons heavy cream (optional)
4 amaretti cookies (purchased), crushed
    into small pieces
2 tablespoons wheat germ
1 tablespoon brown sugar
¼ cup crushed walnuts
salt and pepper, to taste

1 Peel and cut the onion into small, thin slices. Heat a large pot with the oil. Add the onions and cook on low heat, taking care not to burn them, until they become pale and transparent, about 4 to 6 minutes.

2 Add the squash and the chicken stock, and bring to a boil. Cover and let it simmer for 40 to 60 minutes until the squash becomes soft when pierced with a knife.

3 Use a hand blender to blend the squash in the pot with the liquid until it becomes smooth. Remove it from the heat and stir in the cream.

4 In a bowl, mix together the crushed amaretti cookies, wheat germ, brown sugar, and walnuts.

5 Pour the soup into four bowls and sprinkle the crumble mixture on top. Salt and pepper, to taste.

6 Serve warm with whole wheat bread or a baguette.

Roasted Beet Soup and Herring

4 servings

Beets are one of the most powerful root vegetables nutritionally because they contain antioxidants, vitamins, and minerals, including iron, manganese, magnesium, and potassium. Here I combine it with herring, rich in DHA Omega-3. Herring could overpower the delicate flavor of the beet soup, so I use a small portion to give the meal protein and fatty acid. You can serve this as a cold summer soup or warm, with toasted bread on the side.

4 red beets
1 onion
2 tablespoons olive oil
6 cups chicken stock
1 bay leaf
1 teaspoon thyme
1 tablespoon ground nutmeg
¼ teaspoon salt
4 fillets of preserved herring
¼ cup cream
½ cup milk
salt and pepper, to taste
1 slice of whole wheat bread, toasted
1 tablespoon chopped chives

1 Preheat the oven to 375°F.

2 Wash and cut the beets in half; wrap them in foil and roast for 60 to 90 minutes or until they are tender throughout when pierced with a knife.

3 Meanwhile, peel and cut the onion into thin slices. Heat a pan with oil and cook the onions on low heat until they soften and become transparent.

4 When the beets are done, remove them from the oven and let them cool. Peel off the thick rough skin and cut the beets into small cubes. Add them to the onions and sauté for 3 to 5 minutes.

5 Add the chicken stock, bay leaf, thyme, nutmeg, and salt; cover, and bring to a boil. Simmer for 30 to 40 minutes.

6 Add the herring and simmer for 10 more minutes.

7 With a hand blender, blend the soup until completely smooth.

8 Add the cream and milk; salt and pepper, to taste.

9 Pour into soup bowls, and grate the toasted bread on top; sprinkle on a few pieces of chives. Serve immediately.

Potato and Leek Soup with Barley

4 servings

This is a smooth vegetable soup with barley for texture and carbohydrate. For toppings, I have used crushed walnuts, walnut oil, and dried cranberries, similar to an Italian *gremolata*, which is a combination of fruits and nuts used as a topping to meats. You can also use fresh herbs, cheeses, and other kinds of dried fruits.

1 leek
2 potatoes
½ onion
2 tablespoons olive oil
salt and pepper, to taste
6 cups chicken stock
2 tablespoons heavy cream
1 cup cooked barley
¼ cup crushed walnuts
2 tablespoons walnut oil
2 tablespoons chopped dried cranberries

1 Wash the leek carefully by cutting into the dark green part of the leek and fanning it open and running each section under warm water; it often contains hidden sand or dirt. Cut the leek into small pieces.

2 Wash and peel the potatoes, and cut them into small pieces. Cut the onion into small pieces.

3 In a large pot, heat the olive oil on medium heat; add the onions and cook for 3 to 5 minutes, until the onions become transparent.

4 Add the leek, sprinkle with salt and pepper, and stir. Cook for an additional 5 to 7 minutes.

5 Add stock and potatoes, and cover the pot. Bring to a boil, and then simmer for 20 minutes.

6 Use a hand mixer to blend the soup until smooth.

7 Add in the cooked barley, and heat for another 5 minutes.

8 Remove from heat and stir in the heavy cream. Salt and pepper, to taste, and then pour into bowls.

9 Sprinkle on some crushed walnuts, walnut oil, and dried cranberries, and serve.

Egg Drop Soup with Corn and Tofu

4 servings

Egg drop soup is so simple, you can whip this up in less than 15 minutes, and, with the tofu, you have a hearty meal with protein, fatty acids, folic acid, and vitamins.

1 tablespoon canola oil
2 chicken breasts
6 cups chicken stock
1 cup frozen corn, thawed
A pinch of salt and a dash of pepper
3 scallions
1 package silken soft tofu
4 large eggs

1 In a pan, cook the chicken breast in the oil for 7 to 8 minutes.

2 Meanwhile, in a pot, add the stock, corn, salt, and pepper, and bring to a boil. Reduce the heat and let simmer for 3 to 4 minutes.

3 Wash and cut the scallions into small pieces, discarding the white section and using only the dark green section.

4 When the chicken is done, cut it into small pieces, and add it to the stock.

5 Cut the tofu into small pieces and add it with the scallions to the stock; bring the soup to a boil again.

6 In a small bowl, whip the eggs together until they are frothy, about a good minute. Pour them into the soup, and stir the soup quickly—they will become light and fluffy.

7 Serve immediately.

Creamy Pesto Soup with Gnocchi

4 servings

My son adores pesto, and I use it on everything from sandwiches to marinades. This pesto soup is an alternative to doing a rather dry pesto sauce with pasta. It is creamy, and you can use other kinds of pasta, such as orzo, orecchiette, or mini macaroni.

2½ cups fresh gnocchi
1 tablespoon olive oil
4 tablespoons pesto paste
3 cups chicken stock
2 cups milk
½ cup cream
¼ cup grated Parmesan cheese
1 sprig fresh basil
2 tablespoons chia seeds

1 Bring to boil a pot of water with salt. Add the gnocchi and cook according to package instructions. Drain and set aside.

2 In the same pot, heat the oil, add the pesto, and cook for 2 to 3 minutes.

3 Add the chicken stock, and bring to a boil. Simmer uncovered for 20 minutes.

4 Add the milk and cream, and simmer for another 10 minutes, covered.

5 Stir in the cheese; add the gnocchi and cook for 5 minutes.

6 Pour into four large soup bowls. Wash and cut the basil leaves from the sprig of basil and sprinkle it on top, along with the chia seeds.

7 Serve immediately.

Coconut Carrot Soup with Kamut Pasta

4 servings

Earlier in the book I introduced pumpkin coconut soup. Here I modified the spices for a fuller-bodied carrot soup with kamut pasta for a complete meal because your 19-month-old's appetite will be requiring more and more substance in one meal. This is a thick hearty soup full of flavor. Enjoy.

    1 onion
    1 tablespoon canola oil
    6 medium-sized carrots
    1 tablespoon butter
    2 cloves (the dried spice)
    1 cinnamon stick
    1 cardamom pod
    4 cups coconut milk
    2 cups chicken stock
    2 cups kamut elbow pasta
    1 tablespoon chopped fresh cilantro
    1 tablespoon grated bread crumbs
    salt and pepper, to taste

1   Peel and slice the onion into thin strips. Heat oil in a pan on low heat, and slowly cook the onions until they're pale and translucent, about 4 to 5 minutes, sprinkling with a bit of salt.

2   Wash and peel the carrots, and then shred them with a grater into thin slices. Melt butter in a separate pan and add the carrots; cook for about 5 minutes until the carrots begin to soften.

3   Add the rest of the ingredients and bring to a boil. Cover and simmer for about 20 minutes, and then blend the soup with a hand blender until completely smooth.

4   Sprinkle with cilantro, bread crumbs, salt, and pepper, and serve.

Buckwheat Noodle Soup with Kelp/Seaweed and Salmon

4 servings

Buckwheat noodles are a superfood because they are packed with Omega-3 fatty acid, folate, calcium, magnesium, potassium, and other vitamins and minerals. They are a staple in Japanese cuisine and can be paired with any kind of vegetables or protein.

    4 cups water
    14 ounces buckwheat noodles
    2 tablespoons dashi fish stock, dried (if using liquid fish stock, use 4 cups of fish stock instead of water)
    2 tablespoons dried kelp
    1 salmon fillet
    1 tablespoon chopped scallions

1   In a pot of boiling water, cook the noodles according to package instructions, and then drain.

2   In another pot, add the water with stock, kelp, and chunks of salmon, and cook on medium heat until the salmon is completely cooked and flakes apart.

3   In a small bowl, put a portion of the noodles and pour the stock mixture over the noodles.

4   Serve with a small sprinkle of chopped scallions.

Chicken Noodle Soup

4 servings

This is a staple in our weekly menu. The week usually begins with some kind of chicken dish—a roasted chicken or curried chicken thighs—and I keep the bones to roast and use for stock, adding chicken breast later into the soup. Or I start the week with the soup, with chicken legs and thighs, and then the next day, I use the stock to make risotto or noodle soup. This soup is simple—just sauté the ingredients, pour in water, cover, and cook on low heat and forget about it for 2 hours. Add some salt and pepper, a drizzle of olive oil, and maybe a sprinkle of grated Parmesan cheese, and you have a gorgeous soup.

1 onion
4 tablespoons olive oil
4 chicken thighs
2 chicken legs
2 carrots
1 celery rib
8 cups water
1 tablespoon thyme
2 tablespoons flaxseeds
1 bay leaf
2 tablespoons salt
¼ cup grated Parmesan cheese
salt and pepper
2 cups or 8 ounces cooked egg noodles
1 teaspoon oregano

1 Peel and cut the onion into small slices. Wash and peel the carrots and celery and cut them into small pieces.

2 Heat a large pot with 2 tablespoons of olive oil; add the onions and cook on low heat for 3 to 5 minutes until they become transparent.

3 Add the chicken and sauté for 5 minutes on each side until the pieces become golden.

4 Add the carrots and celery into the pot, and sauté for 3 to 4 minutes until they begin to sweat.

5 Pour in the water, thyme, oregano, flaxseeds, bay leaf, and 2 tablespoons salt, and bring to a boil. Cover and simmer on low heat for 2 hours.

6 The chicken should be falling apart, with the meat tender enough to slip away from the bones. Skim the foam and any excess fat that floats to the surface of the soup. Then carefully remove the bones, ligaments, and cartilage from the pot and discard.

7 Add the cheese and remaining olive oil, as well as a good amount of salt and pepper.

8 Divide the cooked egg noodles into four bowls. Pour the soup over them, and serve immediately.

Garbanzo Bean Soup   *6 to 8 servings*

This is one of my favorite soups, and, earlier in the book, I introduced the smooth pureed version of this soup with milder flavors. Now your child is ready for the hearty version, full of strong flavors from the saffron. In this recipe, I make a mild version of the spicy Spanish soup, not using the spicy chorizo sausage but a sweet Italian one instead. I usually make a huge pot of this soup on a weekend and freeze small portions for later use. It may seem like a long cooking period, but it is something that you can start on a Saturday or Sunday morning and let simmer during the day while you play with your kids. I suggest around 80 to 90 minutes total for cooking time, but it won't hurt at all if you decide to let it simmer for several hours.

1 large onion
6 cloves of garlic
1 bunch kale
1 tablespoon olive oil
2 sweet Italian sausages
1 ham shank (with bone)
¾ pound beef short ribs
10 cups water
1 bay leaf
1 package of saffron (or 2 teaspoons)
6 cups garbanzo beans, soaked overnight
2 tablespoons walnut oil
salt and pepper, to taste

1   Peel and chop onions and garlic into small pieces. Wash and chop the kale into small pieces, discarding the hard stems.

2   In a large pot, heat the olive oil and cook the onions and garlic for 2 to 3 minutes.

3   Add the sausage and brown on all sides for 3 to 5 minutes. Remove the sausage; cut it into small pieces; and return it to the pot.

4   Add the ham shank and short ribs, and brown for about 10 minutes.

5   Add water, bay leaf, kale, beans, and saffron, and bring to a boil. Cover and let it simmer for 80 to 90 minutes or longer, skimming the fat from the surface from time to time to "de-fat" (eliminating the fat and the foam that floats to the surface during cooking).

6   Pour into separate bowls, and drizzle with a bit of walnut oil.

7   Serve with bread.

vegetables and salads

....

Roasted Eggplant with Miso

4 servings

This eggplant dish is called *misoyaki*—literally translates to—miso grill.
Miso gives the eggplant a sweetness that is perfect with the soft roasted
eggplant flesh. And it is so easy to make.

- 2 tablespoons miso paste
- 1 tablespoon water
- 2 large eggplants
- 2 tablespoons sesame oil
- 1 teaspoon sesame seeds
- 1 teaspoon of ground flaxseeds

1 Preheat the oven to 375°F.

2 In a small bowl, mix the miso paste with water to thin out the texture.

3 Line a baking tray with aluminum foil. Place the eggplant cut side up
  on the foil and spread the miso paste on top, spreading it evenly.

4 Then drizzle with sesame oil, topping it with the seeds. Bake for
  15 to 20 minutes or until the eggplants are soft and the top is
  carmelized.

5 You can serve it with rice or accompanied with some greens.

Asparagus with Shiitake Mushrooms

4 servings as a side dish

This asparagus recipe combines a salty soy broth with the vegetable. The shiitake mushrooms add a slippery texture to the asparagus, which, if cooked al dente as described below, should be crunchy and crisp. Asparagus is not always a kid's favorite, but you should keep trying to offer it to your children because it is worth the effort. Asparagus is another superfood, with Omega-3 fatty acid, protein, vitamins A, C, and E, folate, calcium, and potassium, among other vitamins and minerals.

5 dried shiitake mushrooms
1 cup water
1 tablespoon cornstarch
1 pound asparagus
1 teaspoon sesame oil
1 tablespoon canola oil
1 garlic clove
1 tablespoon soy sauce
1 tablespoon chia seeds

1 Soak the mushrooms in water for 15 to 20 minutes until they are tender and soft. Remove them from the water, and cut them into small pieces; reserve the liquid.

2 Add the cornstarch to the liquid, and stir until well blended. Set aside.

3 Wash and trim the asparagus—cut off the hard white and pale section on the bottom of each spear.

4 Heat a sauté pan with oil on low heat. Add the garlic and asparagus, and sauté for 5 to 7 minutes.

5 Add the mushrooms with their liquid. Cover and simmer for 7 to 10 minutes, until the asparagus is tender and the sauce thick.

6 Sprinkle with chia seeds and serve immediately.

Broiled Open Cheese Sandwich with Avocado

4 servings

Grilled cheese is such a good way to integrate layers of ingredients into a warm package. Here I combine Emmental cheese with ripe avocado and ground flaxseeds, but you can try different combinations of cheeses and vegetables or sliced meats. I use pesto sauce rather than tons of butter to give it more flavor, and it blends well with the avocado.

1 ripe avocado
4 slices of whole wheat bread
4 tablespoons pesto sauce
2 tablespoons ground flaxseeds
4 thick slices of Emmental cheese
2 tablespoons olive oil
salt and pepper, to taste

1 Heat the oven to medium broil.

2 Peel and remove the pit of the avocado; cut avocado into thin slices.

3 Cover a baking tray with foil, and assemble the sandwiches. Lay four slices of bread on a clean surface and spread with the pesto sauce. Place a few slices of avocado on each piece; sprinkle with flaxseeds; and top each with the cheese.

4 Put the tray on the bottom part of the oven to avoid burning. Cook for 6 to 8 minutes, or until the cheese has completely melted.

5 Serve immediately.

Sautéed Spinach with Chia and Sesame Seeds

4 servings as a side dish

Adding chia seeds is a quick way to add extra DHA Omega-3 to any dish, and this spinach recipe is rich with folic acid, calcium, vitamins C, D, and E, as well as the fatty acid. Fish sauce has a pungent flavor when sampled on its own, but when cooked in a dish, it simply deepens the flavor without adding the tangy edge to it.

1 pound fresh spinach leaves
1 garlic clove
1 teaspoon sesame oil
1 tablespoon peanut oil
1 tablespoon chia seeds
1 tablespoon sesame seeds
1 tablespoon fish sauce

1 Wash and cut the spinach into smaller pieces. Peel and crush the garlic with the side of the knife, but without breaking it completely apart—it will only be used to infuse the dish and will be removed before serving.

2 Heat a pan with the oils on medium heat, and then add the garlic. Cook for 1 minute, and then add the spinach leaves, and cook for 3 to 4 minutes, until they soften and wilt.

3 Remove from the heat and discard the garlic clove.

4 Add the chia and sesame seeds and serve.

Scallion Pancakes

4 servings

I discovered scallion pancakes late in life—it is a Korean dish, and once I discovered it, I could not believe I had gone through life without it. It is dense, moist, salty, crunchy, and a great carbohydrate option for your kids, both for a meal or as a snack.

FOR THE SAUCE
1½ cups low-sodium soy sauce
1 tablespoon rice vinegar
1 tablespoon sugar
1 teaspoon sesame oil
1 teaspoon sesame oil
1 tablespoon ground flaxseeds
1 tablespoon sesame seeds

FOR THE PANCAKES
1 egg
¾ cup water
1 tablespoon soy sauce
1 tablespoon sesame oil
½ cup whole wheat flour
½ cup oat flour
1 tablespoon ground flaxseeds
¼ cup chopped scallions
1 tablespoon cornstarch

FOR THE SAUCE

1 Mix all of the sauce ingredients in a bowl; cover with plastic film; and refrigerate while you prepare the pancakes.

FOR THE PANCAKES

1 In a bowl, mix together the egg, water, soy sauce and sesame oil until well blended.

2 Add the flours and mix well.

3 Stir in the flaxseeds and the scallions.

4 Heat a pan with canola oil and spread it evenly with a paper towel. Pour in half the batter and cook for 2 to 3 minutes until it

is set, and then flip the pancake with a spatula. Cook for another 2 to 3 minutes, and then put it on a plate and set aside—you can cover the plate with foil to preserve the heat. Repeat with the rest of the batter.

5 Cut the pancakes into pizza-like slices, and serve them with the sauce on the side in a small bowl. I don't like to pour the sauce on the pancakes beforehand because I find that the pancakes become too soggy and lose their nice crunch.

....

Baked Artichoke Hearts with Pecorino Cheese and Walnut Oil

4 servings

Artichokes are extremely rich in vitamins and minerals—especially folic acid, zinc, and B vitamins. They also have a mild flavor and an interesting texture, which is great for kids. You can prepare them in a variety of ways, and this is one of the easiest dishes to make as a side dish, or a main dish with toast for a light lunch. Here I use frozen artichoke hearts because it is labor-intensive to work with fresh artichokes for this particular recipe, which requires a large amount.

> 1 pound frozen artichoke hearts
> 1 cup Italian bread crumbs
> 2 tablespoons chopped fresh parsley
> ½ cup grated pecorino cheese
> ½ cup grated Parmesan cheese
> 2 tablespoons ground flaxseeds
> 2 tablespoons ground wheat germ
> 4 tablespoons olive oil
> Zest and juice of one lemon
> salt, to taste

1 Preheat the oven to 375°F.

2 Line a baking dish with foil.

3 Thaw the artichoke hearts and let them drain in a strainer covered with paper towels.

4 Roughly chop the artichoke hearts into smaller pieces.

5 In a large bowl, combine the rest of the ingredients.

6 Toss the artichoke in the bowl with the rest of the ingredients, and blend well.

7 Transfer to a baking dish and bake for 30 to 40 minutes.

8 Serve warm.

Okra with Soy   *4 servings as a side dish*

Okra is an interesting vegetable—soft, gooey, sticky—and in many countries, they are cooked into a stew (gumbo), but in Asia, we eat them as a side dish, fried or boiled. I grew up eating boiled okra and was always entertained by the gooey juice that streams out with the seeds which pop on the tongue. Okra is rich in dietary fiber and contains vitamins A, C, and K, and folate.

> 1 pound okra
> 2 tablespoons soy sauce
> 1 tablespoon chia seeds
> 3 tablespoons dried katsuo fish flakes

1 Wash the okra and let it drain. Bring a large pot of water to a boil with 1 tablespoon of salt, and add the okra. Boil for 6 to 10 minutes until the okra is tender, but not too soft and soggy.

2 When it's done, drain the okra and run cold water on it for a minute to stop the cooking process and to preserve the green color. When it has cooled, cut the okra into small pieces, discarding the edge of the vegetable which contains the stub of a stem.

3 In a large bowl, toss together the okra with soy sauce and chia seeds. Sprinkle on the fish flakes.

4 Serve warm or at room temperature. It is also delicious served cold.

Sweet Moroccan Ratatouille with Dates and Almonds
4 servings as a side dish

Ratatouille is a French vegetable dish from the Province region, traditionally made with zucchini, tomatoes, and eggplant. In Morocco, they have turned this dish into a sweet/savory side dish that is served next to meats and fish and is often sprinkled with fresh mint or other herbs.

> 1 onion
> 1 red pepper
> 1 eggplant
> 2 zucchinis
> 10 pitted dates
> 5 fresh tomatoes
> 1 tablespoon olive oil
> ½ cup almonds, without the skins
> 1 tablespoon ground flaxseeds
> 1 teaspoon sugar
> salt and pepper, to taste

1 Peel and cut the onion into thin slices. Wash and remove the stalks and seeds of the red pepper, and cut it into thin slices. Wash and cut the eggplant first lengthwise, then across so that it is in a half-moon shape. Wash and cut the zucchini into small pieces, discarding the stem ends. Chop up the dates into small pieces. Wash and dice the tomatoes.

2 In a large pan, heat the oil, and add the onions, cooking for 3 to 4 minutes until they soften and become transparent.

3 Add the eggplant, pepper, and zucchini and cook for 3 to 4 minutes.

4 Add the dates, tomatoes, almonds, flaxseeds and sugar, tossing lightly. Cover and cook on low heat for 30 to 40 minutes.

The vegetables should be soft and tender, and the sauce should be sweet.

5 Add salt and pepper to taste.

6 Serve immediately or at room temperature.

Girolle Mushrooms (Golden Chanterelles) with Nori and Shiso

4 servings

Girolle mushrooms are some of the most sought-after and prized mushrooms in France, if not all over the world. When they come in season in the summer months, you see them in a variety of dishes as a sauce or a side dish, but they do not often take center stage. Here, I wrap them with nori and shiso and bake them until they soften and serve it as a main course. You can serve this with brown rice or quinoa and some wilted spinach or kale.

4 cups girolle mushrooms
1 package dry nori seaweed (the kind used for sushi)
5 to 7 large shiso leaves (or the leaves of 5 to 6 mint sprigs and 4 to 5 basil sprigs)
3 tablespoons olive oil
1 tablespoon soy sauce
sea salt, to taste

1 Preheat the oven to 375°F.

2 Line a baking sheet with foil.

3 Clean the mushrooms, and place them on a clean, flat surface. Cut the nori seaweed into thin strips, about 1 inch by 3 inches. Wash and pat dry the shiso leaves (or the basil and mint), and then cut them into thin strips.

4 Taking 2 or 3 mushrooms at a time, wrap them first with the leaves and then with the seaweed, using toothpicks to keep them together. Repeat with all of the mushrooms, taking care to not make too large a bundle at a time.

5 Place them on the baking tray and drizzle the oil, soy sauce, and salt. Bake for 10 to 15 minutes, or until the mushrooms wilt and soften.

6 Remove from the oven and let them rest for a few seconds, and then transfer the bundles to a plate.

7 Serve with rice and greens.

Green Beans with Toasted Sesame

4 serving as side dish

This is my mother's recipe for green beans and was always the favorite among our friends whenever we had dinner parties. It is easy and beautiful, perfect as an accompaniment for roasted fish or chicken. For the green beans, I prefer to use French green beans, which are now available in most grocery stores. They are smaller, thinner and more tender. If you can't find French green beans, make the extra effort when buying the beans— rummage among the beans and choose the smallest, softest ones. It is worth the effort, as my brother will tell you—he spends the most time out of anyone I know picking out the youngest beans at the store.

> ½ **cup sesame seeds (you can use black or beige sesame seeds)**
> 6 **cups of fresh green beans**
> 2 **tablespoons sugar**
> 1 **tablespoon mirin**
> 2 **tablespoons soy sauce**

1 Preheat the oven to 400°F.

2 Line a baking sheet with parchment paper and spread the sesame seeds on top. Roast until they become golden and begin to emit a nice aroma, approximately 3 to 4 minutes. Be careful not to burn them.

3 Take the pan out and let it cool while you prepare the green beans.

4 Wash and cut off the extremities of the beans, then cut them in half. Bring a pot of salted water to a boil, and boil the beans for 5 to 7 minutes (the beans should be a bit crunchy for this particular recipe, unlike the sautéed green beans I evoke later from

French cooking). Run them immediately under cold water to stop the cooking process and drain.

5 In a food processor, add the sesame seeds, sugar, mirin, and soy sauce, and blend until the mixture becomes a paste.

6 In a bowl, toss it together with the green beans.

7 Serve warm or at room temperature.

Rice with Chestnuts, Wild Mushrooms, and Beet Leaves

4 servings

Beets are commonly used in many dishes, but very little use is made of its green leaves, which is an even richer source of antioxidants, folic acid, and vitamin A than the root bulb. It is thought of as a throwaway part of the vegetable, but you will see that it is delicious in its own right and can be integrated into many recipes.

This is a wonderful dish for the fall, when the temperature begins to drop, and the chilly winds render the cheeks of your little ones crimson. If you make beet soup one day, you can keep the beet leaves and make this the following day.

> **Leafy green sections of 4 red beets**
> 3 **shallots**
> 1 **cup various fresh, wild mushrooms (this can be a mix—shiitake, porcini, morels—whatever is fresh and local if possible)**
> 1 **tablespoon canola oil**
> 3 **cups rice**
> 1 **cup chestnuts (sold in jars without any liquid preserving it)**
> 4½ **cups chicken or vegetable stock**

1 Bring to boil a pot of water with 1 table-spoon salt.

2 Peel and cut the shallots into thin strips. Brush clean the mushrooms, and cut into thin pieces.

3 Wash the beet leaves carefully. Add the beet leaves to the pot of water and cook until the leaves and the stalks have softened, approximately 7 to 10 minutes. (The stalks can be quite tough, so you may have to cook them a little longer, but be careful not to overcook—you want them to be tender, but with a slight crunch on the inside.)

4 When done, drain the leaves under cold water and let cool. Then, with your hands, squeeze out any excess water and place them on a paper towel. They should have a shriveled look. Cut them into very small pieces and set aside.

5 In a pot, add oil and shallots; sprinkle a bit of salt; and cook on low heat until the shallots have become soft and transparent. Add the mushrooms and cook for 2 minutes; then add the leaves, rice, and chestnuts, and sauté for 2 to 3 minutes.

6 Pour in the stock and cover with a lid; bring to a boil. Simmer for 20 minutes on low heat.

7 Remove from the heat and serve warm.

Green Apples and Cucumber Salad with Fresh Mint and Fennel Seeds

4 servings

Introducing salads should be an extension of eating raw fruits and vegetables. Kids usually love to nosh on sliced apples and cucumbers, so if you integrate that into a bed of soft, young iceberg lettuce leaves, it tends to work.

2 green apples
1 cucumber
1 sprig of mint
¼ cup yogurt
1 teaspoon fennel seeds
1 tablespoon lime juice
1 tablespoon honey
salt and pepper, to taste
2 heads young mini iceberg lettuce

1 Wash and peel the apples and cucumbers. Core the apples, and remove the seeds from the cucumber; cut them into small pieces. Wash and cut the mint leaves into small pieces.

2 In a bowl, combine the yogurt, fennel seeds, lime juice, honey, and salt and pepper.

3 Toss together with the apples, cucumber, and mint. Cover with plastic and refrigerate for 15 minutes.

4 Wash and drain the lettuce, and place it in four salad bowls.

5 Top with the apple mixture and serve.

 breads

Bulgur Cranberry Bread   *6 to 8 servings*

This is a dense bread with bulgur, spelt flour, whole wheat flour, and crushed walnuts, and it's packed with vitamins and minerals. It is great with some cream cheese and fresh berries, or with jam and butter.

1 cup bulgur
¾ cup boiling water
1 cup whole wheat flour
1 cup spelt flour
1 tablespoon baking powder
1 teaspoon salt
¼ cup brown sugar
1½ cups milk
2 eggs
⅓ cup applesauce
½ cup crushed walnuts
1 cup dried cranberries

1   In a bowl, combine bulgur and hot water. Let soak for 30 minutes, covered. Fluff it with a fork and set it aside while you prepare the rest.

2   Preheat the oven to 350°F.

3   Grease a baking pan (large loaf pan 9x5x3 inches, or 2 small loaf pans 8x4x2½ inches) and dust with whole wheat flour.

4   In a large bowl, stir together the flours, baking powder, salt, and brown sugar until well blended.

5   In another bowl, mix together the wet ingredients—the milk, eggs, applesauce—until completely smooth.

6   Stir in bulgur, cranberries, and walnuts. Then slowly add the wet ingredients to the dry ingredients.

7   Pour into the baking pan, and bake for 1 hour.

8   Serve warm or at room temperature. You can freeze the bread in an airtight container for up to 2 weeks or store it in the refrigerator for 3 to 4 days.

Whole Wheat Pumpkin Bread

6 to 8 servings

This is a hearty bread with eggs, millet flour, pumpkin, walnuts, and applesauce. It is not too sweet and is substantial enough to make a meal when accompanied by some sliced turkey or ham. It is also great with whipped cream and berries as a snack or a dessert.

    2 cups whole wheat flour
    1 cup millet flour
    1 teaspoon baking soda
    1 teaspoon ground ginger
    1½ teaspoons ground cinnamon
    ½ teaspoon cloves
    1 cup sugar
    ½ teaspoon ground nutmeg
    ½ teaspoon salt
    1 cup applesauce
    2 cups pumpkin
    4 eggs
    ⅔ cup water
    1 cup raisins
    ½ cup walnuts

1   Preheat the oven to 350°F.

2   Grease two 8½x4½-inch loaf pans, and dust them lightly with flour.

3   In a bowl, stir together the dry ingredients—whole wheat flour, millet flour, baking soda, ginger, cinnamon, cloves, sugar, nutmeg, and salt.

4   In another bowl, mix together the wet ingredients—applesauce, pumpkin, eggs, and water.

5   Add the dry ingredients slowly into the wet, mixing constantly.

6   Stir in the raisins and walnuts and pour into the loaf pans.

7   Bake for one hour and serve warm or at room temperature.

8   You can also slice the bread and store individual slices in the freezer in an airtight container or bag for up to 2 weeks or in the refrigerator for 3 to 5 days. To reheat, you can use a toaster oven or a stove-top grill, toasting a slice so that it becomes crunchy on both sides.

Cheddar Edamame Cornbread

6 to 8 servings

My son loves cornbread, and I feel like I can put anything into it and he will happily eat it. So I try many different kinds of cornbread, and each time it is an adventure. This cornbread with cheddar and edamame was concocted for the flavor, nutrition, and the beauty of the colors. It is crumbly and light in texture.

> 1 cup cornmeal
> 1 cup whole wheat flour
> ¼ cup sugar
> 3 tablespoons baking powder
> 1 teaspoon salt
> ½ cup oil
> 2 eggs
> ⅔ cup milk
> 1 cup grated cheddar cheese
> 1 cup shelled frozen edamame, thawed

1 Preheat the oven to 400°F.

2 In a bowl, combine the dry ingredients—cornmeal, flour, sugar, baking powder, and salt.

3 In another bowl, mix together the wet ingredients—oil, eggs, and milk. Slowly add the wet ingredients to the dry ingredients and mix.

4 Bake in a 9x9x2-inch pan for 20 to 25 minutes.

Kamut, Hazelnut, and Arugula Bread with Chia Seeds

6 to 8 servings

Using pancake mix is an easy way to bake, since the mix already contains the baking powder and baking soda. You can use it as a foundation to build flavors and interesting combinations. This is a nutty bread with toasted hazelnuts and arugula.

> ½ cup hazelnuts
> 2 cups kamut pancake mix
> 1 cup water
> 1 cup milk
> 2 eggs
> 2 tablespoons applesauce
> 1 teaspoon salt
> 2 tablespoons canola oil
> 3 tablespoons chia seeds
> 1 cup arugula

1 Preheat the oven to 375°F.

2 Line a baking tray with parchment paper and spread out the hazelnuts. Roast them for 3 to 4 minutes until golden and aromatic.

3 In a bowl, mix together the pancake mix with water and milk and blend well.

4 Add the eggs, then the applesauce, salt, oil, and the chia seeds.

5 When all is well blended, add the arugula and hazelnuts.

6 Pour into a loaf pan 8x4x2½ or 8½x4½x2½ inches and bake for 40 to 60 minutes. Check the bread for doneness by inserting a long skewer or a knife into the center of the loaf. If it comes out dry, it is done. If there are bits of dough stuck to it, bake for another 10 minutes.

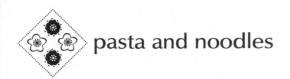 pasta and noodles

....

Linguini with Girolle Mushrooms

4 servings

This is a pasta dish that highlights the rich broth from the golden chanterelle mushrooms with a hint of paprika.

1 tablespoon salt
14 ounces linguine pasta
1 tablespoon olive oil
1 pound girolle mushrooms
3 shallots
1 teaspoon paprika
1 tablespoon oregano
1 cup milk
1 cup cream
1 tablespoon chia seeds
salt and pepper, to taste
2 tablespoons chopped fresh chives

1 Bring to a boil a pot of water with salt. Cook the linguine according to package instructions, and drain. Drizzle on a bit of olive oil, and set it aside.

2 Brush clean the mushrooms and set them aside.

3 Peel and cut the shallots into thin slices. Heat a pan with olive oil on medium heat, and add the shallots. Cook slowly until they turn pale, about 5 to 7 minutes, being careful not to burn them.

4 Add the mushrooms, paprika, and oregano and turn the heat to high, and cover. Cook for 5 to 7 minutes or until the mushrooms have wilted. There should be a soupy stock from the liquid of the mushrooms.

5 Add the milk and cream, and cover again; reduce heat to a simmer.

6 Remove from heat, and add the chia seeds and chives; toss in the pasta and mix well.

7 Salt and pepper to taste, and serve immediately.

Ziti with Salmon, Spinach, and Ricotta

4 servings

This pasta dish is rich in Omega-3, folic acid, calcium, and protein.

14 ounces ziti
1 onion
2 tablespoons canola oil
2 tomatoes
2 wild-caught salmon fillets
½ cup spinach
¼ cup ricotta
3 tablespoons cream

1 In a pot, bring water with salt to a boil; then add ziti and cook according to package instructions.

2 Peel and mince the onion. Heat a pan with oil, and add the onions. Cook on low heat until the onions are transparent but still pale, about 5 to 7 minutes.

3 While the onions are cooking, prepare the tomatoes (peel, seed, and cut into small pieces), and then add them to the pan. Cook for 5 minutes.

4 Cut the salmon fillets into small pieces, and add them to the pan. Cook for 3 more minutes.

5 Chop the spinach into small pieces, and add it to the pan. Raise the heat to high, and add the ricotta; cook for 2 more minutes.

6 Stir the sauce and remove it from the heat; then add the cream.

7 Drain the ziti, and add it to the pan with the sauce, and toss.

8 Serve immediately.

Sautéed Noodles with Zucchini and Chicken

4 servings

Rice noodles are very commonly used for Southeast Asian dishes and absorb broth and sauce well. They are also lighter than the other noodles introduced in this book, such as udon noodles or buckwheat.

14 ounces rice noodles
1 zucchini
2 chicken thighs
A nob of ginger
2 tablespoons canola oil
1 teaspoon sesame oil
3 tablespoons soy sauce
3 tablespoons water
2 tablespoons mirin
1 tablespoon flaxseeds
1 tablespoon sesame seeds

1 Boil a pot of water, and cook the noodles according to package instructions, usually around 5 to 7 minutes.

2 Cut the zucchini into thin strips. Cut the chicken into small pieces. Chop the garlic and ginger.

3 In a pan, heat the canola oil and sesame oil on medium heat. Add the ginger and cook for 3 minutes.

4 Add the chicken, and cook until golden, about 5 to 7 minutes.

5 Add the zucchini, and cook for 5 minutes.

6 Add the soy sauce, water, and mirin, and cook for 3 minutes.

7 Add the cooked noodles, and stir until the sauce coats the noodles evenly.

8 Sprinkle with ground flaxseeds and sesame seeds, and serve.

fish and seafood

Scallops with Pomegranate and Cilantro Chutney   *4 servings*

Scallops are so quick to cook; it literally takes 5 minutes to make this dish. It is rich in protein, vitamin B1, magnesium, Omega-3 fatty acid, and potassium. For an interesting texture combination, I serve this with fresh, raw pomegranates—it gives the scallops an unexpected sweet light crunch. If you can't find fresh pomegranates, you can try it with fresh cubed papaya or mango for that sweet, tangy tropical flavor. If you or your child do not appreciate tropical fruits, you can do this with pears or apples.

½ cup fresh pomegranate seeds
1 tablespoon chopped fresh cilantro
1 tablespoon sugar
2 tablespoons water
salt and pepper, to taste
1 pound fresh scallops
2 tablespoons butter
Zest and juice of one lime

1   In a small bowl, combine the pomegranate seeds, cilantro, lime juice, sugar, water, and some salt and pepper. Cover with plastic wrap and refrigerate while you prepare the scallops.

2   If your scallops have the pink glands attached, cut them off with a knife and discard.

3   Sprinkle the scallops with salt and pepper.

4   Heat a pan with butter, and let it sizzle a bit. Cook the scallops in batches, adding more butter if necessary, in order to not overcrowd the pan. Place them carefully on one side for 3 to 4 minutes, and then flip them onto the other side for the same amount of time.

5   Remove from pan. Place the scallops on four plates.

6   Serve with the chutney in a small bowl for dipping, or drizzle on top as a sauce.

Cumin Shrimp with Cream *4 servings*

This is a very mild curry that is perfect for little ones because it is not spicy, but it has a lot of flavor. You can roast the cumin seeds before using them, popping them in the oven for a few minutes, or use them as is. I like to roast them a bit to give it that extra aroma. I serve this with basmati rice. You can get all of the spices in this recipe in most supermarkets. If not, you can always order them online.

> 1 onion
> 2 tomatoes
> 1½ to 2 pounds shrimp
> 1 tablespoon canola oil
> 2 tablespoons cumin seeds
> 1 tablespoon curcuma powder
> 1 tablespoon coriander powder
> 1 teaspoon ground ginger
> 1 tablespoon chopped fresh cilantro
> 1 tablespoon cumin powder
> ½ cup cream
> 1 cup milk

1 Peel and cut the onion into small pieces. Wash and cut the tomatoes (you can take off the tomato peel by dunking the tomatoes in hot water for a minute, and then removing the skins under cold running water. I simply cook with the skin on in this recipe).

2 Shell and devein the shrimp, putting all of the shells into a small pot—this is what will give the sauce a deep shrimp flavor. Add 1 cup water to the shells; cover the pan and bring to a boil, then immediately take off heat. Remove from heat and drain the liquid into a bowl. Set aside.

3 In a pan, heat the oil and add the onions. Cook for 5 to 7 minutes or until they become translucent.

4 Add the cumin seeds, cumin powder, curcuma powder, coriander powder, and ginger, and sauté for 2 minutes.

5 Add the tomatoes and sauté for 3 to 4 minutes.

6 Add the liquid from the shrimp shells and milk, and bring to a simmer; cook for 5 more minutes.

7 Add the shrimp and cook until pink and plump, about 3 to 4 minutes, being careful not to overcook the shrimp.

8 Stir in the cream, and heat for 1 to 2 minutes.

9 Serve over rice with cilantro sprinkled on top.

Crab Cakes *4 servings*

Crab cakes are a great way to prepare crabmeat, which contain Omega-3 and protein. You can make very small mini crab cakes for snacks as well.

> 3 to 5 tablespoons wheat germ
> 1 pound crabmeat
> ⅓ cup whole wheat bread crumbs
> 3 scallions, chopped
> ⅓ cup chopped red pepper
> ¼ cup canola mayonnaise
> 1 egg
> 1 tablespoon garlic powder
> salt and pepper, to taste
> ½ cup peanut oil

1 Spread the wheat germ evenly on a flat plate.

2 In a bowl, mix together everything else except for the oil. Sprinkle with salt and pepper.

3 Make small patties with your hands, and dust them with the wheat germ.

4 Heat a pan with the oil, and cook the patties on medium heat for 4 to 6 minutes until golden brown.

5 Serve warm with a bit of salt and mayonnaise.

Shrimp and Grits   *4 servings*

Grits are great for toddlers, who tend to love the consistency of mashed potatoes. Grits have the texture of coarsely mashed potatoes, and the flavor is neutral enough to accompany any protein. Here is a simple, creamy recipe for shrimp and grits that your child will love.

FOR THE GRITS
2 cups chicken stock
1 cup cornmeal
1 cup heavy cream
1 tablespoon unsalted butter

FOR THE SHRIMP
1½ to 2 pounds shrimp
2 tablespoons olive oil
1 onion, chopped
1 garlic clove, chopped
3 to 4 slices pancetta (Italian uncured bacon—you can use 2 slices of normal bacon if you don't have pancetta) chopped into small pieces
1 tablespoon cornstarch
¼ cup cream
1 tablespoon chopped fresh chives

FOR THE GRITS

1 In a large pot, add the chicken stock and bring to a boil; then add the cornmeal and blend with a whisk.

2 When the grits begin to bubble up, turn the heat down and simmer, stirring with a wooden spoon, for 10 to 15 minutes. The grits should be thick like pureed potatoes.

3 Remove from the heat, and add the cream and butter; sprinkle with salt and pepper, to taste. Cover with a lid and set aside while you prepare the shrimp.

FOR THE SHRIMP

1 Shell and devein the shrimp. Put all of the shells into a small pot and add 1 cup water. Cover with a lid and bring to a boil. Cook for 2 minutes, and remove from heat. Set aside.

2 Heat a pan with olive oil, and then add the onion and garlic; cook for 3 to 4 minutes on low heat.

3 Add the chopped pancetta, and sauté for 1 to 2 minutes.

4 Drain the shrimp liquid into a cup, and stir in the cornstarch with a spoon until well blended. Add it to the pan, and cook for 5 minutes until the liquid becomes thick.

5 Add the shrimp, and cook for 3 to 4 minutes or until the shrimp turns bright pink. Be careful not to overcook the shrimp.

6 Add the cream, stir and sprinkle with chives.

7 Scoop the grits into four bowls, and pour the shrimp with the sauce on top.

8 Serve immediately.

Norwegian Fish Cakes   *4 servings*

Fish cakes are popular, both in Asia and Scandinavia, and are part of the daily meals in both regions and cultures. There are diverse ways of preparing them, and here is one of the simplest. You can be creative and add fresh herbs, like vervain or dill, or try different kinds of fish, like tuna or mackerel. Here I use olive oil for more flavor, but you can always use canola oil if you prefer something more neutral.

2 wild-caught cod fillets
sea salt, to taste
3 to 4 tablespoons olive oil
4 large potatoes
2 tablespoons parsley
1 egg
Zest of 1 lemon
1 tablespoon wheat germ
1 tablespoon whole wheat flour

1 Preheat the oven to 375°F.

2 Cover a baking tray with foil, and place the cod on top, sprinkling salt and a drizzle of olive oil.

3 Peel and cut the potatoes into small chunks. Bring a large pot of water to a boil, and cook the potatoes for 7 to 10 minutes, until they are tender when pierced with a knife.

4 Meanwhile, bake the salmon for 4 to 6 minutes.

5 Drain the potatoes, and take the salmon out of the oven. Mash the potatoes in the same pot you used to boil them, and then add the salmon and mix until fully integrated.

6 Add the parsley, egg, and lemon zest, and mix well.

7 On a flat plate, mix together the wheat germ and whole wheat flour. Make 4 patties with the potato mixture and pat each on both sides with the wheat germ and flour mixture. Transfer to another plate; cover with plastic wrap; and refrigerate for 45 to 60 minutes, so the patties will be firm when you cook them.

8 In a pan, heat 2 to 3 tablespoons of olive oil, and cook the patties 3 to 5 minutes on each side until they become golden on both sides.

9 Sprinkle sea salt and serve. Many people like to eat the fish cakes with a bit of lemon juice or some kind of mayonnaise. I think they're best with just a touch of salt.

Salmon Frittata
4 servings

One of my favorite ways to eat salmon is to combine it with eggs. Sometimes I simply scramble some eggs into a sautéed fillet of salmon, sprinkle on some chives, and call it a day. This is a little more elegant in its presentation, but it's the same concept. It is an easy weekday meal that can come together quickly and beautifully.

2 salmon fillets
1 tablespoon canola oil
1 tablespoon olive oil
6 eggs
¼ cup cream
2 tablespoons chopped chives
salt and pepper, to taste

1 Salt and pepper both sides of the salmon fillets. In a pan, heat the oils, and add the salmon fillets, cooking them at medium heat for 5 to 6 minutes. Use a wooden fork to separate the fillets so that they are broken up into bite-sized pieces.

2 In a bowl, combine the eggs with cream, salt, and pepper, and whip them together until they become light and frothy, about 2 minutes. Add the cream and whip until fully blended, and then pour the egg mixture into the pan. Bring down the heat to low; cover and cook for 4 to 8 minutes until the eggs set, depending on the consistency that you prefer (I tend to like my eggs runny and very soft, as does my son, so I only cook it for about 5 minutes).

3 Sprinkle the chives and serve warm, cutting it into slices like a pie. You can serve it with some greens, like steamed broccoli, or with some brown rice and wilted spinach.

Baked Salmon with Lemon Zest, Fresh Dill, and Sour Cream
4 servings

Baked salmon is one of the easiest dishes to make, but it is not so simple to make it perfect, with just the right *cuisson*—doneness. Salmon easily becomes very dry if it is not carefully monitored. My chef professors at culinary school would only cook salmon for a maximum of 3 minutes, making it delicate, moist, and almost raw inside. Here I do not suggest raw/rare, but medium rare. That said, the cooking time greatly varies according to the thickness of your salmon steaks, so be careful not to overcook them, and remember that the fish will continue to cook for quite a few minutes after you remove it from the oven.

4 salmon steaks
2 tablespoons of chopped fresh dill
½ cup sour cream
Zest of 1 lemon
¼ cup heavy cream
salt and pepper, to taste

1 Preheat the oven to 375°F.

2 Line a baking sheet with foil. Salt and pepper both sides of the salmon, and place on the baking sheet. Bake the salmon for 5 to 7 minutes. You can check the salmon for doneness by inserting the tip of a knife and peeking inside—if the flesh inside is too red, cook for an extra 2 to 3 minutes, but no longer.

3 In a bowl, combine the rest of the ingredients.

4 Place the salmon on individual plates, and pour the cream sauce on top.

5 Serve immediately.

Calamari and Scallions with Miso

4 servings

Using miso paste as a base for a dressing
or a sauce is a classic Japanese approach
to vegetable, seafood, and meat dishes.
The combination of squid with scallions is
traditional, and I have altered this recipe by
substituting cooked squid for raw squid, and
I cook it in the miso sauce rather than toss
it raw. You will see that it makes for a very
unusual and surprising mix of flavors.

> **4 medium-sized squid, cleaned and cut
> into small pieces**
> **Bunch fresh scallions**
> **3 tablespoons miso paste**
> **2 tablespoons ground sesame seeds**
> **1 tablespoon rice wine vinegar**
> **1 tablespoon sugar**
> **2 tablespoons soy sauce**
> **5 tablespoons water**

1 Personally, I tend to think the squid tentacles
   are the best part, so I chop them up with the
   rest of the squid and cook them. It is up to
   you whether you want to include or discard
   them, but the texture of the tentacles is fun
   and interesting for kids.

2 Wash the scallions, and cut them roughly in
   short pieces, using only the green section.

3 In a bowl, combine the squid with the miso
   paste, sesame, vinegar, and sugar, and let it
   sit in the refrigerator for 10 minutes.

4 In a pot, combine all of the ingredients and
   bring to a quick boil. Cover and simmer for
   5 to 7 minutes, making sure the squid is
   not overcooked (it will become hard and
   rubbery. If the squid is very fresh, it should
   be fluffy and soft).

5 Serve with rice.

chicken, beef, pork, and lamb

Chicken and Seaweed Croquettes   *4 servings*

These chicken croquettes are juicy and packed with flavor, not to mention minerals and vitamins. They are quick to make and can be integrated easily into soups, pastas, or rice dishes because of their neutral flavor. If you are using the croquettes in other dishes, simply omit the sauce when making it.

> 2 tablespoons wakame seaweed, soaked in 1 cup water for 15 minutes
> 1 pound ground chicken
> 1 egg
> 2 tablespoons mirin
> 2 tablespoons soy sauce
> 2 tablespoons ground flaxseeds
> 2 tablespoons wheat germ
> 4 tablespoons whole wheat flour
> 2 tablespoons canola oil
> 2 tablespoons chopped fresh chives

1 Take the seaweed out of the liquid, squeezing out the excess liquid with your hands (reserving the liquid and setting it aside), and chop it into small pieces.

2 In a bowl, mix together the seaweed, chicken, egg, mirin, soy sauce, flaxseeds, and wheat germ until well blended, then make into small balls.

3 On a plate, spread out the wheat flour and roll the balls in the flour to coat.

4 Heat a pan with canola oil, and cook the small balls for 7 to 10 minutes, flattening them out in the pan.

5 Remove from the pan and pour in the remaining soy sauce, mirin, chives, and the seaweed liquid. Bring to a boil and let simmer for 5 minutes, and then add the croquettes back in and cook for 3 to 5 more minutes.

6 Serve warm.

Baked Chicken Tenders with Crushed Hemp Seed and Parmesan Crust

4 servings

Chicken tenders are the easiest for kids to eat, but they often dry if they are not fried. I don't like to fry them because of the fat content and the mess it makes in the kitchen. These baked chicken tenders are simple, quick, and lean. I use buttermilk for this recipe, but I often don't feel like buying a carton of buttermilk for the sake of one recipe. The alternative is to squeeze some lemon juice into a cup of whole milk and let it stand for 15 minutes—the milk will curdle, and it will have a similar effect on the chicken as the buttermilk would, tenderizing the meat. You can serve these tenders on their own or accompanied with tomato marinara for dipping.

1 cup buttermilk
1½ pounds chicken tenders
1 tablespoon olive oil
1 cup grated Parmesan cheese
¼ cup crushed hemp seeds
¼ cup wheat germ
sea salt, to taste

1   In a bowl, combine the buttermilk and chicken tenders and allow to sit for 15 to 30 minutes in the refrigerator.

2   Preheat the oven to 400°F.

3   Cover two baking trays with foil, and drizzle olive oil on the surface to prevent the chicken tenders from sticking.

4   In another bowl, combine the Parmesan, hemp seeds, and wheat germ.

5   Remove the tenders from the milk, and dredge them in the crumbs.

6   Place them on the tray, and bake for 12 to 15 minutes.

7   Sprinkle with sea salt and serve.

Swedish Meatballs with Lingonberry Sauce

4 servings

Swedish meatballs are mild and easy for kids to love, and with lingonberries, which are full of DHA Omega-3, this dish is packed with proteins, whole grains, fatty acids, and minerals. There are many ways you can make Swedish meatballs, but this is the simplest. And if you happen to have leftovers, you can make a great sandwich with a fresh baguette, lettuce, and warm meatballs. You can find lingonberry jam in many grocery stores. If not, you can order it on Amazon.com or find it in the grocery section of an IKEA store.

½ pound ground veal
½ pound lean ground beef
¼ pound ground pork
1 tablespoon garlic powder
1 tablespoon onion powder
2 teaspoons salt
1 egg
1 teaspoon thyme
1 teaspoon oregano
2 tablespoons canola oil
1 cup cold beef stock
4 tablespoons lingonberry jam
1 tablespoon very cold butter
¼ cup cream
salt and pepper, to taste

1   In a bowl, combine the ground meats together, and add the garlic and onion powders, salt, egg, thyme, and oregano; mix well (it is best to use your bare hands to integrate everything well, but you can also use a fork).

2   Take a tablespoon of the meat mixture for each meatball; form small balls and place them on a tray covered with parchment paper.

3   Heat a pan with oil and cook the meatballs, several at a time, making sure the pan is not too overcrowded with the meatballs. When they are done, place them on a plate covered with paper towels. Dab the pan with a paper towel to absorb the fat.

4   Using the same pan, which should still be very hot, pour in the cold beef stock, and use a wooden spoon to scrape off any *suc*—bits of meat that have stuck to the bottom of the pan—this is where all of the flavor will come from for the sauce. The cold stock added to the hot pan will release all of the *suc* very easily.

5   Bring the stock to a boil, and let it simmer and reduce for 10 to 15 minutes, until the stock has reduced to half.

6   Add the jam and cook for another 10 minutes, allowing the sauce to reduce even more.

7   When the liquid has been reduced to a fourth of its original amount, add cold butter, cream, and salt, and pepper, and stir.

8   Transfer the meatballs back to the pan with the sauce, and cook for an additional 2 to 3 minutes.

9   Serve with potatoes or rice.

Meatballs with Sage, Flax, Wheat Germ, and Sweet Soy *4 servings*

I love making different kinds of meatballs because you can include everything you want in them. Meatballs are easy to make and keep well in the freezer. You can make a bunch on a weekend and freeze them for use later in the week. For the beef, I use lean ground grass-fed beef because it is the richest in DHA Omega-3.

> 1 tablespoon cornstarch
> ½ cup water
> 1 pound lean ground beef
> 1 tablespoon ground flaxseeds
> 1 tablespoon wheat germ
> 5 tablespoons soy sauce
> 1 to 2 tablespoons canola oil
> 2 tablespoons mirin
> 1 tablespoon chopped fresh sage
> 1 tablespoon ketchup

1 Mix together the cornstarch and water in a cup, and set aside. In a bowl, mix together the beef, flaxseeds, wheat germ, ketchup, and 2 tablespoons of soy sauce and blend well (best if mixed with bare hands).

2 Taking a tablespoon of the beef mixture at a time, form small meatballs; place them on a plate. Heat oil in a pan over medium heat and cook several meatballs at a time, making sure the pan is not overcrowded. As the meatballs are cooked, place them on a plate covered with paper towels.

3 When the meatballs have been cooked, dab the pan with a paper towel to get rid of the fat. Raise the heat to high heat, and, using the same pan, add the remaining 3 tablespoons of soy sauce, mirin, and the cornstarch mixture. Bring to a boil; then let it simmer for 2 to 3 minutes.

4 Add the meatballs back into the pan and cook for 2 minutes.

5 Take off the heat and sprinkle with sage.

6 Serve immediately.

Braised Ribs with Butternut Squash

4 servings

This is a meal that gets better the longer you keep it on the stove. It is even better the day after when you reheat it because the flavors have sunken in even deeper, which is always the case with stews, curries, and braised dishes. This recipe is always popular among friends and family, with the sweetness of the squash complementing the dark flavor of the ribs.

> 2 tablespoons canola oil
> salt and pepper, to taste
> 2 racks of beef short ribs, cut into
>   individual ribs (4 to 5 pounds)
> 2 onions
> 2 celery ribs
> 2 carrots
> 4 garlic cloves
> 4 cups chopped tomatoes
> 1 bay leaf
> 1 tablespoon thyme
> 2 tablespoons ground cumin

1 Heat a large pot with the oil. Salt and pepper all sides of the ribs, and cook on all sides until dark brown, about 7 to 10 minutes. If your pot is not large enough to accommodate all of the ribs at once, do this in two or three batches, browning only a few at a time, and then putting them on a plate and setting them aside while you brown the rest.

2 Meanwhile, wash and peel onions, celery, carrots, and garlic, and cut them into thin pieces.

3 When the ribs have all been browned well and set aside, dab the bottom of the pot with a paper towel to remove excess fat, and add another tablespoon of canola oil. Add the onions and cook on low heat for 4 to 6 minutes until they become pale and transparent.

4 Add the carrots, celery, and garlic, and cook for 3 to 4 minutes until they soften.

5 Add the ribs back in, and add the tomatoes, bay leaf, thyme, and cumin; fill the pot with enough water to completely cover the ribs. Bring to a boil, and cover.

6 Let the pot simmer for 1½ to 2 hours; skim the foam and excess fat that rises to the top of the pot from time to time, and make sure there is enough liquid covering the ribs at least halfway—add more water when necessary. It is ready when the meat is so tender that it falls off the bones. Serve with bread or some roasted potatoes.

Beef Sukiyaki

4 servings

Sukiyaki is a classic Japanese home-style dish that is a winter staple for all families in Japan. Its sweet soy flavor makes it a favorite among kids, and you can try a variety of meats and vegetables. In Japan, often the hotplate is brought to the dining table with the clay pot, and the dish is cooked while we eat it. We put the sliced meat in the pot, dip it in raw egg, and eat it with steaming rice. When all of the meat and vegetables have disappeared, we pour thick udon rice noodles at the end to cook with the wonderful stock left behind from the cooked meats and vegetables. In this version I use the traditional beef with scallions, enoki mushrooms, Chinese cabbage, and some udon rice noodles, but I've omitted the raw egg dip.

4 beef steaks (New York strip or rib eye)
½ head of white Chinese cabbage
1 bunch enoki mushrooms or button
   mushrooms
1 bunch of scallions
¼ cup soy sauce
½ cup water
1 tablespoon sugar
1 teaspoon ground sesame seeds
1 tablespoon ground flaxseeds
2 eggs
2 cups of cooked udon rice noodles

1   Cover the steaks with plastic, and put them in the freezer for 1 hour—it is easier to slice the beef into thin strips when they are partially frozen. Remove steaks from the freezer, and, with a sharp knife, carefully slice them into very thin slices; place them on a large plate.

2   Wash the cabbage, and rough cut it into small pieces; place them on another large plate. Clean and cut the mushrooms, and place them next to the cabbage. Wash and rough cut the dark green section of the scallions into small pieces, discarding the white parts; place them next to the other vegetables.

3   In a small bowl, mix together the soy sauce, water, sugar, sesame seeds, and flaxseeds.

4   In another small bowl, whip the two eggs together. Set aside.

5   Taking a large pan, place the beef, all of the vegetables, and the udon noodles neatly next to each other. Pour the soy sauce mixture over everything, and turn on the heat. Cover and cook for 7 to 10 minutes.

6   Pour in the eggs, and cover again. Cook for another 2 to 3 minutes.

7   Remove from the heat, and separate into deep plates.

8   Serve immediately.

Marinated Beef with Pears, Roasted Hazelnuts, and Endive   *4 servings*

Endive is bitter by nature, and children tend to have a difficult time with it, but if you combine it with something sweet, like pears or dried fruit, they may like it. I think it is important to introduce toddlers to bitter flavors early on, even if they show initial hesitation because bitter flavors stimulate the palate and the sensory system differently than sweet or savory flavors. Even if my son does not love it, I do try to get him to at least taste bitter flavors found in endive, broccoli rabe, sea cucumbers, etc. This recipe includes endive, but it has other ingredients that your child can enjoy as well, so you are not stuck making a meal that goes completely uneaten.

4 New York strip steaks
1 onion
2 pears
2 medium belgian endive
2 tablespoons canola oil
1 cup hazelnuts, roasted and crushed
2 tablespoons soy sauce
2 tablespoons mirin
2 tablespoons water
salt and pepper

1 Wrap the steaks in plastic, and put them in the freezer for 30 minutes—you will be able to slice them more easily if they are partially frozen.

2 Peel and cut the onion into thin slices. Wash and peel the pears, and slice them into thin flat slices. Wash the endive, and cut them into thin segments.

3 Remove the steaks from the freezer, and cut them into thin slices with a sharp knife. Place the slices on a plate. Heat a pan with oil, and make sure that it is very hot by placing your hand over the pan—if you can feel the heat, it is ready. Cook the beef in batches, so that each piece is seared, about 3 to 4 minutes. Take the slices out, and place them on a plate while you finish cooking the rest. They should be seared and brown on both sides.

4 In the same pan, heat the other tablespoon of canola oil, and sauté the onions on low heat until translucent, about 6 to 8 minutes.

5 Increase the heat to medium, and add the pears and endive. Quickly sauté for 2 to 3 minutes.

6 Add the soy sauce, mirin, and water, and toss and cook for an additional 2 to 3 minutes. Divide the meat and vegetables among four plates.

7 Sprinkle with the hazelnuts, and serve.

Roasted Pork Ribs with Walnuts, Rosemary, and Orange Zest   *4 servings*

This is a very simple way to render pork ribs interesting and aromatic. Just marinate them; pop them in the oven; and serve with rice and some wilted spinach or some other kind of greens.

Zest and juice of 2 oranges
4 tablespoons soy sauce
4 tablespoons honey
1 cup water
2 tablespoons rosemary
1 tablespoon thyme
2 racks of pork ribs, cut into small portions
¼ cup brown sugar
1 cup walnuts
1 tablespoon flaxseeds
1 tablespoon chopped fresh chives
salt and pepper, to taste

1   In a large bowl, combine the orange juice and zest, soy sauce, honey, water, rosemary, and thyme. Add the pork ribs and toss with hands, rubbing the liquid into the ribs. Cover with plastic and refrigerate for at least an hour, and, if possible, overnight (the longer the better).

2   Preheat the oven to 350°F.

3   Cover a baking tray with foil and place the ribs on top. Bake for 60 to 90 minutes, depending on the thickness of the ribs. You can either insert a knife to make sure the meat is well done or use a meat thermometer to check for an internal temperature of 160°F.

4   Meanwhile, heat in a small pot the brown sugar, 4 tablespoons of water, and the walnuts. Cook for 4 to 7 minutes on very low heat so that the walnuts are caramelized by the brown sugar, being careful not to let it burn.

5   Remove the ribs from the oven, and serve them on a large plate with the walnuts, flaxseeds, and chives sprinkled on top. Salt and pepper to taste.

Cheesy Lamb Keftas with Cilantro, Cinnamon, and Cloves   *4 servings*

Lamb *keftas* from the Mediterranean region are usually long patties stuck on a skewer and grilled. And while I love it in its original version, I don't like the idea of serving skewers to my son for obvious safety reasons. This recipe makes small kefta balls with Emmental cheese inside, which are soft and gooey when bitten into. If you can't get Emmental, you can use mozzarella cheese or any other kind of mild cheese that melts well.

  1 pound ground lamb
  1 egg
  1 tablespoon chopped fresh cilantro
  1 tablespoon ground cinnamon
  1 teaspoon ground cloves
  1 teaspoon salt
  ¼ pound of Emmental cheese, cut into small cubes
  ½ cup yogurt
  1 teaspoon chopped cilantro
  salt and pepper, to taste
  2 tablespoons canola oil

1 In a large bowl, mix together the lamb, egg, cilantro, cinnamon, cloves, and salt (it is best if you use your hand to blend everything well, but you can always use a fork).

2 Using the palms of your hands, put 2 tablespoons' worth of the lamb mixture in your palms and flatten it out. Place a cube of cheese in the middle, and then close it up to make a round ball. Repeat until all of the ground lamb has been used. Transfer the balls to a plate; cover them with plastic and refrigerate for at least 30 minutes.

3 In a bowl, mix together the yogurt, cilantro, salt, and pepper; cover with plastic and refrigerate until you have finished cooking the keftas.

4 Heat 1 tablespoon of oil in a pan on medium heat and cook the lamb keftas until they are golden on all sides, around 10 to 12 minutes, tossing them around in the pan with a wooden spoon.

5 Serve with the cilantro yogurt, or on their own with a little sea salt.

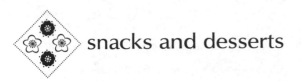

snacks and desserts

Crunchy Cheese Eggrolls

4 servings

These are fun snacks, and you and your child can prepare them together as a food project. You just roll the cheese sticks into the wonton wraps and pop them in the oven. You can eat them with a bit of salt and pepper, or try different dipping options, like soy sauce or marinara sauce.

1 egg
8 mozzarella sticks
8 wonton wrappers
1 tablespoon ground kelp
1 tablespoon sesame seeds
salt and pepper, to taste

1 Preheat the oven to 375°F.

2 Crack the egg into a bowl, and stir with a fork; set aside.

3 Wrap the mozzarella sticks in the wonton wrappers, and brush each wrap on the edges with the egg mixture before closing it up like a package.

4 Brush the smooth top part of the wrapped cheese with the egg mixture, and sprinkle with kelp, sesame seeds, salt, and pepper, and place each one on a baking sheet.

5 Bake for 10 to 13 minutes.

Veggie Desserts

I love making desserts with unexpected vegetables, both for the nutrients and for the taste. Maybe it's because of my Asian heritage; we make many of our desserts from rice (rice flour, sticky rice), legumes (beans), seeds (sesame), plants (tea leaves), vegetables (yams), or nuts (chestnuts). Here are some recipes for a very healthy snack/dessert using ingredients that are unusual and delicious in a sweet dish—beets, asparagus, cherry tomatoes, and lotus roots.

Red Beet Mousse with Pecans

4 to 6 servings

Real mousse is made with raw eggs, but I don't feel very comfortable giving raw eggs to my son. So I make mousse desserts with only whipped cream and light mascarpone cheese, which of course has a different texture, but it's delicious all the same. If you prefer the "real" mousse texture, you can add 3 eggs to this recipe, separating the yolks from the egg whites (mixing the yolk with the beet puree, and beating the egg whites and folding them into the whipped cream).

> 4 red beets
> ¼ cup honey
> 1 cup whipping cream
> 2 tablespoons sugar
> 1 cup mascarpone cheese
> ¼ cup crushed pecans

1 Preheat the oven to 375°F.

2 Roast the beets for an hour until they're very tender. Let them cool, then peel and cut into cubes.

3 In a food processor, blend until smooth; then add the honey, and blend again.

4 In a bowl, whip the cream until light and fluffy.

5 Add sugar.

6 Slowly add the beet mixture to the cream and fold it in carefully.

7 Add the mascarpone and fold it in carefully.

8 Cover with plastic and refrigerate for 1 to 3 hours before serving.

9 Divide among serving bowls and sprinkle with pecans.

Cherry Tomato Ice Treats

Tomatoes are actually a fruit, so it is nice to make desserts with this fruit that is often used as a vegetable. Cherry tomatoes have a particularly high sugar content and are delicious when frozen. You can use other fruits in this recipe, such as cut pears, peaches, or berries.

> 1 cup warm water
> 4 tablespoons agave nectar
> 2 cups cherry tomatoes, cut into halves

1 Mix together the warm water and agave nectar to make a syrup.

2 In a bowl, combine the tomatoes and the syrup. Fill 2 or 3 ice cube trays with the tomato syrup mixture, including a tomato in each cube form.

3 Freeze for 3 hours and serve ice cold.

Sweet Yam and Lotus Root Treats

4 servings

In lieu of potato chips, these treats are made with two vegetables that fit nicely together, in flavor, color, and in texture. The lotus root is an interesting root vegetable, which, when cut, looks like an exaggerated slice of Swiss cheese. The yam is sweet and becomes quite crisp, almost like a chip, when cut thin and roasted.

> 2 cups cut lotus roots, sliced
> 2 cups thinly sliced yams
> 4 tablespoons agave nectar
> 4 tablespoons black sesame seeds

1 Preheat the oven to 325°F.

2 Cover a baking sheet with parchment paper. Spread out the lotus roots and yams. Drizzle the nectar over the vegetables. Sprinkle with sesame seeds.

3 Bake for 40 minutes to 1 hour, until the vegetables are cooked and have become crisp.

4 Let cool and serve.

Baked Banana, Walnut, and Ricotta

4 servings as a snack or breakfast dish

This is a simple snack or a breakfast meal that can be made with ripe bananas. You can serve it warm or at room temperature.

> 4 ripe bananas
> 2 tablespoons butter
> 2 tablespoons brown sugar
> 1 cup ricotta cheese
> 1 tablespoon agave nectar
> ¼ cup ground walnuts
> 1 tablespoon shredded fresh mint

1 Turn the oven to broil.

2 Line a baking sheet with parchment paper. Peel and cut the bananas into half lengthwise, and then cut them again into half sideways. Place them on the baking tray and put small cubes of butter on top of each piece of banana. Sprinkle with brown sugar.

3 Put the baking sheet on the lowest rack of the oven and broil for 5 to 7 minutes. The top should become crispy and brown. Take out of the oven and let them rest.

4 In a bowl, mix together the ricotta cheese, agave nectar, and walnuts.

5 Place each banana on a plate and add a dollop of the ricotta cream mixture.

6 Sprinkle with mint and serve.

Banana, Pine Nut, and Fig Bread Pudding

4 to 6 servings

Bread puddings are the most adaptable and simple desserts you can make, and they can easily be served as a sweet breakfast or brunch dish. I love to make a variety of bread puddings with different combinations of breads and seasonal fruit. Here I combine banana, toasted pine nuts, and dried figs for an interesting mixture of flavor and textures. I bake them on a low temperature for a long time to allow the cream mixture to caramelize and thicken.

4 slices toasted whole wheat bread
1 cup pine nuts
2 eggs
½ cup cream
¼ cup honey or agave nectar
1 cup milk
1 tablespoon almond extract
1 tablespoon ground flaxseeds
½ cup chopped dried figs

1 Preheat the oven to 350°F.

2 Cut the bread into small pieces. On a baking sheet covered with foil, spread the pine nuts and the bread and roast for 3 to 4 minutes, until they become golden and aromatic. Remove from the oven and let cool.

3 In a bowl, mix together the eggs, cream, agave nectar, milk, and almond extract until well blended.

4 In a deep baking dish, distribute the bread evenly, and then pour the egg mixture on top. Sprinkle the pine nuts and flaxseeds.

5 Bake for 60 minutes, and let cool.

6 Serve with a dollop of Greek yogurt or vanilla ice cream if you want to indulge.

Almond Brioche French Toast

4 servings

French toast made with brioche bread comes out lighter and fluffier than the typical version. Try using different breads as well as different kinds of essences—almond extract, but also orange blossom, rose flower, vanilla, or anise essence. If you can't find brioche bread, you can use challah bread or any other kind of fluffy light bread.

2 eggs
1 tablespoon almond extract
2 tablespoons cream
2 tablespoons canola oil
4 slices of brioche bread
2 tablespoons honey

1 In a bowl, combine the eggs, almond extract, and the cream.

2 Heat a pan with oil on medium heat. Dip the brioche into the egg mixture and cook in the pan until the eggs are set, about 2 to 4 minutes on each side. It can be a bit runny and not completely hard.

3 Drizzle with honey and serve warm.

Rose Petal Milk Shake

4 servings

When I first saw and tasted Fauchon's rose petal jam 15 years ago, I was enchanted and inspired by the very concept of eating rose petals. Rose petal preserves have an incredibly delicate scent and flavor that renders any plain dish or recipe into a magical treat for me. This milk shake is a frothy treat that is both beautiful and nutritious with ground hemp seeds, pears, and milk.

> 2 ripe pears
> 4 cups whole organic milk
> 2 cups ice
> 2 tablespoons rose petal preserves
> 2 tablespoons ground hemp seeds
> 1 to 2 tablespoons agave nectar

1 Peel and core the pears, and cut them into small pieces.

2 In a blender, blend the rest of the ingredients together until well blended. The mixture should be frothy.

3 Serve immediately.

Lemon Cake with Chia Seeds

6 to 8 servings

Chia seeds are dense with DHA Omega-3 fatty acid and taste like poppy seeds. This lemon cake with chia is a great alternative to lemon poppy pound cake, with no butter and not much sugar. I make this in a loaf pan, slice it rather thick, and serve it with lemon yogurt.

> ½ cup sugar
> ¼ cup Greek yogurt
> 2 tablespoons lemon zest
> 1 tablespoon chia seeds
> 1¼ cups barley flour

> 1½ cups spelt flour
> 1 teaspoon salt
> ¾ cup applesauce
> 1 egg
> 2 tablespoons confectioners' sugar
> 1 cup sour cream

1 In a bowl, mix together the sugar, yogurt, and 1 tablespoon of lemon zest until well blended. Cover with plastic film and refrigerate until the cake is done.

2 Preheat the oven to 375°F.

3 Grease and dust a loaf pan.

4 In a bowl, mix together the dry ingredients—chia seeds, barley flour, spelt flour, remaining tablespoon of lemon zest, and salt.

5 In another bowl, mix together applesauce, egg, confectioners' sugar, and sour cream.

6 Slowly add the dry to the wet ingredients, and blend well.

7 Pour the batter into the loaf pan and bake for 40 to 60 minutes or until it is baked through—you can check by inserting a long skewer or knife into the middle of the cake. If it comes out dry, it is done.

8 Remove from the oven and let cool for a few minutes; then unmold from the pan and slice on a plate.

9 Top with the lemon yogurt and serve immediately.

Carrot Cake

6 to 8 servings

This carrot cake has fresh carrots, whole grains, and a rich cinnamon flavor that is satisfying and healthy without butter, which often makes carrot cake very heavy. Here I use oat flour, which gives the cake a nutty flavor. You can top it with a cream cheese frosting for special occasions, or serve it plain. It is sweet enough to enjoy as is. The cream cheese frosting recipe follows.

  4 cups grated carrots
  2 cups oat flour
  2 teaspoons baking soda
  2 teaspoons baking powder
  2 tablespoons ground wheat germ
  2 tablespoons ground flaxseeds
  2 teaspoons ground cinnamon
  ½ teaspoon salt
  ½ teaspoon allspice
  4 eggs
  ¾ cup canola oil
  ¾ cup brown sugar
  ½ cup sour cream

1 Preheat the oven to 350°F.

2 Grease and dust a 9-inch square pan.

3 In a bowl, mix together the dry ingredients—flour, baking soda, baking powder, wheat germ, flaxseeds, cinnamon, salt, and allspice.

4 In another bowl, mix together the wet ingredients—eggs, oil, sugar, and sour cream.

5 Slowly add the dry mixture to the wet, and mix until well blended. Fold in the grated carrots.

6 Pour into the pan and bake for 40 to 60 minutes or until it is baked through—you can check by inserting a long skewer or knife into the middle of the cake. If it comes out dry, it is done. Take out of the oven and let cool for a few minutes, and then slice on a plate.

Cream Cheese Frosting

  3 tablespoons butter, softened
  1 pound cream cheese, softened
  1 cup confectioners' sugar
  2 teaspoons vanilla extract

1 Beat together the butter and cream cheese until it becomes light and fluffy.

2 Add sugar and vanilla extract.

3 With a rubber spatula, spread the frosting on top of the carrot cake as desired.

Millet Honey Bon Bons   *6 to 8 servings*

I call these snacks bon bons because they can be rolled into small balls that resemble candies or truffles.

  ½ cup dried apricots
  ½ cup dried cranberries
  ½ cup raisins
  ½ cup dried figs
  ½ cup crushed walnuts
  1 tablespoon sesame seeds
  1 cup cooked millet
  1 tablespoon ground flaxseeds
  2 tablespoons applesauce
  2 tablespoons honey
  1 teaspoon almond extract

1 Chop all of the dried fruit into small pieces.

2 On a flat plate, mix the walnuts and the sesame seeds.

3 In a bowl, combine all of the remaining ingredients and integrate well.

4 Form into small balls, and then roll them in the walnut/sesame mixture to coat.

Orange, Carrot, and Cinnamon Rice Pudding   *4 to 6 servings*

Rice pudding is the most popular snack in Norway, and my husband grew up eating it as a child. Here I include oranges and carrots to add more vitamins and beta-carotene, and it combines beautifully with cinnamon. I also use agave nectar instead of refined sugar. You can try this recipe with brown rice, which would be a more nutritious option, but for the texture, white rice comes out more tender. I prefer to use cinnamon sticks in the milk, but if you don't have any, you can always use ground cinnamon.

 2 cups rice
 6 cups milk
 2 cinnamon sticks (or 1 tablespoon ground cinnamon)
 1 tablespoon agave nectar
 1 grated carrot
 1 organic orange, peeled and sliced into 4 parts
 2 tablespoons brown sugar
 1 teaspoon cinnamon for topping

1 Put the rice in a bowl and wash it under cold water until the water becomes clear, not murky. Drain.

2 In a pot, combine the rice, milk, cinnamon sticks, agave nectar, carrot, and orange, and bring to a boil. Cover and simmer for 15 minutes. Use tongs to remove the orange slices.

3 In a small bowl, combine the brown sugar and the cinnamon.

4 Pour the rice pudding into individual bowls and sprinkle with the brown sugar topping.

5 Serve warm.

Almond Barley Pudding   *4 to 6 servings*

Because barley is full of protein, folate, Omega-3, calcium, iron, and other vitamins and minerals, this pudding is a solid snack or a good sweet dish for a brunch.

 3 cups milk
 ¼ cup honey
 3 tablespoons cornstarch
 1 teaspoon salt
 3 egg yolks
 1 cup cooked barley
 2 teaspoons almond extract
 ¼ cup crushed walnuts
 ¼ cup powdered almonds

1 In a pan, combine the milk, honey, cornstarch, and salt, and bring to simmer, whisking constantly until the mixture thickens. Remove from heat.

2 In a bowl, whisk egg yolks, and then add a ladleful of the cooked milk mixture and stir.

3 Add the whole mixture into the pan, bringing it to a simmer and constantly whisking.

4 Stir in the barley, almond extract, walnuts, and powdered almonds and transfer to a container.

5 Cover with plastic wrap, allowing the wrap to touch the surface of the pudding to prevent a filmy skin from developing.

6 Refrigerate for a minimum of 4 hours, and up to 12 hours, before serving.

Yogurt Honey Sponge Cake with Buckwheat Flour and Flaxseeds

6 to 8 servings

This is a Middle Eastern dessert that is moist and delicious, with a dense consistency from the buckwheat flour. It contains no butter and no eggs. This sponge cake has very little sugar, and the main sweetness comes from the lemon/honey syrup. This cake can also be used as a base for birthday cakes with icing (recipe follows).

½ cup honey
2 cups water
Zest of 1 lemon
Juice of ½ lemon
1 teaspoon baking soda
2 teaspoons cake flour
2½ cups buckwheat flour
2 cups Greek yogurt
2 cups milk
2 tablespoons ground flaxseeds
½ cup chopped dried apricots

1 Preheat the oven to 375°F.

2 Grease a cake mold with butter or canola oil.

3 In a small pan on medium heat, whisk the honey, water, zest, and the juice until well blended. Simmer for 5 minutes, without boiling, until the syrup has thickened. Set aside.

4 In a separate bowl, mix the baking soda and the flours. Incorporate the yogurt, milk, and flaxseeds. Whip with an electric hand mixer for 2 minutes on medium speed and then for 5 minutes on high speed until fluffy.

5 Pour batter into the cake mold and bake for 45 to 60 minutes, or until done. To check if the cake is done, stick in a knife or a long toothpick in the middle of the cake; it should come out clean.

6 As soon as the cake is done, remove it from the oven and quickly pour on half the syrup; let it cool for 10 minutes.

7 Turn the cake mold upside down onto a plate to release the cake and pour on the rest of the syrup. Garnish with apricots.

Variation: Icing for Yogurt Honey Sponge Cake

6 to 8 servings

This is a delicious alternative to buttercream frosting for cakes. Very little butter is used, but the cake is coated like a sugar-glazed doughnut.

2 cups confectioners' sugar, sifted
4 tablespoons butter, melted
4 tablespoons milk
1 teaspoon vanilla extract

GARNISH
½ cup blueberries, ½ cup strawberries, or ½ cup black raspberries

1 Combine all ingredients.

2 More milk can be added for a thinner consistency.

3 Pour on top of the cake and smooth out with a spatula.

4 Garnish with fresh berries.

Walnut and Prune Kamut Cookies

Makes 4 dozen

These light, flaky cookies are from Lebanon, and they are perfect for an energy-boosting snack.

½ cup canola oil
1 cup prunes, pureed in a blender
½ cup brown sugar
2 cups kamut flour
½ cup crushed walnuts
½ cup brown sugar
1 teaspoon cinnamon

1 Preheat the oven to 350°F.

2 Grease a baking sheet with canola oil.

3 In a bowl, whip the oil, prune puree, and brown sugar. Add the kamut flour and mix until well blended and dough-like in texture—this is the cookie dough.

4 In a separate bowl, mix the walnuts, sugar, and cinnamon—this is the filling.

5 To assemble, roll the dough into small balls. Press down to flatten. Then make a well in the center of the balls with the tip of your index finger. With a small spoon, fill the well with the walnut mixture.

6 Bake for 12 to 15 minutes.

7 Cool the cookies on a rack and serve.

Apple, Blueberry, and Strawberry Oat Crumble   *6 to 8 servings*

I love making warm crumbles for dessert. They are so simple to make and such a comfort dessert, infusing the entire house with its wonderful aroma. You can make a ton of crumble and freeze it, using it over any kind of fresh or frozen fruit, any time you want a nice warm, healthy dessert for your little one.

1 apple
1 teaspoon lemon juice
2 cups blueberries
2 cups strawberries (fresh or frozen)
2 tablespoons honey
½ stick butter, softened
½ cup oat flour
½ cup oats
¼ cup brown sugar
¼ cup crushed walnuts

1 Preheat the oven to 350°F.

2 Peel the apple, cut it into small cubes, and sprinkle it with lemon juice. Add the blueberries and strawberries whole, and drizzle the fruit with the honey. Mix well and set aside.

3 In a separate bowl, mix the butter with the flour, oats, sugar, and crushed walnuts with your hands. Mix until it resembles small crumbles with a meal-like texture.

4 In a baking dish, layer in the fruit mixture, and then sprinkle the crumbles to cover the top of the fruit. Bake for 45 minutes.

5 Serve warm with ice cream or Honey Yogurt Sauce (page 189).

Honey Yogurt Sauce

This is a higher protein alternative to using cream or ice cream with baked desserts or fruit salad.

½ cup Greek yogurt
2 tablespoons honey
1 teaspoon vanilla

1 In a small bowl, mix all ingredients until smooth.

2 Serve with fresh fruit or with baked desserts, like the Apple, Rhubarb, and Strawberry Oat Crumble.

Kiwi Jam   *Makes 2 cups*

Kiwi is full of DHA Omega-3, as well as other vitamins and minerals. Raw kiwi can be at times very tart, making it difficult for kids to enjoy. This cooked version adds sweetness and can be used as a spread on toast or waffles, as a base for frozen treats or drinks, or with baked desserts. If it seems too labor intensive to do 12 kiwis, make half the recipe for 1 cup of jam.

12 kiwis
1 tablespoon lime juice
1 apple
1 cup brown sugar
1 teaspoon vanilla

1 Wash, peel, and crush the kiwis, and put them in a bowl. Add the lime juice.

2 Wash, peel, and cut the apple into small chunks. Mix with the kiwi, and then add the brown sugar and vanilla.

3 Mix well. Put the mixture into a medium-sized pot and cook for 10 to 15 minutes until the apples are very tender.

4 Remove the jam from the heat and transfer it to jars. If you don't vacuum seal the jars, the jam will keep in the refrigerator for up to 1 week; it can be frozen for up to 1 month.

Kiwi Banana Ice Pops

Kiwi is a good source of Omega 3, as well as vitamin C. This icy treat is very simple to make and is a good alternative to purchased ice pops, which often contain a lot of sugar.

½ banana
1 cup Kiwi Jam (previous recipe)
½ cup water

1 Peel the banana, and cut it into small pieces.

2 In a bowl, mix the kiwi jam with the banana and water.

3 Pour into ice pop molds and freeze for 6 hours.

4 Serve cold!

Grilled Watermelon with Pine Nuts and Honey   *4 to 6 servings*

The first time I tasted grilled watermelon was in Gambia. A wonderful chef and owner of a tiny restaurant made one of the most memorable meals I had ever eaten and then finished it off with grilled watermelon with a liqueur-based syrup. My son loves watermelon, and I make shakes, ice pops, granitas, gelatins, jams, and anything else I can make with the fruit. This is an unexpected way to prepare and eat watermelon; it's fantastic with the crunch of toasted pine nuts.

½ cup pine nuts
½ large watermelon (4 to 6 large, thick slices)
2 tablespoons honey
2 sprigs fresh mint, cut into thin strips

1 Preheat the oven to 375°F.

2 Line a baking tray with parchment paper and spread out the pine nuts evenly. Roast for 3 to 4 minutes until they become golden and aromatic. Remove from the oven and let cool.

3 Cut the skin off of the watermelon, and slice it into thick segments.

4 Heat a stove-top grill or an outdoor grill on medium heat. Place the watermelon slices on the grill. Cook for 2 to 3 minutes, and then flip them over and cook on the other side for 2 to 3 minutes—they should have grill marks on both sides.

5 Place on a large plate.

6 Sprinkle with pine nuts, honey, and mint.

7 Serve warm.

Fresh Melon, Vervain Leaves, and Sesame Fruit Salad   *4 to 6 servings*

Yes, this seems like a strange combination, but it works beautifully. I love the combination of unusual flavors, and so does my son. It is funny to watch him try different flavors and textures, and this is a challenge to any palate, let alone a little toddler's. Vervain is a fragrant herb that is usually dried and used in tea infusions, but if and when you can get the fresh kind, it's a gorgeous herb to use. It is closer to sage than anything else, so if you can't find vervain, you can use fresh sage leaves.

¼ cup sesame seeds
1 cantaloupe melon
2 sprigs fresh vervain or sage leaves
½ cup water
1 tablespoon honey

1 Preheat the oven to 375°F.

2 Line a baking sheet with parchment paper and spread out the sesame seeds. Roast for 2 to 3 minutes until they are golden and aromatic. Remove from the oven and let cool.

3 Cut the skin off of the melon, and then slice it into thin, flat slices. Place in a deep baking dish or bowl.

4 Wash and cut the vervain leaves and add to the melon.

5 Add the water, sesame seeds and honey, and cover with plastic. Refrigerate for at least 1 hour, tossing the mixture around from time to time. This allows the flavors to soak in.

6 Serve chilled.

seven

25 to 36 months and beyond
Having Fun with Food

Now your toddler can eat like the big people—more flavor, more variety. All of these recipes are family meals that are mild, interesting, and stimulating for a toddler, yet flavorful enough for the parents to enjoy.

Try these unusual flavor combinations, and have fun as a family tasting them together.

This is the time when cognitive development picks up pace in terms of memory, thought processes, and learning capacities. There will be developmental milestones regarding linguistic developments as well. At this stage, your child is developing more and more of her personality and her particular likes and dislikes. Her pickiness may become stronger, or it may fade away after a few months. She may develop mood swings or bursts of temper to test her boundaries. It is important to keep in mind that this phase, thankfully, does not last forever!

How Much Should They Be Eating and Drinking?

Your child should now be eating three meals a day, plus one or two snacks. In general, she should be consuming somewhere between 1,000 and 1,700 calories per day. She can now eat the same food as the adults in the family, and she will be able to use a fork or a spoon and eat independently. You can encourage this by simply being patient and letting your child lead the pace during meals. This is also the time to switch from giving full-fat milk to 2% milk because your child does not need as much fat as before.*

Feeding Guide:[†]

- Grains: 3 ounces (1 ounce equals 1 slice of bread, 1 cup of ready-to-eat cereal, or ½ cup of cooked rice, cooked pasta, or cooked cereal).

- Vegetables: 1 cup to 1½ cups per day

- Fruits: 1 cup

- Milk and Dairy: 2 cups (milk, yogurt, cheese)

- Protein and Legumes: 2 ounces to 3 or 4 ounces (1 ounce equals 1 ounce of meat, poultry, or fish, ¼ cup cooked dry beans, or 1 egg).

Sample Menu for a 2-Year-Old

BREAKFAST:

¾ cup 2% milk, ½ cup iron-fortified cereal or 1 egg, ½ cup juice or ½ cup strawberries, ½ slice toast, ½ teaspoon margarine

SNACK:

1 ounce cream cheese, 4 whole wheat crackers, ½ cup juice

LUNCH:

½ cup 2% milk, ½ sandwich with whole wheat bread, 2 teaspoons salad dressing, 1 ounce meat, 1 or 2 carrot sticks, 1 small oatmeal cookie

SNACK:

½ cup 2% milk, ½ cup grapes or ½ cup orange segments

DINNER:

½ cup 2% milk, 2 ounces meat, ½ cup pasta, 2 tablespoons vegetable, 1 teaspoon margarine

* AAP states that, while fat is crucial for brain and body development in the first 2 years of life, your children need less fat as they get older.

[†] AAP: Caring for Your Baby, Ibid., p. 318.

Family Meals

In most traditional cultures, eating together is a daily ritual, a big part of the day for families. Sadly, in many modern and urban cultures, parents and children often eat separately, and sometimes they don't even spend time talking to each other while sitting down at a table to eat. This not only erodes family bonding, but also healthy eating habits.

Just before my son turned two, we began to shift our mealtimes as a family so that we could sit down and eat together for dinners on week-nights and lunches and dinners on the weekend. Before that, I was feeding my son before my husband and I had our dinners. At two, we transitioned my son to a high chair that pulled up directly to the table, and we made a decision to eat together every night—very early dinners together. This changed my son's attitude during mealtimes because it became an interactive experience for him, and he became more and more interested in what we were eating and how we were eating it. Eating together encouraged the whole feeding process at a time when he was becoming less interested in food and more interested in run-ning and walking about. By watching us eat, he also overcame much of his pickiness—while he refused to eat carrots before, he watched me eat raw carrots sticks every day for two weeks, and one day, he simply picked one up and began to eat it. And he now loves raw carrot sticks. So I can say from experience that it's a great way to share, stimu-late, and inspire good eating habits, while spending time together as a family.

Continuing to Stimulate the Brain

As an adult, it becomes more and more unusual to be able to taste new flavors or to experience new sensations through food. It is always an unexpected pleasure, and the entire culinary business is built on the fact that chefs are trying to create new recipes and develop new ways for us to experience foods. The key is to keep challenging, stimulating, and surprising the taste buds and sensory organs in the mouth. For kids at this stage, even as they approach this phase of independence and pickiness, it is important to keep introducing a variety of flavors and textures, even if your child takes one bite and spits it out. Cultivating the palate is just as important as getting the nourishment into the growing body. Each new taste experience leaves an imprint of that flavor, which can then be built upon for future acceptance of that particular flavor or texture (bitter, slippery, crunchy, etc.).

 soup

Spring Vegetable Soup *4 servings*

This is a beautiful and simple soup that can be made with fresh vegetables of the season. I think fresh peas really enhance the flavor, but you can always use frozen. Otherwise, you can improvise and add any of your favorite vegetables. I like to use pancetta, or unsmoked bacon, since it leaves room for more flavor for the vegetables. You can also use Canadian bacon instead, or if you prefer a vegetarian version, do without the bacon altogether.

¼ pound pancetta or unsmoked bacon
1 onion
½ daikon radish
1 medium-sized zucchini
2 carrots
½ cup fresh peas
2 to 3 tablespoons olive oil
salt and pepper, to taste
Piece Parmesan cheese crust (the size of
    your thumb)
8 cups water
Parmesan cheese to grate for serving

1 Cut the pancetta into small pieces. Peel and mince the onion into fine, small pieces. Wash, peel, and cut the radish, zucchini, and carrots into similar, small bite-sized pieces. Shell the peas and wash.

2 In a soup pot, heat the olive oil on low heat. Add the pancetta and cook slowly, making sure not to burn—otherwise it will make the entire soup bitter.

3 When the fatty parts of the pancetta become translucent and the flesh tightens up after 3 to 5 minutes, add the onions and cook slowly until they become translucent for about 3 to 5 more minutes.

4 Then add the daikon, carrots, and zucchini, and cook for 5 minutes, tossing the vegetables around with a wooden spoon. At this point, add a little salt and pepper.

5 Add the cheese crust and water, and cover the pot and bring to a boil.

6 Add the peas and simmer for 15 to 20 minutes.

7 When all of the vegetables are tender when pierced with a fork, add salt and pepper, to taste.

8 When serving, sprinkle with a little grated Parmesan cheese and a drizzle of olive oil. Serve with crusty bread or whole wheat krispbread.

Crab Porridge with
Whipped Eggs and Chives   *4 servings*

This is a dense version of an egg-drop soup. The crabmeat adds the Omega-3 along with the eggs, and the soupy texture is perfect for a casual weekend dinner, perhaps paired with steamed vegetables.

>1 cup rice
>6 cups dashi stock or chicken stock
>2 eggs
>3 to 4 chive stalks
>½ pound crabmeat
>2 tablespoons sesame seeds, roasted
>salt and pepper, to taste

1 Rinse the rice under cold water and drain. In a pot, add the rice and stock and bring to a boil. Reduce the heat to low; cover the pot and cook for 20 minutes.

2 In a small bowl, whip the eggs until foamy and completely blended.

3 Wash and chop the chives into small pieces.

4 Add the crabmeat to the rice, and crumble it into small pieces with a wooden spoon. Cook for 2 to 3 minutes.

5 Add the eggs to the pot of rice, stirring the rice constantly so that the eggs become integrated into the rice. Allow to cook for a minute or two, until the eggs become solidified, but not hardened.

6 Add the chives, sesame seeds, salt, and pepper, and serve immediately. This dish is great accompanied by some salted cucumbers or radish.

Warm Avocado Soup
with Lime and Mint   *4 servings*

We usually see avocado raw in salads or guacamole. This recipe is a great way to use avocados in a rich warm soup.

>4 ripe avocados
>6 cups chicken stock
>½ cup cream
>Zest of ½ lime
>1 tablespoon minced mint leaves
>salt and pepper, to taste

1 Cut the avocados in half and remove the pit. Scoop out the flesh of the avocados and puree in a blender.

2 In a soup pot, add the stock and avocados. Heat gently until warm, and then add the rest of the ingredients.

3 Serve warm or room temperature with crunchy bread or crackers.

Soft Udon Noodle Soup
with Sardines and Chives   *4 servings*

Udon noodle soup, with its silkiness unlike any other type of noodle, has become comfort food for my son. Every time I make it for him and his little friends, it is, without fail, a huge hit. The best thing about this soup is that you can include almost anything—fish, poultry, meat, veggies—and it always turns out divine. You can find udon noodles, in dry form, in most Whole Foods stores. If you have an Asian grocery store nearby, you can find the fresh refrigerated kind. You can also order either kind online at Amazon.

> 5 to 6 pieces of dried kombu
> ¼ cup dried bonito flakes
> 4 cups udon rice noodles (around 1 pound)
> 4 tablespoons soy sauce
> 4 to 6 sardine fillets (with the bones carefully removed)
> 4 eggs
> 3 tablespoons chopped fresh chives
> 2 tablespoons pomegranate seeds (optional)

1   Soak the kombu and bonito flakes in 3 cups water, making sure the kombu pieces are well soaked. Set aside while you prepare the rest.

2   Boil the udon noodles according to package instructions, usually around 6 to 8 minutes. I tend to like udon noodles overcooked, so that they are very tender; I don't hesitate to let them boil a bit over the required time. Drain, and run cold water over the noodles to stop the cooking process.

3   For the soup stock, drain the kombu and bonito through a strainer, catching the liquid in a pot; and add the soy sauce. Heat on medium heat, and let it begin to simmer.

4   Add the sardine fillets, breaking them into small pieces in the stock.

5   In a small bowl, whip up the eggs for a minute until they become frothy and pale. Pour into the simmering stock and stir so that the eggs cook in a uniform way in the stock.

6   Add the chives, then the pomegranate seeds, if desired.

7   Divide a portion of the noodles among four separate bowls, and then pour the stock over them evenly.

8   Serve immediately.

Miso Noodle Soup
with Mackerel and Egg   *4 servings*

Udon noodles are so versatile, and, no matter how you cook them—in a soup or sautéed—they are always a big hit with children. Here is an Omega-3–packed recipe with mackerel and eggs.

4 cups udon rice noodles
6 cups water
2 tablespoons miso paste
1 kombu seaweed
1 tablespoon dried wakame
2 tablespoons dried bonito flakes
2 mackerel (cleaned)
2 to 4 scallions, chopped (white part only)
4 eggs

1 Preheat the oven to 375°F.

2 Fill a large pot with water and bring to a boil. Add the rice noodles and cook according to package instructions, around 5 to 7 minutes. The noodles should be soft and tender. Drain and run under cold water; set aside.

3 In a smaller pot, bring the 6 cups of water to a boil. Add the miso paste, kombu, wakame, and bonito flakes, and simmer for 15 minutes.

4 Add the eggs, cracking them one at a time into the simmering water, and cook for another 5 minutes; the water should keep simmering lightly to cook the eggs to a light and fluffy texture.

5 Line a baking sheet with foil and roast the mackerel for 7 to 10 minutes.

6 Remove it from the oven, and take the cooked flesh off the bones, making sure no small bones are attached to the fish pieces. Add the pieces to the soup stock.

7 Divide the cooked noodles among four soup bowls and pour the soup stock over them, putting one egg into each bowl. Sprinkle with chopped scallions.

8 Serve immediately.

Chicken Asparagus Soup
with Macaroni and Cream   *4 servings*

This mild soup is well liked by toddlers, even if they usually have a difficult time accepting asparagus on its own.

2 onions
1 garlic clove
1 tablespoon canola oil
4 chicken thighs
2 cups chopped asparagus
6 cups chicken stock
½ cup cream
1 tablespoon ground flaxseeds
salt and pepper, to taste
4 cups cooked kamut or whole wheat
    macaroni

1 Peel and slice the onions into thin slices. Crush and chop the garlic.

2 In a large pot, add the oil and heat on medium heat. Add the chicken and sauté until the pieces are browned on all sides, about 6 to 8 minutes.

3 Add the onions and sauté for another 5 minutes.

4 Add the asparagus, and sauté for another 3 minutes.

5 Add the chicken stock and garlic, and bring to a boil. Cover and simmer for 30 minutes, skimming the surface of the stock from time to time to eliminate the fat and foam that floats to the top.

6 Remove the chicken and cut it into small pieces, discarding the bones.

7 Add the chicken back in, and then with a hand blender, blend the entire soup so that it becomes smooth.

8 Remove it from the heat, and add the cream.

9 Stir; sprinkle salt, pepper, and flaxseeds into the soup.

10 Divide the macaroni into 4 bowls, and pour the soup on top.

11 Serve immediately.

Thai Tom Yam Shrimp Coconut Soup

4 servings

Tom Yam soup is a national dish of Thailand—fragrant, rich, and satisfying—and very easy for kids to love with its tomato broth. Here I added coconut milk for a milder version of this soup. I don't like to use the Tom Yam paste that many use as a base for this soup, since it almost always contains MSG. This recipe is from scratch, and as you will see, it is not difficult. Lemongrass stalks are now available in most supermarkets and Whole Food stores. If you can't find the Kaffir lime leaves, you can order them online, or substitute the zest of one lime.

1 pound fresh shrimp
2 lemongrass stalks
2 garlic cloves
1 red pepper
1 cup button mushrooms
8 cups chicken stock
2 limes or 4 lime leaves
4 tablespoons nuoc nam fish sauce
2 tomatoes, peeled and cut into segments
4 cups coconut milk
2 tablespoons chopped fresh cilantro
salt and pepper, to taste

1 Peel and devein the shrimp, putting the shells into a small pot with ½ cup water. Cover and bring to a boil. Remove from the heat and let cool.

2 Meanwhile, wash the lemongrass, cut off the bulb—the lower white section—and chop the stem. Peel and crush the garlic, and mince it into small pieces. Wash and cut the red pepper into small pieces. Brush clean the mushrooms, and cut them into thin pieces.

3 In a large stock pot, combine the chicken stock, the zest of the lime or lime leaves, and the lemongrass. Bring to a boil.

4 Add the garlic and mushrooms, fish sauce, tomatoes, coconut milk, the shrimp liquid, and red pepper. Simmer for 10 to 15 minutes.

5 Add the shrimp and cook for 4 to 5 minutes, or until the shrimp turn pink, shiny, and plump.

6 Sprinkle with cilantro and serve immediately.

Sautéed Lotus Roots and Arugula *4 servings as a side dish*

If you've never had lotus roots, you should definitely give them a try. They are crunchy, light, and neutral enough to adapt to a variety of dishes. They contain high amounts of fiber, vitamins C and B6, potassium, thiamin, and copper, among other vitamins and minerals. You can get them fresh or in cans at an Asian grocery store, or even in some super-markets. You can also order them online. Otherwise, you can use canned water chestnuts or jicama, which are easier to find and have a similar crunchy texture.

> 2 cups sliced lotus root (canned or fresh)
> 2 cups fresh arugula, washed and chopped
> 1 teaspoon sesame oil
> 1 tablespoon canola oil
> 1 tablespoon sesame seeds
> 1 tablespoon soy sauce
> 1 tablespoon mirin
> 1 tablespoon ground flaxseeds

1 Heat a pan with the sesame and canola oil. Add the lotus root and stir-fry for 3 to 4 minutes, tossing the slices around with a wooden spoon, making sure all sides are cooked and browned.

2 Add the rest of the ingredients and cover. Simmer for 20 minutes.

3 Serve immediately.

Crunchy Grilled Vegetables with Orange Zest *4 to 6 servings as a side dish*

With a stove-top grill, this is something that can be prepared very quickly any time of the year. Just gather your favorite vegetables together; brush them with olive oil; and grill them over very low heat. It is as simple as that.

> 1 bunch asparagus
> 2 zucchinis
> 2 red peppers
> 2 tomatoes
> 1 eggplant
> 2 tablespoons olive oil
> sea salt, to taste
> Zest and juice of 1 orange
> 2 tablespoons chia seeds

1 Wash and cut the asparagus in half, discarding the white bottom part. Wash and cut the zucchini into thin round pieces. Wash and cut the peppers into small pieces, discarding the seeds. Cut the tomatoes in half. Wash and cut the eggplant into small pieces.

2 In a bowl, toss the vegetables in batches with olive oil, sea salt, and the zest and juice of an orange.

3 The order is important here because each type of vegetable requires a different length of cooking time. First, oil the eggplant pieces and put them on the grill, then the peppers, then the zucchinis, then the tomatoes, waiting 3 to 4 minutes before adding the next batch.

4 Place vegetables on a serving plate and sprinkle with chia seeds.

5 Serve immediately or at room temperature.

Roasted Fennel and Cherry Tomatoes with Fennel Seeds
4 servings as a side dish

Fennel is a wonderful vegetable that is often overlooked. It has a fragrant licorice scent that is a great complement to any protein dish or works well on its own with some bread and cheese.

> 2 fennel bulbs
> Bunch fresh basil
> 2 cups cherry tomatoes
> 1 tablespoon fennel seeds
> 2 anise stars
> 2 tablespoons olive oil
> ¼ cup grated Parmesan cheese
> salt and pepper, to taste

1 Preheat the oven to 350°F.

2 Wash and cut the fennel bulbs into thin strips. Wash and remove the leaves of the basil. Wash the tomatoes and drain.

3 Line a baking sheet with foil. Spread the cut fennel and tomatoes on the baking sheet.

4 Toss together the rest of the ingredients and sprinkle over fennel and tomatoes.

5 Bake for 30 to 40 minutes or until the fennel is tender.

6 Serve warm.

Couscous with Fava Beans, Peas, and Artichoke Hearts   *4 servings*

This is a light and elegant couscous that is adaptable to the seasons. In the spring, these vegetables, along with other fresh picks of the season, can be used; in the fall, you can add squash, mushrooms, pears, or apples. The foundation is a vegetable stock made with sautéed onions and shallots. You can always add as much variety as desired. Sometimes my son only likes to eat the fava beans out of the medley of vegetables. Other times, he will eat everything on the plate. Don't despair—just keep trying.

1 onion
2 shallots
2 tablespoons olive oil
2 cups fresh fava beans (if frozen beans, thawed)
2 cups fresh green peas (if frozen peas, thawed)
2 cups shelled edamame, (if frozen, thawed)
4 artichoke hearts (if frozen, thawed)
4 cups vegetable stock
3 cups cooked couscous
2 sprigs of mint

1 Peel and slice the onion and shallots into thin slices. In a pot, heat the olive oil, and add the onion and shallots. Cook until tender and transparent, about 3 to 4 minutes.

2 Add the fava beans, peas, edamame, artichokes, and stock. Bring to a boil and cover. Simmer for 10 to 15 minutes.

3 Season with salt and pepper, and sprinkle with mint.

4 Divide the couscous among 4 bowls.

5 Pour the stock and pea mixture on top, and serve immediately.

Zucchini and Mozzarella Cheese Gratin   *4 servings as a side dish*

You can't get any simpler than this. This delicious side dish takes 2 minutes to prepare and is a perfect accompaniment to a fish or a meat dish. Or you can add chicken tenders for a more substantial meal.

4 zucchinis
1 cup grated mozzarella cheese
1 cup grated Parmesan cheese
1 cup milk
¼ cup cream
2 tablespoons ground flaxseeds
1 garlic clove
2 tablespoons olive oil
salt and pepper, to taste

1 Preheat the oven to 350°F.

2 Wash and cut the zucchini into thin rounds.

3 In a deep baking casserole dish, combine the zucchini and the rest of the ingredients; mix well.

4 Bake for 30 to 40 minutes, or until the zucchini is tender.

5 Serve warm.

Whole Wheat Toasts with Brie and Fig Jam

4 servings

My son is not very open to trying different kinds of soft cheeses, especially the strong cheeses of France, like Camembert or Saint Marcelin. My friend Agathe's kids, on the other hand, can't get enough of the strongest cheeses imaginable. Agathe tells me it's in her kid's genes to love French cheeses, but I think it's about how much and how often they eat it as a family. I want Magnus to appreciate the subtle flavors and textures of all kinds of cheeses, so I try to use them in dishes. This toast with the mild Brie cheese is something that he has come to like after several attempts.

    4 slices whole wheat bread
    2 tablespoons fig jam
    4 slices of brie cheese—enough to spread
        on the bread
    2 tablespoons ground flaxseeds

1   Preheat the oven to 375°F.

2   Line a baking tray with parchment paper, and place the bread on the sheet. Spread each slice of bread with a bit of fig jam.

3   Add a slice of Brie so that it covers the bread entirely. Bake for 5 to 7 minutes, or until the cheese has melted.

4   Sprinkle with flaxseeds, and serve immediately before the cheese stiffens.

Snap Peas with Pecorino Cheese

4 servings as a side dish

Snap peas are a perfect snack for little ones—they are sweet, crunchy, and interesting to eat with its pods and skin. They can either nosh on them plain, or you can prepare them as a side dish. I usually always prefer snap peas raw, as they change flavor if you cook them. Here, I simply toss them with cheese and olive oil.

    1 pound fresh snap peas
    ½ cup grated pecorino cheese
    2 tablespoons ground flaxseeds
    2 tablespoons olive oil
    salt and pepper, to taste

1   Wash and "devein" the peas—pop one side of the peas and take off the stringy fiber that runs along both sides.

2   Put them in a bowl and toss with the remaining ingredients.

3   Serve at room temperature.

French Potato Gratin   *4 to 6 servings*

When my son turned 2, he stopped eating potatoes. From one day to the next, he would not eat potatoes in any shape or form—mashed, baked, or sautéed. But he began to eat potatoes again after I introduced this potato gratin.

1 onion
4 large potatoes
2 cups milk
1 cup cream
2 tablespoons ground flaxseeds
2 cups grated Emmental cheese
salt and pepper, to taste

1   Preheat the oven to 375°F.

2   Wash and peel the onions, and cut them into thin slices. Wash, peel, and slice the potatoes into thin slices (ideal would be to use a vegetable slicer); and soak them in a bowl of cold water to remove the starch. Drain.

3   In a bowl, combine the milk, cream, and flaxseeds.

4   In a deep baking dish or casserole dish, cover the bottom of the dish with a layer of the potatoes. Sprinkle with cheese and onions, and pour in some of the milk mixture. Layer again and repeat until all of the potatoes and milk mixture have been used.

5   Bake in the oven for 40 to 60 minutes, or until the potatoes are completely soft when poked with a toothpick or knife.

6   Serve warm.

Snap Peas with Sesame and Lime Zest Pesto

4 to 6 servings as a side dish

In this recipe, I use cooked snap peas, but if your child prefers the crunchy texture of raw snap peas, by all means, you can toss everything together without cooking the peas.

¼ cup sesame seeds
¼ cup cashew nuts
1 pound fresh snap peas
2 tablespoons ground flaxseeds
1 teaspoon soy sauce
1 teaspoon brown sugar
1 teaspoon mirin
1 tablespoon chopped mint leaves
1 tablespoon lime juice

1   Preheat the oven to 300°F.

2   Line a baking sheet with parchment paper and pour the sesame seeds evenly over the sheet. Roast for 3 to 5 minutes, until the seeds are aromatic and golden (being careful not to burn—every oven is different, so the time can be shorter or longer). Let the seeds cool completely.

3   Repeat with the cashew nuts, roasting them a bit longer (4 to 6 minutes).

4   Meanwhile, bring to boil a pot of water with salt.

5   Wash and trim the snap peas, snapping off the edges and removing the fiber that runs along the side of the peas. Boil the peas for 5 to 7 minutes, being careful not to overcook them (you don't want soft, mushy peas—they should be crunchy, but softened enough to soak up the pesto). Drain, and run the peas under cold water.

6 In a food processor, blend together the rest of the ingredients until well blended.

7 In a bowl, toss together the peas and the pesto.

8 Serve warm or at room temperature.

Roasted Cauliflower with Cranberries and Parsley

4 servings as a side dish

Earlier in the book I introduced sautéed cauliflower with dates. Here the cauliflower is crunchy and crisp, and this recipe gives a different experience to eating this superfood. It is packed with vitamins C and Bs, folates, Omega-3, protein, phosphorus, and more. It is recommended that these cruciferous vegetables be a regular part of a child's diet— with three servings a week, minimum.

   3 sprigs of parsley
   1 head of cauliflower
   2 tablespoons olive oil
   ¼ cup dried cranberries
   ½ tablespoon sea salt

1 Preheat the oven to 400°F.

2 Wash and chop the parsley into small pieces. Wash and trim the cauliflower into florets, discarding the thick hard stems. Line a baking sheet with foil.

3 Toss the cauliflower with oil, cranberries, and parsley. Bake on the sheet for 20 to 30 minutes.

4 Serve warm or at room temperature.

Zucchini with Tofu and Mushrooms

4 servings

This is a very simple tofu dish that can be served as a side dish, or as a main with brown rice or other carbohydrate. My son usually loves tofu with anything, so even when he does not feel up to eating zucchini, he tends to get a few bites with the tofu and the soy stock.

   2 zucchinis
   1 cup fresh mushrooms
   1 tablespoon canola oil
   1 teaspoon sesame oil
   ½ package silken soft tofu
   1 tablespoon ground flaxseeds
   1 tablespoon ground sesame seeds
   1 tablespoon soy sauce
   1 tablespoon mirin

1 Wash and cut the zucchinis into thin round slices. Wipe the mushrooms with a cloth, and slice into small slices.

2 In a pan, heat the canola and sesame oils on medium heat. Add the zucchinis and cook for about 5 to 7 minutes, or until they soften.

3 Add the mushrooms and cook together for another 3 to 4 minutes, tossing the vegetables around with a wooden spoon.

4 When the mushrooms soften and begin to release liquid, add the tofu, mashing it up with the spoon and mixing it with the vegetables.

5 Add the rest of the ingredients, and cook for another 2 to 4 minutes.

6 Serve warm with rice.

Asparagus with Miso-Ae   *4 servings*

You've already seen several recipes that combine miso with a protein or a vegetable. Miso-ae is a pesto-like condiment made with miso, sesame, and vinegar, and it is tossed with vegetables or seafood and accompanied by rice. This is a lighter version of the classic recipe and has very little vinegar, which is much more palatable for kids.

> ½ pound asparagus
> 1 tablespoon miso
> 1 tablespoon water
> 1 teaspoon vinegar
> 1 tablespoon ground sesame seeds
> 1 teaspoon sugar

1 Wash and cut the asparagus spears in half; remove the end pieces where the skin is white and tough. Using a vegetable peeler, peel off the outer layers of the asparagus.

2 Fill a large pot with water and bring it to a boil. Add 1 tablespoon of salt and then the asparagus. Boil for 5 to 6 minutes, or until the asparagus is tender, but not too soft. Drain, and run cold water on the asparagus for a few seconds to stop the cooking process.

3 In a bowl, mix together the miso, water, vinegar, sesame, and sugar until well blended.

4 Toss the asparagus with the miso mixture until well blended.

5 Serve warm or at room temperature.

Succotash with Fresh Basil and Crabmeat   *4 servings*

Succotash is a great dish that includes a beautiful array of vegetables in a thick broth. I usually add a protein to make it a complete meal and serve it with bread or quinoa for a simple light dinner. Here is a crabmeat version, which gives great flavor to the broth and adds Omega-3 fatty acid.

> 1 onion
> 1 tablespoon olive oil
> 1½ cups cherry tomatoes
> 1½ cups frozen edamame, thawed
> 1½ cups frozen corn, thawed
> 1 tablespoon thyme
> 2 cups vegetable stock or chicken stock
> ½ pound crabmeat
> 1 tablespoon chopped fresh basil
> salt and pepper, to taste

1 Peel and cut the onion into thin strips. Wash and cut the cherry tomatoes in half.

2 Heat a pan with oil, and add the onions. Cook for 3 to 4 minutes until the onions become pale and translucent.

3 Add the edamame, tomatoes, corn, thyme, and stock. Cover and let simmer for 15 minutes, stirring from time to time with a wooden spoon. The sauce should thicken, and the tomatoes should have softened.

4 Add the crabmeat, breaking up the flesh with the wooden spoon. Cook for 7 to 10 more minutes, tossing everything together.

5 Sprinkle with chopped basil, salt, and pepper.

6 Serve immediately.

Cucumbers, Papaya, and Crab Salad with Green Lime Cilantro Dressing

4 servings

Papaya has a gorgeous sunny flavor without being too sweet, which is often the case with tropical fruit. It is great combined with savory dishes, particularly with seafood. It is full of beta-carotene and vitamin C, and the texture is smooth and soft, which is a nice contrast to the crunch of the cucumbers in this dish. The best way to buy a papaya is to touch it. It should not be too firm, but soft like a ripe avocado.

½ ripe papaya, chopped into small pieces
1 green lime
1 cucumber
½ pound crabmeat
3 to 4 sprigs cilantro
salt and pepper, to taste

1 Peel the papaya. Using a spoon, scoop out the dark seeds of the papaya. Cut into small cubes and put into a bowl.

2 Squeeze in the juice of the lime. Toss.

3 Cut the peel off the cucumber, and chop it into similar sized cubes as the papaya; toss together.

4 Mix in the crabmeat and cilantro; sprinkle with salt and pepper.

5 Serve immediately (papaya tends to become rather mushy if left out too long—it is best when eaten right away). Serve with crunchy bread or crackers.

Salted Crunchy Cucumber and Radish

4 to 6 servings as a condiment

These are fresh "pickles"—without the nitrates that are used for most store-bought pickles. They add a crunchy texture to an otherwise "soft" meal, such as noodles, porridge, or rice dishes. You can add olive oil and try other kinds of vinegar, but I usually like to keep it very simple with salt, rice wine vinegar, and some cerfeuil leaves. If you can't find dried cerfeuil leaves, you can use oregano. They will keep in the refrigerator in an airtight container for up to 3 to 5 days, so you can save any leftovers from this recipe.

2 cucumbers
1 daikon radish
2 tablespoons rice wine vinegar
1 teaspoon sugar
1 teaspoon salt
1 tablespoon dried cerfeuil leaves
1 tablespoon dried oregano

1 Wash and peel the cucumbers and radish (remember that daikon radish has two layers of skin, so rotate it twice to get to the more delicate flesh).

2 For the cucumbers, remove the inner core with the seeds, and cut them into quarters lengthwise, then into small pieces.

3 Cut the radish into similar-sized pieces.

4 In a small bowl, mix together all of the ingredients. Cover with plastic wrap and refrigerate for 1 hour to allow the flavors to mingle.

5 Serve cold or room temperature, as an accompaniment.

Grilled Peach and Feta Salad *4 servings*

Feta cheese is tangier and saltier than goat cheese, and it is nicely balanced in this recipe by the sweetness of the peaches, which are even sweeter when grilled. This is a nice refreshing salad for the summer months when peaches are in season.

    4 peaches
    1 tablespoon olive oil
    ¼ cup feta cheese
    ¼ cup Greek yogurt
    1 teaspoon chopped fresh basil

1   Peel the peaches, then wash and cut them in half; remove the pits, and slice peaches thinly.

2   Lightly oil the peach slices with olive oil, and cook for 3 to 4 minutes on a grill (outdoor or stove-top grill pan).

3   In a bowl, combine the feta cheese with the yogurt, and mix well.

4   Put the peaches on a plate and pour the yogurt mixture on top.

5   Sprinkle with basil, and serve.

Goat Cheese Balls with Red Pepper, Crushed Walnuts, and Chives *4 Servings*

These goat cheese balls are festive and easy to make, and you can make them as a project with your child by rolling the cheese into balls and covering them with a variety of toppings. Here are three options, but you can use any kind of vegetable, dried and fresh fruits, and herbs.

    1 cup soft goat cheese
    3 tablespoons chopped chives
    3 tablespoons chopped red peppers
    3 tablespoons chopped or
       crushed walnuts

1   Taking a tablespoonful of goat cheese at a time, place the cheese in the palm of your hand, and slowly roll into a ball. Continue until all of the cheese has been rolled into small balls.

2   Place the three toppings on separate plates.

3   Roll the cheese balls in the toppings until well covered.

4   Serve immediately.

chutney, tapenade, and pesto

These chutney/tapenade/pesto recipes are easy to make, and they keep in the refrigerator for up to 10 days, making any of them an easy addition that adds the extra brainfood boost and flavor to your child's meals.

Mango Chutney
4 to 6 servings

Mango chutney is the classic Indian condiment for spicy dishes. I love the sweet and savory combinations and think it is a very stimulating meal when you have a good mixture of both. This chutney is inspired by the traditional mango chutney, but it doesn't have as much sugar or the usual amount of vinegar. It integrates brainfood elements of flaxseed and walnut oil.

> 3 medium apples, peeled, cored, and chopped
> 2 large mangos, peeled and chopped
> 2 tablespoons brown sugar
> 1 tablespoon vinegar
> 1 tablespoon lemon juice
> 1 teaspoon walnut oil
> 1 tablespoon chopped and peeled ginger
> ½ teaspoon each: ground nutmeg, cinnamon, and salt
> 1 teaspoon ground flaxseeds

1 In a pot, combine all of the ingredients; cook on low heat covered for 20 minutes or until all of the ingredients have been cooked to a soft texture.

2 Remove from the heat, and serve at room temperature with meat, tofu, or vegetable dishes.

Prune and Date Chutney with Walnuts and Cinnamon   *4 to 6 servings*

Prunes are definitely a superfood. They contain high amounts of Omega-3 fatty acids, vitamins C and A, calcium, iron, magnesium, potassium, and folate. In the U.S., prunes are not used much in cooked recipes, but they are very commonly used in North African savory dishes, with lamb, duck, and other meats. This chutney is a wonderful way to enjoy dates and prunes, and they can be served as a snack or cooked with meats, grilled or stewed together to infuse a sweetness in savory dishes. You can also eat it as a jam on toast or crackers or as a topping for yogurts or ice cream. Using it is a great way to add extra vitamins and minerals to a dish.

> 2 tablespoons brown sugar
> 2 tablespoons ground cinnamon
> 1 cup water
> Zest and juice of 2 oranges
> 2 tablespoons ground walnuts
> ½ pound pitted prunes
> ½ pound pitted dates
> 8 ounces ground walnuts

1 In a bowl, stir together the brown sugar, cinnamon, water, zest and juice of the 2 oranges, and the ground walnuts.

2 With a knife, open up the center of each prune and date, and insert a walnut.

3 Place the fruit in a large, heavy pan, and cover with water and the sweetened juice. Cover and cook on low heat for 20 to 30 minutes.

4 Remove from the heat, and serve warm or at room temperature.

Olive Flaxseed Tapenade   *4 to 6 servings*

Olives contain antioxidants and phytonutrients, which can protect cells from damage. They also contain calcium, vitamin A, and DHA Omega-3. Olives usually contain a high amount of sodium, so it is good to use small portions for a spread or a dip. Tapenade is usually made with raw garlic and capers, but because I find raw garlic too strong for kids, I have omitted these and added some flaxseeds, wheat germ, and ground pine nuts.

> ½ cup pitted black olives
> ½ cup pitted green olives
> 2 tablespoons olive oil
> 1 teaspoon lemon juice
> 1 teaspoon ground flaxseeds
> 1 teaspoon ground wheat germ
> 1 teaspoon ground pine nuts

1 In a food processor, blend all of the ingredients until smooth.

2 Serve with crackers or bread.

3 Stored in an airtight container, the tapenade will keep up to 3 to 5 days in the refrigerator and up to 1 month in the freezer.

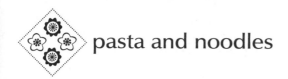 **pasta and noodles**

Mini Ziti with Tuna, Capers, and Tomatoes   *4 servings*

This is a simple pasta dish that even my husband (who can only make coffee) can whip up in a few minutes. Capers give a salty tang to this sauce without overpowering the dish. I like to cook the tuna separately before mixing it into the sauce, just to give it extra tenderness.

> 2 garlic cloves
> 2 tablespoons olive oil
> 2 cans tuna preserved in olive oil
> 4 cups peeled and chopped tomatoes
> 1 teaspoon sugar
> 1 tablespoon capers
> 1 tablespoon salt
> 14 ounces whole wheat mini ziti

1   Peel and crush the garlic, and cut into small pieces. In a small pot, heat 1 tablespoon olive oil, and add half of the crushed garlic. Cook for 1 minute, and then add the tuna. Cover and simmer while you prepare the tomato sauce.

2   In another pot, heat the other tablespoon of olive oil, and add the rest of the garlic. Let it cook for 1 minute, and then add the tomatoes, sugar, and capers. Cover and let simmer for 30 to 40 minutes.

3   Add the tuna to the tomato sauce.

4   Bring to a boil a pot of water with 1 tablespoon salt. Cook the ziti according to the package instructions.

5   Drain, and toss together with the tomato sauce.

6   Serve immediately.

Angel Hair Pasta with Light Anchovy and Broccoli Sauce   *4 servings*

You may think that the flavor of anchovies is too strong for kids. But as you will see in this recipe, when anchovies are cooked well, almost caramelized in olive oil, and tossed together with pasta and other elements, like broccoli, the strong flavor of the fish dissipates, and you are left with nutty, salty remnants, which enhance any vegetable pasta dish.

1 large head of broccoli
14 ounces of whole wheat angel hair pasta
4 tablespoons olive oil
1 garlic clove, crushed
8 slices of anchovies soaked in olive oil
salt and pepper, to taste

1   Wash and cut up the broccoli, separating the florets from the stems, but keeping all of it. Bring a pot of salted water to a boil. Put in the broccoli stems, and let them boil for 5 minutes. Then add the florets, and boil for 3 to 4 minutes.

2   With a spoon, carefully remove the broccoli and put it into a bowl of ice water to stop the cooking process and to preserve the green color. Drain and set aside.

3   In the same water that you used to boil the broccoli, boil the pasta following the instructions on the package. When done, drain and set aside.

4   In a pan, heat the olive oil on medium to low heat; add the garlic and sauté for 1 to 2 minutes.

5   Add the anchovies and cook for 2 to 3 minutes, until they dissolve into the oil.

6   Add the broccoli and toss; then add the pasta and toss together.

7   Salt and pepper to taste, and serve immediately.

Cauliflower Fusilli with Cranberries and Roasted Pumpkin Seeds   *4 servings*

Cooking pasta in the same water as a vegetable used in the same dish infuses the pasta with the scent and flavor of that vegetable, enhancing the flavors of the entire dish. Here the pasta is cooked in the same cooking liquid as the cauliflower, which has a strong flavor. The dried berries add color and an unexpected tang in an otherwise salty dish that is based on anchovies.

1 full head of fresh cauliflower
14 ounces whole wheat fusilli pasta
3 tablespoons olive oil
4 anchovy fillets
3 tablespoons dried cranberries or
    lingonberries, roughly chopped
½ cup grated Parmesan cheese
½ cup pumpkin seed kernels
2 tablespoons dried oregano
salt and pepper, to taste

1   Bring to a boil a large pot of water with 1 tablespoon salt.

2   Meanwhile, wash and cut the cauliflower into small pieces, separating the florets, peeling the outer layer of the stalk, and chopping the stock into small pieces. Boil the cauliflower in the salted water for 7 to 10 minutes, until it becomes very tender when pierced with a knife (it should go right through).

3　When done, remove the cauliflower with a slotted spoon and drain in a strainer. Set aside.

4　Boil the pasta in the cauliflower liquid, following the instructions on the package.

5　In a pan, heat the olive oil; add the anchovy fillets and cook until they dissolve.

6　Add the berries, oregano, Parmesan cheese, cauliflower, and the pumpkin seeds, tossing it all together until well blended.

7　When the pasta is done, take it out with a slotted spoon and put into the pan, allowing some of the cooking liquid to be included in the cauliflower mixture. Toss well.

8　Sprinkle with salt and pepper, and serve.

Chicken Carbonara with Peas

4 servings

My favorite carbonara sauce recipe is from the mother of a dear Italian friend; it is made with raw eggs, Parmesan, and pancetta, and it is divine. But for kids, I hesitate to serve raw eggs. In this recipe, the eggs and Parmesan cheese are cooked with the pasta in the pan. The flavors are still great, and you can feel safe serving it to your little ones.

1 garlic clove
4 to 5 thin slices of pancetta (or bacon, if there is no pancetta)
1 tablespoon olive oil
6 chicken thighs
14 ounces spaghetti
2 cups peas
2 eggs
½ cup grated Parmesan cheese
1 tablespoon chopped fresh parsley
salt and pepper, to taste

1　Bring to a boil a pot of water with a tablespoon of salt. Peel and smash the garlic with the side of a knife, taking care to leave it intact. Cut the pancetta slices into small pieces.

2　In a pan, heat the oil, and then add the pancetta and let it cook for 2 to 4 minutes.

3　Add the chicken thighs and the garlic; cover and cook for 20 to 30 minutes.

4　Meanwhile, boil the pasta according to the package instructions.

5　Place the chicken on a cutting board, and cut it into small pieces, discarding the bones; return it to the pan and add the peas. Cook for 3 to 5 minutes, tossing the ingredients together.

6　In a bowl, mix together the eggs and the grated Parmesan cheese.

7　When the pasta is done, drain and pour it into the pan with the chicken; then pour in the egg mixture, tossing quickly so the pasta is coated with the egg mixture. Cook it in the pan for 2 minutes, or until the eggs are firm and cooked through.

8　Sprinkle with parsley, salt, and pepper, and serve.

Pasta with Butternut Squash and Walnut Cream Sauce   *4 servings*

This light pasta is easy to make and is perfect when butternut squash comes into season in the fall. The squash is sweet, and the nutty flavor of walnuts blends well. This recipe contains beta-carotene, folate, vitamin C, Omega-3, carbohydrates, and calcium. You can also use pumpkin instead of butternut squash. To save time, I often buy the pre-cubed organic butternut squash from Whole Foods, as the squash is quite difficult to peel.

2 cups butternut squash, cubed
1 teaspoon sage
1 cup chicken stock
¼ cup warm cream
½ cup crushed walnuts
1 tablespoon of butter
14 ounces kamut or whole wheat linguini pasta
salt and pepper, to taste

1 In a medium-sized pot, combine the cubed squash with the sage and chicken stock, and bring to a boil; then simmer for about 15 minutes or until the squash is tender when pierced with a fork.

2 Remove from heat and mash the squash with a fork (or use a hand mixer for better smoothness).

3 In a small pot, heat the cream until close to boiling. Then add the crushed walnuts and butter to the cream. Heat it for 4 to 6 minutes.

4 Add the mashed butternut squash and mix well. Take off the heat. Set aside.

5 Fill a large pot with water and bring it to a boil. Add 1 tablespoon salt. Add the pasta and cook following the instructions on the box.

6 Drain the pasta, and then fold into the cream sauce. Sprinkle with salt and pepper to taste.

Spaghetti with Caviar, Edamame, and Lemon Zest   *4 servings*

This is a beautiful light pasta dish that is super simple and packed with Omega-3 fatty acid, complex carbohydrates, and protein. Kamut is a great source of protein, and you can find the pasta version in most stores. If you have difficulty finding it, you can always use whole wheat pasta.

14 ounces kamut or whole wheat spaghetti
1 cup edamame
2 tablespoons fresh chopped chives
2 tablespoons olive oil
Zest of 1 lemon
salt and pepper, to taste
½ cup salmon roe, tobiko, or other kind of caviar

1 Boil the spaghetti according to the package instructions. Drain.

2 Toss together with all of the other ingredients, except for the salmon roe.

3 Sprinkle the salmon roe on top and serve immediately.

Sautéed Buckwheat Noodles with Cabbage and Pork

4 servings

This is a very popular noodle dish called *Yakisoba*—sautéed noodles—that is often sold as a street snack in Japan. Here I use buckwheat noodles with pork and cabbage. If you prefer to do a vegetarian version of this, you can add bean sprouts and mushrooms instead of pork.

14 ounces buckwheat "soba" noodles
1 onion
2 garlic cloves
1 carrot
½ head of cabbage
1 tablespoon canola oil
1 teaspoon sesame oil
4 pork chops
½ cup soy sauce
¼ cup water
2 tablespoons Worcestershire sauce
2 tablespoons chili paste
2 garlic cloves, chopped

1. Bring to a boil a large pot of water. Add the noodles, and cook according to the package instructions. Drain and set aside.

2. Peel and slice the onion and garlic. Wash and peel the carrot, and, with a grater, shred into thin strips. Wash and cut the cabbage into thin strips.

3. Heat a large pan with canola oil and sesame oil. Add the onion and garlic, and cook for 3 to 4 minutes.

4. Add the pork chops, and cook for 6 to 8 minutes, until the pork is golden on both sides.

5. Remove the pork from the pan and cut into small cubes. Return it to the pan. Add the carrots and cabbage, and cook for 6 to 8 minutes until they soften.

6. Add the soy sauce, water, and Worcestershire sauce, and then add the noodles. Cook for 3 to 4 minutes, tossing very well so that the noodles are coated with the sauce.

7. Serve immediately.

Flaxseed Noodles with Corn, Green Beans, and Mushrooms *4 servings*

There are several noodle recipes in this book, and I am including more varieties, since they are often the most preferred dish for kids. Noodles are like pasta, and they lend themselves to infinite combinations and cooking methods.

1 cup green beans
5 large shiitake mushrooms
1 cup water
14 ounces egg noodles
1 onion
2 tablespoons canola oil
1 red pepper
1 cup corn
3 to 4 sprigs scallions
5 tablespoons soy sauce
3 tablespoons ground flaxseeds
1 tablespoon grapeseed oil

1   Wash and trim the green beans. Bring a pot of water to a boil, and add the green beans. Cook for 5 to 7 minutes until tender. Dunk them into an ice bath, or drain and run them under cold water. Set aside.

2   In a small bowl, soak the mushrooms in the cup of water.

3   Boil a pot of water and cook the noodles, following the instructions on the package (usually 4 to 6 minutes—egg noodles cook fairly quickly). Drain; run cold water on the noodles for a few seconds, and toss with tongs or a fork to prevent them from sticking. Set aside.

4   While the noodles are cooking, slice the onions into thin slices, and heat a pan with canola oil. Cook the onions slowly on very low heat, making sure not to burn them.

5   Cut the green beans into small pieces. Wash and remove the seeds of the red pepper, and cut pepper into small pieces. Add the green beans, corn, and red pepper to the pan with a bit of salt.

6   Wash and chop the scallions, and add to the pan. Cook for 5 to 7 minutes until they soften.

7   Meanwhile, take out the mushrooms that have been soaking in the water (keep the water), and chop into small pieces; and add to the pan. Pour the water into the pan; add the soy sauce, and cover. Simmer for 5 minutes.

8   Remove from heat, and add the flaxseeds and grapeseed oil. Toss the noodles into the pan, making sure they are covered in the sauce (if you prefer it to be more moist, add another tablespoon of soy sauce and canola oil).

9   Serve immediately.

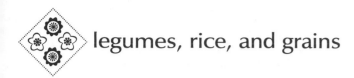

legumes, rice, and grains

Mediterranean Sautéed Navy Beans *4 servings as a side dish*

This is usually a spicy dish, stewed for hours on the stove. Here, I soak the beans overnight with raw onions and carrots for flavor, and the sauce is without the usual spice, keeping only the rich Mediterranean flavors of fresh tomatoes, parsley, a bit of garlic, and a touch of brown sugar sweetness that your child will love. This is also great for a snack with toast or crackers.

> 2 cups dried navy beans
> 1 onion, peeled and cut into rough pieces
> 1 carrot, cut in large pieces
> 2 onions
> 2 garlic cloves
> 6 fresh tomatoes
> 2 tablespoons olive oil
> 1 tablespoon brown sugar
> 1 tablespoon chia seeds
> 2 tablespoons chopped fresh parsley
> salt and pepper, to taste

1 In a large bowl, combine the beans, cut onion, and carrot; fill with water. Cover and let stand overnight in the refrigerator.

2 Drain the beans, and discard the onion and carrot. In a large pot, cover the beans completely with water. Bring to a boil; cover and simmer for 40 to 50 minutes, or until the beans are very tender. Drain and set aside.

3 Peel and chop the onions into small pieces. Crush and chop the garlic. Bring another pot of water to a boil; dunk the tomatoes for a few seconds, and peel the skin off under cold, running water. Cut the tomatoes into small pieces.

4 Heat a large pot with oil and cook the onions for 3 to 4 minutes until they soften.

5 Add the garlic and cook for 2 minutes.

6 Add the tomatoes and sugar; stir and cook for 2 to 3 minutes; add the beans and cover. Simmer for 30 to 40 minutes.

7 Divide the beans among four plates. Sprinkle with chia seeds and fresh parsley; salt and pepper to taste.

8 Serve.

Sautéed Rice with
Green Beans and Ham   *4 servings*

Sautéed rice is a great way to integrate vegetables and protein which may otherwise be difficult for your child to accept. If your child usually dislikes green beans, this recipe calls for the beans to be chopped into very small pieces.

1 cup green beans, frozen or fresh (if frozen, thawed; if fresh, cooked in salt water for 7 to 10 minutes, then drained, then finely chopped)
4 to 5 slices of Serrano or Parma ham
1 garlic clove
3 tablespoons canola oil
2 eggs
2 tablespoons butter
4 cups brown or white rice (preferably cooked the day before and refrigerated—this makes for a better sautéed rice)
1 tablespoon dried seaweed flakes
salt and pepper, to taste

1   Dice the green beans into small pieces. Cut the ham into small pieces. Peel and crush the garlic clove to flatten it, not breaking it completely apart—it will be used to infuse the oil while cooking and taken out before serving.

2   In a pan, heat 1 tablespoon of canola oil. Break the eggs into a bowl, and whip vigorously for 1 minute; pour into the pan. Allow the eggs to settle and cook for 2 to 3 minutes until they set; then flip to the other side and cook for another 2 minutes. This should make a thin, crepe-like egg pancake. Remove from the pan and slice into thin pieces. Set aside.

3   In the same pan, heat the 2 tablespoons of canola oil on medium heat. Add the garlic and cook for 1 minute, tossing it in the oil.

4   Add the butter, and then the ham, and cook for 2 to 3 minutes, making sure it does not become too crispy.

5   Add the green beans, cooking for a further 2 minutes.

6   Add the rice and toss well, while cooking on the heat for about 5 minutes.

7   Add the sliced egg crepe and toss, sprinkling the seaweed flakes on top. Salt and pepper to taste.

8   Serve immediately.

Shiitake Mushroom Rice   *4 servings*

Rice infused with mushrooms is a typical autumnal dish, and there are many variations—rice infused with bamboo shoots, chestnuts, red beans—often made for festive occasions. It is very easy to make.

4 dried shiitake mushrooms
2 cups short grain rice
1 carrot
3 cups water
1 tablespoon fresh chopped chives

1   In a small bowl, soak the mushrooms in ½ cup of water for 10 minutes.

2   Wash the rice carefully until the water is no longer murky. Drain the water. Remove the mushrooms, reserving the liquid. Cut off the stems and discard; chop the mushrooms into small pieces.

3   Wash and peel the carrot, and dice into small pieces.

4   In a pot, combine the rice, carrot, water, mushrooms, and the liquid from soaking the mushrooms. Bring to a boil, and then quickly lower the heat to low. Cover, and simmer for 20 minutes.

5   Serve warm.

Sweet Peas, Roasted Pine Nuts, and Fresh Mint with Quinoa

2 to 4 servings as a side dish

Quinoa is delicious in cold dishes as well as warm. This recipe has a nice combination of fresh herbs and vegetables. You can use any kind of vegetable, such as zucchini, peppers, or eggplant.

Sprig of fresh mint, finely chopped
½ cup pine nuts
2 cups cooked quinoa
1 cup frozen peas, thawed, or fresh
**   sweet peas (boiled in salted water**
**   for 5 minutes, drained)**
1 tablespoon olive oil
1 teaspoon lemon juice
salt and pepper, to taste

1   Preheat the oven to 300°F.

2   Wash and finely chop the mint.

3   Line a baking sheet with parchment paper, and roast the pine nuts for 4 to 6 minutes, tossing them around with a wooden spoon after 2 minutes until slightly golden, making sure not to burn them (they burn quickly).

4   In a large bowl, mix together the quinoa, peas, olive oil, lemon juice, and salt and pepper.

5   Add the nuts and mint.

6   Serve room temperature with toast or with a protein.

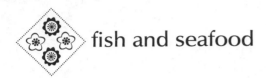

fish and seafood

Tuna Tataki with Cilantro Soy Dressing   *4 servings*

Tataki is a Japanese term that means to hit, and when it is used as a cooking technique (as in maguro tataki, a dish from the South of Japan where my mother is from), it means to sear the fish fillets with heat and take them off right away to avoid overcooking. This is the quickest and, for me, the most delicious way to eat a tuna steak—cooked medium rare, seared on both sides for no more than 1 to 2 minutes. The core should be pink or red, depending on your preference. For adults, you can use an ample amount of freshly cracked pepper, but for the kids I don't use salt or pepper because the cilantro soy dressing contains enough sodium.

> **salt and pepper, to taste**
> **4 tuna steaks (they must be extremely fresh and quite thick)**
> **3 to 4 sprigs of cilantro**
> **3 tablespoons soy sauce**
> **1 tablespoon sesame oil**
> **1 tablespoon walnut oil**

1 Heat a ridged, nonstick grilling pan on the stove top (or heat a grill if you are working with a real grill oven) on high heat.

2 Salt and pepper the tuna steaks for adults.

3 While the pan is being heated, wash and chop the cilantro, and combine in a bowl with the rest of the ingredients. Mix well and set aside.

4 When the pan is hot enough (you can put the palm of your hands over the top of the pan, and, if you can feel the heat coming off, it is ready), sear the tuna fillet on one side for 1 to 2 minutes—you will be able to see the color of the tuna steak turn from red to brown as it cooks. Flip to the other side as the brown color reaches halfway, making sure not to overcook the steak. Tuna, when overcooked, becomes dry and flaky; we want it to be moist and juicy.

5 As the color of the tuna steak turns brown on this other side, remove it from the grill, and let it rest for 5 minutes.

6 Pour the dressing over the top, and serve with quinoa, rice, or pasta.

Roasted Salmon with Orange-Infused Spinach

4 servings

This is a simple way to make salmon with a bit of a twist—orange zest adds a different layer of flavor, and the color combination of a pink salmon steak and bits of orange skin makes for a gorgeous dish when served on a bed of dark green spinach.

> 3 cups frozen spinach or 6 cups fresh spinach
> 1 tablespoon soy sauce
> Zest and juice of 1 orange
> 1 tablespoon water
> 1 tablespoon mirin
> 4 salmon steaks
> salt and pepper, to taste

1 Preheat the oven to 375°F.

2 Thaw the frozen spinach (if using fresh spinach, wash it and boil in salted water for 3 to 4 minutes until soft; then drain and set aside).

3 In a small bowl, combine the soy sauce, the zest of the orange (wash the orange well, then grate the skin with a grater or a peeler), the juice of the orange, water, and mirin.

4 Place the salmon steaks on a baking tray lined with parchment paper. Sprinkle the soy mixture on top, and place the spinach on the tray next to the salmon. Bake for 5 to 7 minutes, depending on the thickness of the salmon. This may seem like very little time, but fish cooks very quickly and can dry out quickly as well. The fish will continue to cook even after you take it out of the oven.

5 Making sure that the spinach is also warm enough, take the tray out of the oven; let it rest for 2 to 3 minutes.

6 Add salt and pepper, to taste, and then serve with rice, couscous, or quinoa.

Peruvian Clams with Shiso Leaves, Cherry Tomatoes, Whole Wheat Croutons and Cucumber   *4 servings*

At one of my favorite restaurants in Paris, I had a phenomenal dish called Leche de Tigre by Chef Enoki, which means the liquid of ceviche, from the Latin American dish of raw mixed seafood. This recipe is a cooked clam version, which is a safer option for kids, and uses the delicious liquid of the clams to flavor the croutons and cucumbers.

> **4 slices whole wheat bread**
> **3 tablespoons olive oil**
> **2 pounds fresh little neck clams**
> **1 cucumber**
> **2 cups cherry tomatoes**
> **2 chopped fresh shiso leaves (if you can't find shiso leaves, use the leaves of 4 sprigs of fresh mint and the leaves of 2 sprigs of fresh basil, and chop into thin strips)**
> **4 tablespoons water**
> **salt and pepper, to taste**
> **Zest and juice of one lime (optional)**

1   Cut the whole wheat bread into small cubes and put on a foiled-covered baking tray; drizzle with olive oil, and sprinkle some salt; bake in a toaster oven (or in the oven) for 5 to 7 minutes until they are golden and hard. Crush them slightly so they become croutons.

2   Wash and clean the clams by running them under cold water, scrubbing them with a hand brush. Soak them in a bowl of salt water; cover the bowl with a plate and allow it to sit for 5 to 7 minutes (this allows the clams to spit out any sand they may be retaining).

3   Remove the green outer skin of the cucumber and cut it in half. Remove the seeds with a spoon, and cut the cucumber into small cubes.

4   Drain the clams.

5   In a pan, heat the olive oil on medium heat and add the clams, tomatoes, cucumber, and the leaves with 4 tablespoons water; cover with a heavy lid. Cook for 5 to 7 minutes until the clams open. Discard any clams that fail to open.

6   Pour the opened clams plus vegetables into a large bowl; add the croutons, salt, and pepper, and serve immediately into smaller bowls with chunky bread to soak up the liquid. Sprinkle with the zest and juice of the lime (optional).

Marinated Octopus with Green Olives and Lemon Confit   *4 servings*

Octopus with lemon and olives is a typical Mediterranean dish, but it's often cooked in a thick spicy tomato or wine sauce, which is not great for children and tends to mask the delicate flavor of the octopus. This dish is simply cooked in vegetable stock, allowing the sauce to be flavored with the natural stock of the octopus.

Lemon confit, or pickled lemon, adds a salty flavor that enhances fish and seafood in a great way. If you can't get it at your local grocery store, you can order it online, and it keeps well for a few months.

> **1 pound octopus**
> **1 onion**
> **2 garlic cloves**

2 pickled lemons
2 tablespoons olive oil
2 cups vegetable stock
2 potatoes
Zest and juice of 1 lemon
½ cup pitted and chopped green olives
salt and pepper, to taste

1 Bring a large pot of water to a boil. Add the octopus and simmer for about 15 minutes. Drain and let cool. Cut it into small pieces.

2 Slice the onions, and crush the garlic cloves; then cut them into small pieces. Wash and cut the potatoes into thin small pieces. Cut the pickled lemons into small pieces.

3 In a pan, heat the oil; add the onions and garlic and cook for 3 to 4 minutes.

4 Add the stock, potatoes, zest and juice of a lemon, olives, and the octopus. Cover and simmer over low heat until potatoes and octopus are tender, about 45 minutes.

5 Serve with pasta or bread.

Crispy Salmon Potato Cakes

4 to 6 servings

These salmon potato cakes can be addictive. They are traditionally fried and made with onions, but I think onions can be a bit over-powering, and I bake in the oven instead of frying for great flavor without all the fat. You can serve them with sour cream or some crème fraiche on the side.

1 salmon fillet
1 pound potatoes
1 egg
2 tablespoons ground flaxseeds
2 tablespoons oat flour
1 teaspoon baking soda
1 teaspoon salt
1 tablespoon chopped chives
2 tablespoons olive oil
salt and pepper, to taste

1 Preheat the oven to 375°F. Cover a baking sheet with foil and place the salmon skin-side down on the sheet. Bake for 6 to 9 minutes, depending on the thickness of the salmon.

2 Once it's done, cool the fillet; use a fork to break up the salmon into small pieces. Set aside.

3 Wash and peel the potatoes. Dunk them into cold water, and, using a grater, shred them into fine pieces. Place the shreds on a paper towel. In order to remove the moisture from the potatoes, cover them with another layer of paper towels and squeeze the potatoes on both sides with your hand.

4 In a bowl, combine the egg, salmon, flaxseed, oat flour, baking soda, salt, and chives. Sprinkle salt and pepper.

5 Add the potatoes and mix well.

6 With an ice-cream scoop, portion out the potato mixture into patties, one at a time, onto the baking sheet, flattening it out. Bake for 15 to 20 minutes.

7 Sprinkle with salt and pepper, and serve immediately.

Roasted Sardines with Lemon Peel Chips and Crunchy Parsley *4 servings*

I was introduced to the beauty of sardines during a trip to the coastal towns in Portugal. There, the folks I met—children as well as adults—ate sardines every day, grilling them on their balconies overlooking the Mediterranean Sea. I learned to eat them with sea salt, or with olive oil and boiled potatoes, or fried and served with fresh tomato sauce. Sardines have a deep flavor, not as rich as mackerel, but similar. This fish, which is rich in DHA Omega-3, is versatile and easy to cook. Most fishmongers will carry them, and you can cook them whole, with the head intact or without.

>   4 cups of canola oil for cooking
>   2 lemons
>   Bunch of parsley (I prefer the curly rather than flat for this recipe)
>   1 to 2 tablespoons coarse sea salt
>   12 small to medium-sized sardines
>   2 to 3 tablespoons olive oil

1   Preheat the oven to 350°F.

2   Heat the canola oil. Wash and peel the lemons with a peeler, making thin slices; set them aside for frying. Wash and carefully dry the parsley on a paper towel. Fry the lemon peels in the oil for 1 to 3 minutes depending on the thinness of the lemon peel until they become crispy, taking care not to burn them. Place them carefully on a plate lined with paper towels.

3   Then fry the parsley very quickly—a few seconds—several sprigs at a time. They will stiffen and curl up, making crispy leaves. Place them on a plate lined with paper towels, and sprinkle salt on top.

4   Place the sardines on a foil-covered baking sheet. Roast for 7 to 10 minutes.

5   Place them on a cutting board, and, with a knife and a fork, remove the skin of each fish.

6   Place them on a large tray, one next to the other. Drizzle with the olive oil, then sprinkle the sea salt, lemon peel, and fried parsley on top.

Warm Smoked Salmon Panini Sandwich with Dill and Sour Cream

4 servings

Warm pressed panini sandwiches are a perfect way to integrate leftovers, both the bread and the filling, into a quick hot meal. If you don't have a panini press, you can use a pan or a large pot full of water, covered on the bottom with foil to press down the bread. For this recipe, wild-caught salmon should be used because it contains less mercury and is richer in DHA Omega-3.

>   4 tablespoons olive oil
>   4 tablespoons sour cream
>   8 slices of whole wheat baguette or sliced bread
>   4 slices wild-caught smoked salmon
>   2 tablespoons chopped fresh dill
>   salt and pepper, to taste

1   Heat a ridged grill pan on the stove top or a normal nonstick pan on medium heat, and add 2 tablespoons olive oil.

2   Assemble the sandwich—spread the sour cream on one side of each slice of bread; place the salmon; sprinkle the dill; and finally, add salt and pepper.

3 Close the sandwich and place on the pan; cover with foil and press down with a panini press or a pan. (Before I bought a panini press, I used to put a gallon of water on the pan and then press it down for a few minutes. I have a friend who puts a piece of brick covered with foil. You can be creative and use anything that will weigh it down.)

4 Cook for 5 minutes, and then flip the sandwiches over. Drizzle the other 2 tablespoons of olive oil, and then let them cook for another 5 minutes, or until the bread becomes golden and crispy on the outside.

5 Serve immediately.

....

Polenta Cakes with Dill and Smoked Salmon   *6 to 8 servings*

Polenta cakes are a great side dish or on their own. It is a denser, moister, and savory version of a cornbread. This has smoked salmon and dill, which makes it a complete meal and perfect to take along for a picnic or an al fresco meal.

1 tablespoon canola oil
2 to 3 smoked salmon fillets
2 cups milk
2 cups water
1 tablespoon chopped fresh dill
1 teaspoon salt
1 cup cornmeal
½ cup cream
1 tablespoon chia seeds
salt and pepper, to taste
2 tablespoons butter,

1 In a pan, heat oil over medium heat, and then add the salmon. Cook the salmon fillets for 2 to 3 minutes, until they become light pink, as opposed to the dark pink when simply smoked.

2 When the fillets are done, put them on a plate, and, with a fork, mash them into small flaky pieces; let the salmon rest.

3 Separately, in a pot, bring milk, water, dill, and salt to a boil. Add the cornmeal and reduce the heat to low, whisking constantly for about 10 minutes until the mixture thickens and bubbles up from the bottom.

4 Mix in the salmon and remove from the heat. Stir in the cream and chia seeds.

5 Pour the mixture into a plastic-wrap-lined 9x9-inch baking dish and refrigerate for an hour.

6 Remove it from the baking dish, and cut the polenta into shapes using a cookie cutter. Toast it in the oven for 5 minutes, or pan fry it with a tablespoon of olive oil.

7 Serve warm.

Mackerel with Ginger and Dried Figs

4 servings

This recipe was the result of a spur-of-the-moment inspiration, when I had just come home with fresh mackerel and happened to see a jar of dried figs that my husband had brought home from the market. Together, with the spike of fresh ginger, this dish has become one of our staples, and because mackerel is a great source of DHA Omega-3, it is a perfect "brainfood" dish. Just be careful with mackerel because it contains quite a few bones within the flesh—make sure they are all removed before you give it to your child.

> 4 whole mackerel gutted and cleaned,
>   with or without the head
> ¼ cup soy sauce
> ½ cup water
> ¼ cup mirin
> 10 small dried figs
> Stub of fresh ginger
> 2 tablespoons chopped fresh cilantro

1 Cut each mackerel in half, diagonally if preferred. Place on a nonstick pan. Add the rest of the ingredients and toss lightly in the pan.

2 Cover and heat on medium heat. Simmer for 7 to 12 minutes, taking a spoon to coat the fish on all sides as it cooks.

3 When the flesh of the fish turns from red to dark brown, it is ready. You can serve it with rice or quinoa, pouring the sauce over whichever carbohydrate you decide to accompany the mackerel. You can eat the fish with or without the outer silvery skin. I tend to like it, but many don't, so it is up to you.

Hawaiian Halibut with Macadamia Nut and Flaxseed Crust

4 servings

This is a typical way to prepare fish and seafood in Hawaii, with its abundance of macadamia nuts. These mild nuts contain protein, calcium, potassium, and fiber and make a rich crust on the fish.

> 1 cup macadamia nuts
> ½ cup panko-style bread crumbs
> 1 tablespoon wheat germ
> 2 tablespoons walnut oil
> 1 tablespoon flaxseeds
> 2 tablespoons canola oil
> 4 halibut steaks
> salt and pepper, to taste

1 Preheat the oven to 375°F.

2 In a bowl, mix together the nuts, bread crumbs, wheat germ, walnut oil, and flaxseeds.

3 Cover a baking tray with foil, and brush it with canola oil. Place the halibut on the baking tray, and sprinkle it with salt and pepper on both sides. Bake for 2 to 3 minutes.

4 Remove the pan from the oven, and spread the nut mixture on top of the fish; pat it down.

5 Bake for another 4 to 5 minutes. The topping should be golden brown.

Shrimp, Scallops, and Squid with Ginger, Coriander, and Cumin

4 to 6 servings

This is a lovely, yet simple, seafood dish, which is inspired by a fusion of Indian and Algerian dishes I had with shrimp and fresh ginger. You can serve it with couscous, quinoa, or chunky bread to soak up the sauce.

1 nub fresh ginger
1 garlic clove
1 medium-sized squid
6 large scallops
1 pound shrimp
2 tablespoons olive oil
1 tablespoon cumin seeds
1 teaspoon ground curcuma
1 teaspoon paprika
1 tablespoon coriander seeds
2 tablespoons chopped fresh cilantro
sea salt, to taste

1 Peel and chop the ginger and garlic into small pieces. Clean the squid and cut into small pieces, including the tentacles. Remove the glands, if any, from the scallops. Peel and devein the shrimp.

2 In a pan, heat the oil and add garlic, ginger, cumin seeds, curcuma, paprika, and coriander; cook for 3 minutes.

3 Add the squid, shrimp, and scallops, and cook over high heat for 3 to 5 minutes until the shrimp turn pink and the scallops and squid have become opaque.

4 Sprinkle with cilantro and sea salt.

5 Toss well and serve immediately.

Grilled Sardines with Paprika and Tomatoes

4 servings

I think sardines are best when grilled, but you can't grill all year round in most places, so this is a quick stove-grill alternative that you can do any time. I prepare the fish whole, with the head intact. My son loves to gaze at the entire fish; we talk about how sardines are different from other kinds of fish. But you can prepare this without the head, asking your fishmonger to fillet the fish.

2 fresh tomatoes
2 tablespoons chopped fresh cilantro
1 teaspoon paprika
1 teaspoon cumin
1 teaspoon ginger
3 tablespoons olive oil
8 sardines
salt and pepper, to taste

1 Wash and cut the tomatoes into small chunks, and put them into a bowl. Add the cilantro, paprika, cumin powder, ginger powder, and olive oil, and mix well. Cover with plastic and refrigerate for 15 minutes.

2 Cut the sardines open so that they are flat. Place the sardines, skin side down on a stove-top nonstick grill, and spread the tomato mixture on top. Cook for 3 to 5 minutes.

3 Place the sardines on a plate and drizzle with the tomato mixture.

4 Serve immediately.

chicken, turkey, and duck

Chicken, Watercress, and Tofu over Rice

4 servings

This is another domburi dish, a variation on the chicken and egg combination that I shared with you earlier. The watercress adds a nice crunch and provides folate, iron, and zinc.

½ pound fresh watercress
1 nub fresh ginger
1 package firm tofu
1 tablespoon canola oil
2 tablespoons soy sauce
2 tablespoons mirin
1 tablespoon sugar
½ cup water
2 chicken thighs, meat cut from the bone into small pieces
2 eggs
4 cups cooked brown rice
2 garlic cloves

1 Wash and cut the watercress in small pieces. Peel and slice the ginger into very thin slices, and then dice it into even smaller pieces. Rinse the tofu under cold water, and cut into cubes.

2 In a pan, heat the oil. Add the chicken and cook for 8 to 10 minutes, until golden.

3 Add the watercress, and sauté for 4 to 5 minutes.

4 Add the soy sauce, mirin, sugar, and water, and cover. Let simmer for 20 minutes.

5 In a bowl, whisk the eggs together and pour over the chicken in the pan. Cover immediately and simmer for 30 to 40 seconds. The eggs should be set, but still a bit runny and soft. You don't want them to be too firm and overcooked.

6 Divide the rice among four bowls, and pour the chicken mixture over it.

7 Serve immediately.

East African Chicken Curry

4 servings

This is a mild, sweet curry with tomatoes as the base. To save time, I use store-bought tomato marinara sauce and add the spices.

1 onion
1 tablespoon canola oil
3 tablespoons water
2 tablespoons brown sugar
1 tablespoon turmeric
1 teaspoon cumin seeds
1 tablespoon cumin powder
1 tablespoon ground mustard
1 tablespoon ground ginger
1 teaspoon ground cardamom
6 chicken legs
2 chicken breasts
3 cups tomato marinara sauce
1 tablespoon chopped fresh cilantro
8 cups chicken stock
1 tablespoon chia seeds

1 Peel and slice the onion into thin strips. In a pan, heat the oil on medium heat. Add the onion, water, and brown sugar. Cook until the water has evaporated and the onions are tender, golden, and caramelized, about 5 to 7 minutes.

2 Add all of the spices, except the chia seeds. Stir and cook 2 to 3 minutes.

3 Add the chicken, and stir to coat the chicken pieces with the spices and onions. Cook for 3 minutes, and then add the chicken stock and the marinara sauce.

4 Cover with a lid, bring to a boil, and then simmer on low heat for 1 to 2 hours, or until the meat of the chicken is falling off the bones.

5 Serve with chopped cilantro and chia seeds and rice.

Ghanaian Cashew Nut Chicken with Kale

4 to 6 servings

This is a rich and substantial chicken dish from Ghana. The thick broth can be eaten as a soup or with rice. It is usually made with palm oil and is quite spicy, but I make it with lighter canola oil. It contains a good amount of protein, folate, and fatty acids and has a great aroma from the roasted cashew nuts.

2 cups cashew nuts
2 onions
1 garlic clove
1 cup frozen kale, thawed
1 tablespoon canola oil
salt and pepper, to taste
1 pound chicken thighs
6 fresh tomatoes
1 tablespoon brown sugar
½ cup organic cashew butter
8 cups chicken stock
1 tablespoon chopped fresh cilantro

1 Preheat the oven to 375°F.

2 Line a baking tray with parchment paper and spread out the cashew nuts. Roast for 3 to 4 minutes until they become golden and aromatic. Let cool. In a food processor, grind the nuts until they become powder.

3 Peel and slice the onions into thin slices. Crush the garlic, and chop into small pieces. With your hands, wring out the kale to drain any excess liquid, and chop it into small pieces.

4 Heat a large, heavy-bottomed pot on medium-high heat, and add the canola oil. Salt and pepper the chicken on all sides. Add the chicken to the pot and brown on all sides, about 6 to 8 minutes.

5 Remove the chicken to a plate, and dab the bottom of the pot with a paper towel. Add another tablespoon of oil; add the onions and cook on low heat until soft, about 5 to 6 minutes.

6 Return the chicken to the pot; add the tomatoes and brown sugar, and cook for 2 minutes.

7 Add the ground cashew nuts, cashew nut butter, chicken stock, and kale, and bring to a boil. Cover and simmer for 60 to 90 minutes, or until the chicken is tender and falling off the bone, skimming the surface from time to time to eliminate the foam and the fat that floats to the top.

8 Serve with cilantro and rice.

Turkey with Tarragon and Mushroom Gravy

4 servings

Turkey is always an easy alternative to chicken, and it combines well with a creamy mushroom sauce, in which I often mix finely chopped hard boiled eggs for the extra fatty acid, protein, and thickness in the sauce. As in many recipes, the chicken stock should be cold, so that when it hits the hot pan in which the meat and onions were cooked, the temperature shock to the pan will release the *suc* (the bits of meat) stuck on the bottom of the pan to make a more flavorful sauce. Tarragon is a very light and mild herb and goes perfectly with the subtle flavors of the turkey.

1 tablespoon cornstarch
1 tablespoon water
1 onion
1 tablespoon canola oil
4 turkey breasts
1 cup cold chicken stock
2 cups mushrooms
3 tablespoons chopped fresh tarragon leaves
½ cup cream
1 tablespoon chopped fresh chives
2 hard boiled eggs, chopped into small pieces
salt and pepper, to taste

1 In a cup, mix together the cornstarch with the tablespoon of water. Set aside.

2 Peel and cut the onion into thin slices.

3 Heat the oil in a pan; add turkey breasts and brown on both sides, about 4 to 5 minutes on each side. Transfer to a plate; cover with foil; and set aside while you prepare the sauce.

4 In the same pan, add the onions and cook for 3 to 4 minutes until they soften.

5 Pour the cup of cold chicken stock into the pan, scraping the bottom of the pan with a spatula to enhance the flavor of the gravy. Add the mushrooms, cornstarch, and tarragon. Let the stock simmer on medium heat until it begins to thicken, about 4 to 5 minutes.

6 Cut the turkey into bite-sized pieces and return it to the pan.

7 Add the cream, chives, and chopped hard-boiled eggs and combine well. Cook for 3 to 4 minutes and serve with rice or potatoes.

8 Salt and pepper, to taste.

Duck with Blackberries and Pears

4 servings

Blackberries are a superfood, containing an extraordinary amount of antioxidants; they are an anti-carcinogen, anti-viral, and anti-bacterial wonder. They also contain Omega-3 fatty acid, vitamins A, C, and E, calcium, magnesium, potassium, and folate. On top of all of that, they are a beautiful fruit with an incredible color so strong that it was used as a natural dye. I find that raw blackberries can be a bit sour for children, so I love to cook them with dark meats or in desserts to round out the tanginess. Here is a wonderful combination of sweet and savory with pears and duck, cooked until the meat falls off the bone and the braising liquid is sweet and mild.

2 onions
2 pears
2 tablespoons olive oil
4 duck legs with skin
8 cups chicken stock
½ cup blackberries
1 tablespoon brown sugar
1 teaspoon cinnamon
1 tablespoon agave nectar
1 tablespoon cornstarch
½ cup water
salt and pepper, to taste

1 Preheat the oven to 375°F.

2 Peel and slice the onions into thin slices. Wash, peel, and core the pears, and cut into medium-sized cubes.

3 In a deep Dutch oven or heavy-bottomed pot, heat the oil, and cook the onions until tender, about 3 to 4 minutes.

4 Add the duck and cook so that all sides are nice and golden, about 7 to 10 minutes.

5 Add the stock, pears, blackberries, sugar, cinnamon, and agave nectar. Cover and roast in the oven for 60 to 90 minutes, or until the meat on the bone is very tender.

6 Meanwhile, in a cup, mix together the cornstarch with water with a spoon until completely dissolved. After the duck has been in the oven for at least 90 minutes, remove from the oven and pour in the cornstarch liquid; cook for 10 more minutes on the stove top.

7 Serve with couscous, quinoa, or bread.

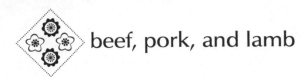

beef, pork, and lamb

Beef with Persimmons, Kale, and Water Chestnuts   *4 servings*

The combination of sweet and savory in a one-dish meal is always wonderful, producing unexpected flavors. This recipe is perfect for an autumn day, when the silky, plump persimmons are in season. They are a real superfood, a good source of beta-carotene, vitamins C and B6, and fiber, as well as manganese, and plenty of phytonutrients.

If it is difficult to get persimmons in your area, try the same recipe with 1 cup dried apricots instead. Water chestnuts are a good source of dietary fiber, riboflavin, vitamin B6, potassium, copper, and manganese, and have a great crunchy texture that is between a crisp pear and a cashew nut. For a saute dish like this, ready-made oyster sauce would be ideal to use, but most of them contain MSG, so this recipe gets its hint of sweetness from honey.

> **2 ripe persimmons**
> **1 bunch kale**
> **1 cup water chestnuts**
> **2 New York strip steaks**
> **1 tablespoon canola oil**
> **3 tablespoons dashi stock or chicken stock**
> **2 tablespoons water**
> **2 tablespoons soy sauce**
> **1 teaspoon honey**

1 Peel the persimmons, and cut them into small chunks. Wash and cut the leaves off the hard stem of the kale, and then chop the leaves into thin, short strips. Drain and wash the water chestnuts. Cut the steaks into small thin strips, and sprinkle them with salt and pepper on both sides.

2 In a pan, heat the oil on high heat. Sear the beef on all sides, tossing with a wooden spoon (about 5 minutes); transfer to a plate.

3 Using the same pan, lower the heat, and add the kale and cook for 5 to 7 minutes, until the leaves begin to wilt.

4 Add the persimmons, stock, water, soy sauce, and honey, and cook for 3 to 4 minutes.

5 Return the beef to the pan and toss.

6 Remove from heat, and serve with brown rice.

Mabo Tofu with Rice

4 servings

Mabo tofu, or mapo tofu, is a Chinese dish that blends ground meats with tofu and scallions. It is traditionally a very spicy dish, but this is a modified version suitable for kids. While Mabo tofu is usually made only with pork, I use more beef than pork, since it makes for a leaner dish. It is a complete meal, with protein, fiber, folate, vitamins, and minerals. It keeps well, so you can make a large batch and freeze leftovers for later. There are ready-made mabo tofu pastes, but they always contain MSG, so it is worth it to make this from scratch.

1 bunch of fresh scallions
1 red pepper
1 tablespoon cornstarch
2 tablespoons water
2 tablespoons canola oil
1 tablespoon sesame oil
¼ pound ground pork
½ pound ground beef
2 cups tofu
2 cups chicken stock
4½ teaspoons soy sauce
salt and pepper, to taste

1 Wash and cut the scallions into small pieces, discarding the white section toward the bulb. Wash the pepper and remove the seeds.

2 In a cup, mix together the cornstarch and water.

3 In a pan, heat the canola oil and the sesame oil on high heat. When the oils become very hot, add the pork and beef, and, with a wooden spoon, break up the meat and cook well for 5 to 6 minutes, until it has all browned.

4 Add the tofu, scallions, and pepper, and cook for 2 minutes.

5 Add the stock, soy sauce, and cornstarch. Toss again and cover. Simmer for 10 to 15 minutes, or until the sauce thickens.

6 Serve next to or over a bowl of rice.

Szechuan Eggplant with Pork

4 servings as a side dish

This recipe is from the Szechuan region and is usually a spicy vegetable dish flavored with pork. For children, I think it is an ideal dish to combine the soft texture of the stewed eggplants together with chewy ground pork and crunchy peanut. Here I have left out the spicy peppers, and it is great with rice or another grain, like quinoa.

> 1 tablespoon cornstarch
> 1 tablespoon water
> 2 large eggplants
> 1 garlic clove
> 1 tablespoon canola oil
> 1 tablespoon sesame oil
> ¼ pound ground pork
> 2 cups chicken stock
> 4 tablespoons soy sauce
> 1 teaspoon rice vinegar

1 In a cup, mix together the cornstarch and water. Set aside. Wash and cut the eggplant into small pieces. Soak in water for 5 minutes; drain and squeeze the excess liquid out with your hands. Set aside on a paper towel. Peel and crush the garlic.

2 In a pan, heat the canola oil and sesame oil. Add the pork, and, using a wooden spoon, break it up into small pieces; brown for about 5 to 7 minutes.

3 Add the eggplant and sauté for 5 minutes.

4 Add the chicken stock, soy sauce, cornstarch mixture, garlic, and vinegar. Bring to a boil, and cover. Simmer for 10 to 15 minutes, or until the eggplant is soft and tender.

5 Serve with rice.

Pork with Fresh Cherry and Mint Sauce

4 servings

When cherries come into season, it is wonderful to combine them with savory flavors—it makes for a surprising dish. I like cherries particularly with pork, as they sweeten up the meat and add an interesting, plump, soft texture to a meat that can often be dry.

> 1 shallot
> 4 pork chops
> 1 teaspoon thyme
> 2 tablespoons canola oil
> 2 cups cold chicken stock
> 1 cup pitted fresh cherries
> Few sprigs of fresh mint
> 1 tablespoon grated walnuts
> salt and pepper, to taste
> ¼ cup heavy cream (optional)
> 1 tablespoon walnut oil
> 1 tablespoon olive oil

1 Peel and chop the shallots into small pieces. Sprinkle the pork chops with salt and pepper, then thyme.

2 Heat a pan with 1 tablespoon canola oil on high heat. Sear the pork chops on both sides, 3 minutes each side, and then lower the heat to medium low, continuing to cook the pork for 4 to 6 minutes on each side. Pork should not be pink inside, so you will need to make sure the pork chops have been completely cooked through to white inside (145°F internal temperature). Transfer the pork to a plate, and dab the pan with a paper towel to absorb excess fat.

3 Add another tablespoon of canola oil on medium heat. Add the shallots and cook on low heat, until they become soft, being careful not to burn them, about 3 to 5 minutes.

4 Add the chicken stock, and cover. Simmer for 15 minutes.

5 Add the cherries, and cook for 5 more minutes.

6 Then chop the mint leaves, and add to the sauce with walnuts, salt, and pepper. Remove from the heat.

7 Stir in the heavy cream. Place one pork chop on each plate, and drizzle the sauce on top; then drizzle the walnut oil.

8 Serve with rice, pasta, or quinoa.

....

Braised Bamboo Shoots, Kombu Seaweed and Pork

4 servings

Bamboo shoots are a good source of fiber, protein, vitamin B6, copper, and zinc. But very often, the canned bamboo shoots are high in sodium, so I boil the shoots first, before I cook with them. I discard the cooking water, thus getting rid of a good amount of salt contained in the shoots.

2 cups bamboo shoots
2 cups water
2 dried kombu seaweed, chopped into
    small pieces
6 pork chops with bone
1 tablespoon canola oil
1 teaspoon sesame oil
1 tablespoon sake
2 tablespoons soy sauce
½ cup water
2 tablespoons chopped scallions

1 Bring a pot of water to a boil. Add the bamboo shoots, and boil for 3 minutes. Drain and set aside.

2 In the same pot, add 2 cups water, and add the kombu. Bring to a boil, and simmer for 20 to 30 minutes, covered. Cool by putting the pot into a large bowl of ice-water.

3 Cut the meat off the pork chops, and cut it into bite-sized pieces. Keep the bones. In a pan, heat the canola and sesame oils on medium heat. Add the bone and the pieces of meat, and cook for 4 to 6 minutes, tossing until the meat is golden on all sides.

4 Pour in the kombu with its liquid, and add the bamboo shoots, sake, soy sauce, and scallions; bring to a boil. Simmer for 10 minutes.

5 Remove the bones, and serve with rice.

Roasted Flaxseed-Thyme Crusted Lamb with Mini Fingerling Potatoes

6 to 8 servings

Roasted lamb is a simple yet impressive meal for a family gathering. The tender meat of lamb is often easier for kids to chew than beef, which often can be tough and even stringy if not cooked properly. In some countries, like France, lamb is cooked very rare, while in others, like Greece, it is cooked for hours until the meat falls off the bone. I tend to like it between the two extremes—roasted slowly in the oven for about an hour and a half, depending on the size and thickness of the piece of meat. I find that rare lamb is not the most desired consistency for kids, while the very cooked version tends to dry out the meat.

> 1 bulb of garlic
> 6 anchovy fillets
> 4 tablespoons olive oil
> 2 tablespoons water
> 2 tablespoons thyme
> 1 cup of crushed flaxseeds
> 1 leg of lamb with bones (6 to 7 pounds)
> 1 tablespoons sea salt
> ½ cup honey
> Fresh chopped sage leaves
> 1 pound of mini potatoes

1 Preheat the oven to 450°F.

2 Peel and remove the core of the garlic; put the garlic into a food processor, and process until it becomes a paste.

3 Drain the anchovies, discarding the oil in which they're preserved. Add the anchovies into the processor. While the processor is blending, add the olive oil, then the water, thyme, and ½ cup of the crushed flaxseeds. The mixture should become a thick paste. Set aside while you prepare the lamb.

4 On a foil-covered baking sheet, place the lamb on one side, and, with a sharp knife, make several holes into the flesh at varied depths. These holes will serve as "pockets" into which the garlic-anchovy-flax paste will be inserted. Using a small spoon, insert small portions of the paste into the pockets. Turn the lamb around and repeat until almost all of the paste has been inserted (leave about 2 tablespoons worth of paste). Rub the entire lamb leg with the remaining paste. Sprinkle with sea salt and the remaining crushed flaxseed, and then drizzle with honey.

5 Place the lamb in the oven and roast for 20 minutes, and then turn down the oven to 350°F and roast for another 60 to 90 minutes. You can use a meat thermometer to check for doneness (it should read 130 to 135°F).

6 Take the lamb out of the oven, and let it rest for 15 to 20 minutes. Cut it into thin slices on a cutting board, and place the entire sliced lamb on a large plate.

7 Sprinkle with 2 tablespoons sea salt and chopped sage, and serve.

Gorgonzola Cheese Sticks
4 to 6 servings as a snack

This is a super simple snack, as kids tend to love all that is crunchy. These cheese sticks have the crunch of a potato chip without the fat, and they are full of flavor, calcium, and DHA Omega-3.

½ cup gorgonzola cheese
½ cup cream cheese, softened to room temperature
1 tablespoon milk
1 package pizza dough
2 tablespoons chopped chives
2 tablespoons chia seeds
1 tablespoon flaxseeds
2 tablespoons wheat germ

1 Preheat the oven to 325°F. In a small bowl, mix together the cheeses and the milk. Sprinkle a clean work surface with flour. Spread out the pizza dough and spread the cheese on top. Top with the chives, chia seeds, flaxseeds, and wheat germ.

2 Cut the dough into thin pieces. You should have 10 to 12 thin strips from one package of pizza dough. Twist the dough a few times to make a Twizzler-like shape. Bake for 15 to 20 minutes, or until the sticks are golden. Remove from the oven and let cool on a wire rack.

3 Serve as a snack or as an appetizer.

Multigrain Mini Yam Cakes with Cinnamon Maple Syrup Sour Cream
2 to 3 servings

I spent days and days trying out the best way to make these mini yam cakes. I tried them without egg, with some ricotta or cream cheese, without flour, or with butter, but this seems to be the most popular version with the children who tasted them in my circle of friends and family. This is truly a health snack, with the sweetness coming from the yam and a bit of maple syrup, and they're chewy.

2 sweet potatoes or yams
½ cup multigrain flour
1 egg
1 teaspoon cinnamon
1 teaspoon ground flaxseeds
1 teaspoon wheat germ
2 tablespoons milk
1 tablespoon butter
4 tablespoons sour cream
1 teaspoon maple syrup (can add more for more sweetness)
1 teaspoon canola oil

1   Preheat the oven to 375°F.

2   Wash and wrap the sweet potatoes in foil, and roast for 1 hour, or until tender when poked with a knife. Take the potatoes out of the oven and unwrap the foil; scoop out the flesh into a bowl.

3   Add the flour, eggs, ½ teaspoon of the cinnamon, flaxseeds, wheat germ, and milk; mix well until blended completely.

4   In a pan, heat the butter on low heat. Take a spoonful of the potato mixture, add it to the pan, and flatten it out to make a pancake—but not too thin. Cook for 3 to 4 minutes or until golden; flip to the other side for 3 to 4 minutes more, until golden and crispy on the outside.

5   Remove from the pan and let it cool on a plate covered with a paper towel to soak up the extra oil.

6   In a small bowl, mix together the sour cream with maple syrup and ½ teaspoon cinnamon.

7   Serve on the side. Makes about 20 cakes.

Grapefruit with Cinnamon, Walnuts, and Mint

4 to 6 servings

This is a great light dessert after a heavy meal or as a light afternoon snack. The longer you soak the cinnamon sticks in the grapefruit mixture the better, so you can make it well ahead of a get together or a dinner party with other little ones. It is also good combined with yogurt, ice cream, or crème fraiche. Pink grapefruit is usually sweeter than yellow, so I prefer it when I make this for my son.

- 5 large pink grapefruits
- 3 large cinnamon sticks
- 1 tablespoon agave nectar
- 2 tablespoons ground walnuts
- 2 sprigs of mint, washed and chopped into thin strips

1 Peel the grapefruit, and, with your hands, carefully remove the grapefruit segments from the skin; place them into a large bowl.

2 Add the cinnamon sticks and nectar, and toss carefully.

3 Cover with plastic wrap and refrigerate for at least 1 hour.

4 Divide among 4 to 6 serving bowls.

5 Sprinkle with the ground walnuts and mint leaves, and serve.

Passion Fruit Salad with Basil and Blackberries

4 servings

While blackberries can be considered too sour for children, I began to give my son blackberries around 24 months, and he ate them when they were wild and fresh. Blackberries contain perhaps the highest level of Omega-3 fatty acid in a fruit, and this is an elegant and simple fruit salad. When passion fruit is in season, the ripe fruit infuses the entire kitchen with its gorgeous scent. The colors in this salad are extraordinary, and the flavors are unexpected and refreshing.

- 2 Fuji apples
- 2 bananas
- 1 cup blackberries
- 4 passion fruits
- 2 teaspoons agave nectar
- Zest and juice of 1 small lime
- 1 sprig of basil

1 Wash and peel the apples, and then cut them into small, bite-sized pieces. Cut the bananas into similar-sized pieces. Wash the blackberries, and let them sit on a paper towel after draining.

2 Cut the passion fruits in half, and scoop out the orange flesh with a spoon; put the flesh into a bowl. Add all of the other fruit, and toss gently.

3 Add the agave nectar and the zest and juice of one lime. Cut the basil leaves into thin strips, and sprinkle them on top. Toss all together.

4 Allow the salad to sit for 10 to 15 minutes in the refrigerator in order to infuse the flavors before serving.

Blueberry Cheesecake
8 servings

The Place Monge cheesecake is one of my favorite desserts, found at the famous small Maison Kayser bakery on Rue Monge in Paris. This version is very simple and uses blueberries, which many children prefer (the original contains tangy berries). (But if you do have an occasion to go to Paris, you should try the original version.)

FOR THE CRUST
½ **stick butter**
¼ **cup brown sugar**
¼ **cup spelt flour**
¼ **cup oat flour**
½ **cup crushed walnuts or almonds**

FOR THE FILLING
3 **8-ounce packages of cream cheese**
¼ **cup honey**
¼ **cup cream**
3 **eggs**
1 **teaspoon vanilla extract**

FOR THE TOPPING
2 **gelatin leaves (or one teaspoon of**
  powdered gelatin dissolved in
  1 tablespoon warm water)
½ **cup water**
3 **cups blueberries**
2 **tablespoons honey**

1 Preheat the oven to 350°F.

2 Lightly oil an 8 inch tart pan.

FOR THE CRUST

1 In a bowl, mix the butter and sugar until well mixed and fluffy. Add the flours and walnuts, and mix. Press the mixture onto the bottom of the tart pan. Bake for 15 to 20 minutes. Let cool.

FOR THE FILLING

1 In a bowl, combine the cream cheese and honey, and beat together until well combined. Add the cream, eggs (one at a time), and the vanilla extract. Pour into the cooled crust, and bake in a bain marie for 30 to 40 minutes. Meanwhile, make the topping.

FOR THE TOPPING

1 In a small bowl, combine the gelatin leaves with the ½ cup water. Let soften.

2 In a pan on medium heat, cook the blueberries with honey for 3 to 4 minutes until the berries have softened. Take off heat and let cool.

3 Integrate the softened gelatin, and stir together, making sure all of the gelatin has been incorporated. Set aside.

4 When the cake is done, remove it from the oven and let cool. Pour on the topping.

5 Chill in the refrigerator for at least 2 hours before serving.

Coconut, Fig, and Garbanzo Bean Bars

4 to 6 servings

These bars are a high protein snack or dessert. They will keep for up to 10 days in an air-tight container in the refrigerator.

1 cup dried fig
2 cups water
1 cup garbanzo bean flour
½ cup crushed walnuts
1 teaspoon baking soda
1 teaspoon baking powder
2 sticks butter, softened
½ cup brown sugar
2 eggs
1 tablespoon vanilla extract
2 cups rolled oats
1 cup dried coconut
1 cup sweetened condensed milk

1 Preheat the oven to 350°F.

2 In a small pan, add the dried fig and water, and bring to a simmer. Cook for 20 minutes.

3 Put into a food processer and puree. Set aside.

4 In a bowl, combine the bean flour, walnuts, baking soda, and baking powder, and mix.

5 In a separate bowl, whip together the butter and the brown sugar. When well integrated, add eggs and vanilla extract.

6 Slowly combine the flour mixture with the butter mixture, and mix with your fingertips to a mealy texture. Add the oats and mix.

7 On a buttered or oiled baking dish, press the mixture into the pan, and then add the dried fig and the dried coconut on top. Drizzle with honey, followed by condensed milk. Bake for 20 minutes.

8 Remove from the oven, and let cool in the pan.

9 Cut into thin bars.

Almond Barley Bake with Lingonberries

4 to 6 servings

Barley, a superfood with its Omega-3, folate, protein, and iron, is a great base for a dessert, since you get so many vitamins and minerals in one food. This bake is simple yet super-healthy.

3 cups milk
¼ cup honey
3 tablespoons cornstarch
1 teaspoon salt
1 teaspoon almond extract
1 tablespoon butter
1 cup cooked barley
1 cup slivered, unsalted almonds
¼ cup lingonberry jam

1 Preheat the oven to 350°F.

2 In a large saucepan, heat the milk until bubbles form at the edges, but not boiling.

3 In a bowl, combine the honey, cornstarch, and salt. Pour into the milk, a little at a time. Continue to cook on low heat until the mixture thickens, being careful not to let it burn or boil.

4 Remove from heat, and stir in almond extract, butter, barley, and almonds, and pour into a buttered baking dish. Bake for 45 to 60 minutes.

5 Spread with lingonberry jam on top, or serve it on the side.

Sweet Walnut and Pear Dessert Soup with Quinoa

4 servings

This is a soup inspired by a walnut dessert soup served at French Laundry. This recipe is a lot less labor-intensive, contains no alcohol, and integrates the cooked walnuts into the soup rather than straining them. I wanted to keep the idea of walnuts and pears together in a creamy soup, and I thought that quinoa would be a nice way to provide carbohydrate and protein.

2 cups walnuts
4 cups milk
5 tablespoons agave nectar
½ cup heavy cream
1 vanilla pod
4 ripe pears
1 cup cooked quinoa

1 Preheat the oven to 375°F.

2 Line a baking sheet with parchment paper. Place the walnuts on the sheet and roast for 3 to 5 minutes, until they become aromatic and golden, being careful not to burn them. Take them out and cut them into small pieces.

3 In a pot, add the walnuts, milk, 3 table-spoons agave nectar, and the cream. Cut open the vanilla pod, scoop out the seeds with the tip of a knife, and add the seeds to the pot; also add the vanilla bean. Cover and simmer for 45 minutes on low heat.

4   Wash and peel the pears, and slice them into small pieces, discarding the hard core section with the seeds. In another pot, add the pears and 2 tablespoons of agave nectar, and fill it with enough water to cover the pears. Bring to a boil and simmer for 15 to 20 minutes, until they become very tender. Remove from the heat and let the pears cool for a few minutes.

5   Prepare a food processor or blender. With a slotted spoon, take the pears out of their pan and put them into the processor, and add ½ cup of the cooking liquid. Remove the vanilla bean from the walnut/cream mixture. Add the cream mixture to the pears and cooking liquid. Blend everything until it becomes completely smooth. Stir in the cooked quinoa. Serve cold or warm.

Baked Apples with Prunes, Walnuts, and Raisins   *2 to 4 servings*

This is a perfect autumn dessert, especially when served warm with a scoop of vanilla ice cream.

> **4 apples**
> **¼ cup prunes, pitted and cut into small pieces**
> **½ cup raisins**
> **¼ cup walnuts**
> **Zest of ½ lemon**
> **1 teaspoon freshly grated ginger**
> **2 tablespoons honey**

1   Preheat the oven to 375°F.

2   Cut the apples in half and take out the core, making a well in the center. Chop up the prunes, raisins, and walnuts.

3   In a pan, add the dried fruits, nuts, and the lemon zest, and mix. Add the ginger and honey and simmer for 5 minutes.

4   In a baking dish, place the apples, cut side up; fill in the well in each half with the fruit mixture and pour the liquid on top. Bake for 20 minutes.

Oatmeal Banana Spelt Cookies

6 to 8 servings

I can't help but make different versions of oatmeal cookies. They are so nutritious and so good, and without the butter and all the sugar that is usually found in most cookies. Spelt flour makes it nuttier and gives a crunchier texture. One of these cookies can also be served as an energy bar for a quick breakfast. I like to add cardamom rather than cinnamon to give it a twist.

2 cups spelt flour
1 teaspoon baking soda
½ teaspoon salt
1 teaspoon ground cardamom (optional)
2 cups mashed bananas
½ cup brown sugar
2 eggs
1 teaspoon vanilla
¼ cup canola oil
3 cups old fashioned oats
1 cup raisins
½ cup chocolate chips

1 Preheat the oven to 350°F.

2 In a bowl, mix together the spelt flour, baking soda, salt, and cardamom. In another bowl, whip up the bananas and the sugar. When integrated, add the eggs, vanilla, and oil.

3 Slowly incorporate the dry ingredients into the wet. Then fold in the oats, raisins, and chips.

4 Drop tablespoonfuls of dough onto an ungreased baking sheet, and bake for 10 to 13 minutes.

5 Cool on a plate or wire rack, and serve.

No Butter Spelt Almond Cookies

Makes 4 dozen cookies

This is another healthy cookie recipe based on spelt flour and ground almonds. Rather than using butter, this recipe calls for oil and banana for moisture and sweetness.

2 cups spelt flour
2½ cups ground almonds
1 teaspoon baking soda
½ teaspoon salt
½ cup applesauce
½ cup mashed banana
½ cup brown sugar
2 eggs
4 tablespoons canola oil
1 teaspoon almond extract

1 Preheat the oven to 350°F.

2 In a bowl, mix together the spelt flour, ground almonds, and baking soda. When mixed well, add the salt.

3 In a separate bowl, whip together the applesauce, banana, and the brown sugar. Then add eggs, oil, and the almond extract.

4 Slowly incorporate the dry ingredients with the egg mixture until well blended.

5 Drop tablespoonfuls of dough onto an ungreased baking pan, and bake for 10 to 13 minutes.

6 Cool on a plate or wire rack for a few minutes before serving.

Ginger Cookies with Barley and Oats

Makes 4 dozen cookies

This is a twist on a traditional German ginger cookie, made with barley flour and ground flaxseeds. I actually prefer the taste of barley flour to normal white flour, and it gives the baked goods a bit more coarse texture.

½ teaspoon allspice
1 teaspoon cinnamon
2 teaspoons ground ginger
1½ cups barley flour
1 teaspoon baking soda
2 sticks of butter, softened
½ cup brown sugar
2 tablespoons ground flaxseeds
8 tablespoons water
1 teaspoon vanilla
½ cup applesauce
3 cups old fashioned oats
1 cup white chocolate chips (optional) or 1 cup raisins

1 Preheat the oven to 350°F.

2 In a bowl, mix together the allspice, cinnamon, ginger, barley flour, and baking soda.

3 In a separate bowl, whip together the butter and brown sugar. When the mixture becomes fluffy, mix in the flaxseeds, water, vanilla, and applesauce.

4 Slowly incorporate the dry flour mixture into the wet mixture until well mixed. Fold in the oats and the chips or raisins.

5 Drop rounded tablespoonfuls of dough onto an ungreased cookie sheet. Bake 10 to 13 minutes, or until golden brown and slightly soft to the touch for chewy cookies.

6 Cool 1 minute, and then transfer to a plate or wire rack.

Cardamom-Infused Chilled Cherry Cucumber Soup

4 servings

When cherries come into season, I love to find a variety of ways to present them to my son. They have such a beautiful, rich color and flavor. This soup is a simple and elegant dessert, perfect for a warm summer day. Cucumber adds an unexpected crunch and was inspired by a fruit salad I once had in Senegal—exotic fruits with tiny bits of cucumber—which seemed funny but it works.

2 cardamom pods
3 tablespoons agave nectar
4 cups water
3 cups fresh cherries, seeded and cut in half
½ fresh cucumber (peeled, seeded, and cut into very small pieces)
2 tablespoons crème fraiche (optional)

1 In a pot, add the cardamom pods, agave nectar, and water, and bring to a boil.

2 Simmer for 10 minutes, and then add the cherries.

3 Simmer for 5 minutes, and then add the cucumber. Remove from the heat.

4 Let cool, and add the crème (optional).

5 Serve at room temperature or chilled. The cherries should be tender, and the cucumbers should be crunchy.

Azuki Bean Paste

Azuki beans are at the heart of East Asian pastries. Because there was traditionally no cream, butter, or cheese to use in cakes, cookies, or pastries, many of the sweet recipes in East Asia are based on sticky rice, fruit, and sweetened beans or legumes. It is a nice source of protein, as well as a complex carbohydrate. This paste is versatile and can be used for many sweet recipes. It is great on toast as an alternative to a peanut butter and jelly sandwich, or it can be mixed with ice cream or used as a filling for cakes and puff pastries. These beans can be a bit time consuming, but they are worth the effort. They contain high amounts of fiber, folic acid, iron, zinc, copper, magnesium, and B vitamins. In Asia, they are used as the foundation of desserts and pastries, and there are infinite ways you can prepare these beans.

> 2 cups dried azuki beans
> Pinch of salt
> ½ cup brown sugar
> ½ cup honey

1 Wash and drain the beans. In a pot, add water to the top and add the beans; bring to a boil, and drain. Do the same again: fill the pot with water and add the beans plus the pinch of salt; again bring it to a boil. Then cover and simmer until the beans are completely soft, approximately 40 to 60 minutes.

2 Take off the heat and drain. Pour the beans into a bowl, and, with a hand blender, puree the beans until they're completely smooth. Add the sugar and honey, and blend a bit further.

3 Depending on what texture you want, add water to make it soupy, or leave it thick like a paste.

4 The paste will keep for about 3 to 4 days in an airtight container in the refrigerator and up to 2 months in the freezer.

Azuki Bean Cookies   *6 to 8 servings*

These cookies are made with azuki beans as a base, without butter and quite low in sugar content. It is a good source of proteins and makes for a great snack.

> 2 cups azuki beans, soaked overnight
>   in water
> ¼ cup olive oil
> 1 egg
> ¾ cup organic applesauce
> 1 teaspoon vanilla extract
> ¼ cup brown sugar
> 3 tablespoons cocoa powder
> 1 cup oat flour
> 1 teaspoon cinnamon
> 1 teaspoon baking soda
> ¼ cup carob chips (chocolate chips,
>   almonds, or walnuts)
> 3 tablespoons ground flaxseeds (optional)

1 Preheat the oven to 350°F.

2 Drain the presoaked azuki beans. Fill a large pot with water and add the azuki beans and bring to a boil. Drain the water, then add fresh water to the beans and bring to a boil again. Cover and simmer for 40 to 50 minutes or until the beans are tender. Drain.

3 In a mixer, blend the beans, olive oil, egg, applesauce, and vanilla until smooth.

4 In a bowl, combine the sugar, cocoa powder, flour, cinnamon, and baking soda.

5 Slowly add the flour mixture into the wet mixture and blend well in the mixer. When well blended, stir in the chips and flaxseeds.

6 Drop the mixture onto a baking sheet lined with parchment paper and bake for 10 to 12 minutes.

Azuki Bean Crumble with Vanilla Ice Cream   *4 to 6 servings*

Here I use Azuki beans to make an American-style dessert which my son loves, topped with vanilla ice cream for special occasions.

1 stick butter, softened and room temperature
½ cup whole wheat flour
½ cup brown sugar
½ cup oat flour
½ cup rolled oats
½ cup crushed walnuts
½ cup crushed hazelnuts
2 cups cooked azuki bean paste
1 teaspoon cinnamon
4 to 6 scoops vanilla ice cream

1 Preheat the oven to 375°F.

2 In a bowl, combine the butter with the wheat flour, brown sugar, oat flour, rolled oats, cinnamon, walnuts, and hazelnuts, and mix together with your fingers until the mixture become mealy in texture.

3 In a deep baking dish, put the azuki bean paste on the bottom, and then cover with the crumble mixture on top. Bake for 30 to 40 minutes, or until the crumble becomes golden and crunchy.

4 Serve with the ice cream.

Azuki Soup   *6 to 8 servings*

Azuki soup is a very traditional way to enjoy these beans. In Japan, we add mochi rice cakes or jellies, as well as preserved fruits. We eat it cold or warm, as a thin soup, or as a thick, solid, almost stew-like soup. You can adjust the consistency to suit your taste. My son loves it all kinds of ways.

1 cup azuki beans
8 cups water
1 cup brown sugar

1 In a large bowl, add the beans and fill it with water; soak overnight.

2 Drain, and in a large pot, add the beans with 8 cups of water, and bring to a boil. Cover and simmer for 90 minutes, or until the beans are soft.

3 Stir in the sugar.

4 Using a hand blender, blend the beans until completely smooth.

5 You can serve the soup warm or chilled, with a bit of crème fraiche or vanilla ice cream.

Panna Cotta with Yuzu Coulis

4 servings

Panna cotta is a rich creamy Italian dessert, and it's usually served with a berry coulis, which my son is not too crazy about. So this is an Asian twist, with a coulis made of yuzu—a very tart citrus from Japan. With brown sugar, honey, or agave nectar, yuzu juice and zest becomes a beautiful syrup that is perfect for desserts. The juice is sold in most Asian grocery stores or is available online. It may be a bit difficult to find, but it's certainly worth the trouble. If you can't find it, you can substitute lime juice in this recipe.

> 1 cup milk
> 1 tablespoon gelatin powder
> 3 cups cream
> 1/3 cup agave nectar
> 1 vanilla pod
> 2 tablespoons yuzu juice
> 4 tablespoons honey
> 5 tablespoons water
> 1 tablespoon chia seeds

1 In a heavy-bottom pot, add the milk and the gelatin powder, and stir together. Let the mixture sit for 5 minutes.

2 Heat the pot on medium heat—do not bring it to a boil—heat it while stirring for 5 minutes.

3 Add the cream, agave nectar, and the inside of the vanilla bean (with the tip of a knife, scoop the inside of the vanilla bean into the pot). Stir and cook for 3 to 4 minutes, and remove from the heat. Let cool for 3 to 4 minutes.

4 Pour the mixture into 4 to 6 cups or ramekins, and cover with plastic. Refrigerate overnight.

5 For the coulis, add the yuzu juice, honey, and water to a small pot, and bring to a boil. Simmer for 5 minutes, and remove from the heat.

6 Pour a spoonful over the panna cotta, and serve with a sprinkle of chia seeds.

Fresh Figs with Mascarpone, Honey, and Pistachio Nuts   *4 Servings*

This is a simple dessert that highlights the intricate flavor and texture of fresh figs—soft and creamy with a popping crunch from the seeds.

> 4 whole figs
> 2 tablespoons honey
> 4 tablespoons mascarpone cheese
> 2 tablespoons chopped pistachio nuts

1 Wash and cut the top stem off the figs. Then cut across the top of the fruit and slowly open it with your hands until the deep crimson center appears.

2 To each fig, add a tablespoon of mascarpone cheese, then drizzle in 1/2 tablespoon honey, then sprinkle on 1/2 tablespoon nuts.

3 Serve immediately.

appendix

What to Have in Your Pantry

So much of what you can cook at any given time depends on how well your pantry is stocked. As long as you have a few essentials on your shelves, you can add some fresh vegetables and a protein source and whip up a meal without too much fuss. Here are some basics that are always in my pantry:

Soy sauce
Mirin
Ground flaxseeds
Chia seeds
Walnuts, whole and ground
Wheat germ, ground
Walnut oil
Grapeseed oil
Kombu seaweed
Nori seaweed
Sesame seeds
Sesame oil
Rice wine vinegar
Olive oil
Seaweed flakes
Tahini
Dried soy beans
Puffed wheat
Puffed kamut
Dried shiso flakes
Hemp oil

Pumpkin seeds
Rice vinegar
All kinds of dried fruits and nuts—cranberries, raisins, strawberries, figs, dates, almonds, cashews, peanuts, etc.
Dried shiitake mushrooms
Raspberry vinegar
Oregano
Cloves
Basil
Pine nuts
Egg noodles
Soybean noodles
Rice noodles
Short grain white rice
Brown rice
Organic, low sodium chicken stock
Prepared tomato sauce

acknowledgments

I have been extremely lucky to have had enormous support from so many people who helped me turn my simple idea into a reality.

I am deeply indebted to my late attorney, mentor, and, most of all, a very dear friend, Keven Davis. This book would not have happened without his careful guidance, deep commitment, and his belief in this project. I know he would have been the happiest to see this book come to life, and I dedicate this book to him. I am grateful to Keven's gifted legal team at GBS Law who collaborated on this project—Hilary Hughes, Theresa Simpson, and Maureen Look.

I thank my literary agent, Laura Dail, who immediately grasped the raw idea of this book and tackled the project with impressive force and determination. I am extremely grateful to Katie McHugh at Perseus/Da Capo Press, who took a great leap of faith in a concept and, with vision, precision, and expertise, shaped this book into something real and complete. Thank you for giving me this opportunity to share my passion.

I would like to express my gratitude to the pediatrician, friend, and writer, Dr. Lisa Stern, who was recommended to me by the leading liver specialist at UCLA as the "best pediatrician in the entire Los Angeles area and the best doctor I know." Thank you for your support and friendship and for writing a foreword to the book. To Bonnie Modugno, the nutritionist who guided me throughout the entire book, thank you for your expertise. Thank you Beatrice Peltre for bringing such beauty to the book with your photographs. And to Meirav Sakalowsky, thank you for writing the preface, for embracing my "baby brain food" idea from the very beginning, and for allowing me to give guidance on Isabella's meals; I am so happy to have watched her grow and thrive.

Dr. Paul Crane, Dr. Marvin Ament, Dr. Balfour, and the nurses at Cedars-Sinai who guided us through very difficult times; I thank you all very much. My deep appreciation goes to Donna Hollarin and her Baby Group in Santa Monica and the Pump Station in Santa Monica for giving me a much-needed place of comfort in those trying first months of my son's life.

I am grateful to Halona, for always being there to encourage and guide me in everything I do; to Belle, for the incredible friendship, support, and kindness during the toughest times of my life and for constantly sharing new recipes and food ideas with me—this book was inspired by the conversations we had together since Magnus was 3 months old. And to my friends and family who encourage and inspire me: Kira, Lisa, Laura, Moufida, Feriel, Somesha, Herbie, Gigi, Jessica, Melinda, Tom, Cheri, Karon, Kahlil, Noa, Nancy, Ben, Daniel, Cynthia, Pedramin, Agathe, Patricia, Leandro, Mirjam, Staci, Aarti, and Jennifer.

And most importantly, my family—my mother, who taught me to cherish food and to persevere in all that I tackle; my brother, for looking out for me and our family; my little Magnus, for being such an incredible light in my life; and Kjetil, for believing in me and supporting me in everything I do and cheering me on to go further—thank you for always being there for me. None of this would have been possible without you.

index

recipe index

Please turn to page 265 for an index of age-appropriate recipes.

age-appropriate recipes